James Mackintosh

The Roman Law of Sale, with Modern Illustrations

Digest xviii, 1 and xix, 1

James Mackintosh

The Roman Law of Sale, with Modern Illustrations
Digest xviii, 1 and xix, 1

ISBN/EAN: 9783744773256

Printed in Europe, USA, Canada, Australia, Japan

Cover: Foto ©ninafisch / pixelio.de

More available books at **www.hansebooks.com**

THE ROMAN LAW OF SALE

WITH MODERN ILLUSTRATIONS.

DIGEST XVIII. 1 AND XIX. 1.

PRINTED BY MORRISON AND GIBB

FOR

T. & T. CLARK, LAW PUBLISHERS, EDINBURGH

GLASGOW, . . . J. SMITH AND SON.
LONDON, ... STEVENS AND SONS.
,, ... STEVENS AND HAYNES.

THE ROMAN LAW OF SALE

WITH MODERN ILLUSTRATIONS.

DIGEST XVIII. 1 AND XIX. 1 TRANSLATED

WITH NOTES AND REFERENCES TO CASES

AND THE

Sale of Goods Bill.

BY

JAMES MACKINTOSH, B.A., ADVOCATE,
LATE SCHOLAR OF EXETER COLLEGE, OXFORD.

EDINBURGH:
T. & T. CLARK, LAW PUBLISHERS.
1892.

PREFACE.

THE civil law has been so dominant a factor in the development of the common law of Scotland that, apart from its intrinsic merits, it must always remain an essential part of a liberal professional training in Scots law. Although its influence upon the law of England has been neither so direct nor so considerable, there are signs there also of a growing practical interest in its study, if one may judge from the frequency with which it is referred to in the recent volumes of the Law Reports, and from the higher standard of attainments now enforced at the Universities and by many legal bodies. In many cases candidates for legal examinations are now very properly required, in addition to showing a general knowledge of the traditional and somewhat tedious text-book, the *Institutes* of Justinian, to profess some special subject as treated in the *Digest*, and are thus introduced to an acquaintance with the most interesting and characteristic monument of the Roman genius for law.

The principles of the law of sale, as stated in the Titles *De Contrahenda Emptione* and *De Actionibus Empti Venditi*, seemed to me well adapted to serve as a specimen of the remains of the great jurists of the Classical period. Unfortunately the compilers of the *Digest*, in the hasty execution of their task, threw together the materials that lay to their hands without sufficient regard to subject or to orderly arrangement; there is, therefore, a want of logical sequence in the discussion of topics, and a constant necessity for cross-reference to other titles in the *Corpus*

Juris relating more or less closely to the same subject. I hope the Notes and the Index will obviate this disadvantage to some extent. I found it would be impossible, within the limits of a short book, to find room for a connected sketch of the whole Roman law of Sale, co-ordinating the chief texts, and filling up the gaps in these two titles. There are many foreign books written on this plan; and English readers may now be referred to Dr. Moyle's *Contract of Sale in Roman Law*, which appeared as the last sheets of this book were passing through the press.

The attempt at a comparative treatment of the civil and the common law is somewhat of a novelty, but it possesses obvious advantages both from an educational and a practical point of view. I have constantly referred to Pothier's Treatise on Sale, which is still a standard authority in our Courts, and has done more than any other book to give currency to the civil law in modern practice. To facilitate the comparison with English law, I have thought it worth while to print as an Appendix the Sale of Goods Bill, in the shape in which it was introduced in the House of Lords this year, embodying the amendments made in Committee in previous years. This draft code is an ably executed condensation of the common law; and it may be anticipated, after the criticism it has already undergone, that it will receive legislative sanction in the near future without material alteration.

A desire has been expressed by some legal and public bodies that the Bill should be extended to Scotland, but this appears to be a proposal of doubtful expediency, under present circumstances. The application to Scotland of a Bill based exclusively on English case law, with a few saving clauses interjected, would be productive of more confusion than advantage. If the legitimate desire of the mercantile community for an assimilation of the law of sale in the two countries is to be given effect to in a satisfactory manner, it is essential that there should be adequate inquiry and mature consideration before a consolidating statute is passed. There were two Commissions of Inquiry prior to the passing of the Mercantile Law Amendment Act of 1856, although the changes then in contemplation were not so far-reaching, and it may be hoped that Parliament will not be more precipitate on the present occasion.

I am indebted to Professor GOUDY for the suggestion of this book, and for much kind help while it passed through the press. I have also to thank Mr. W. GALBRAITH, W.S., who has been good enough to revise most of the proof sheets, and make several corrections. I have been greatly aided in the selection of English cases by the excellent commentary on the Sale of Goods Bill, lately published by His Honour Judge CHALMERS, the accomplished draughtsman of the Bill.

EDINBURGH, *June* 1892.

CONTENTS.

	PAGE
TABLE OF CASES, .	xiii
DE CONTRAHENDA EMPTIONE (DIGEST XVIII. 1), .	1
DE ACTIONIBUS EMPTI VENDITI (DIGEST XIX. 1),	140
SALE OF GOODS BILL, .	237
INDEX TO THE LATIN TEXT AND NOTES,	259

ADDENDUM.

The Sale of Goods Bill, as amended on Report and ordered to be printed on 17th May, contains the following changes:—

Arrangement.—§ 10 is transposed, and appears as § 57. This alters the numbering of the sections from 11 to 41, so that § 11 appears as § 10, and so on.

New Clauses.—Add to § 14, (1): 'and that in the case of an agreement to sell he will have a right to sell the goods at the time when the property is to pass.'

Add to § 31, (1): 'Apart from any such contract, express or implied, the place of delivery is the seller's place of business, if he have one, and if not, his residence: Provided that, if the contract be for the sale of specific goods, which to the knowledge of the parties when the contract is made are in some other place, then that place is the place of delivery.'

Add to § 34 a new sub-section (3): 'Unless otherwise agreed, where goods are sent by the seller to the buyer by sea, under circumstances in which it is usual to insure, the seller must give such notice of shipment to the buyer as may enable him to insure them, and, if the seller fails to do so, the goods shall be deemed to be at his risk.'

Application of the Bill to Scotland.—It is now proposed to extend the Bill to Scotland.

The changes introduced for this purpose are mainly (1) a number of saving clauses, and (2) certain new clauses.

Savings.—The provisions of § 4 (embodying the Statute of Frauds); of § 12 (fresh consideration required to support warranty given after sale completed); of § 24 (rule of market overt); of § 26 (revesting of property in stolen goods on conviction of offender); of § 28 (effects of writs of execution) are not to apply to Scotland. It is declared by § 50 (3) that 'nothing in this section shall prejudice the right of the seller in Scotland to recover interest on the price from the date of the tender of the goods, or from the date on which the price was payable, as the case may be'; by § 54 (5) that 'nothing in this section shall prejudice the buyer's right of rejection in Scotland as declared by this Act'; and by § 63 (4) and (5) that 'the provisions of this Act relating to contracts of sale do not apply to any transaction in the form of a contract of sale which is intended to operate by way of mortgage, pledge, charge, or other security,' and 'nothing in this Act shall prejudice or affect the landlord's right of hypothec or sequestration for rent in Scotland.'

New Clauses.—In place of § 13 (1) (2) (3), the following clauses are proposed for Scotland :—

'(*a*) Where a contract of sale is subject to any condition to be fulfilled by the seller, the buyer may waive the condition or elect to treat the breach of such condition as a breach which may give rise to a claim for damages: (*b*) Failure to perform any material part of a contract of sale is in general a breach of contract which entitles the party not in fault to reject the goods and treat the contract as repudiated, and it depends on the circumstances and equities of each case whether the contract can be treated as repudiated or the breach complained of falls to be satisfied by damages.'

A clause, numbered § 41, is proposed allowing attachment by seller in Scotland. 'In Scotland a seller of goods may attach the same while in his own hands or possession by arrestment or poinding; and such arrestment or poinding shall have the same operation and effect in a competition or otherwise as an arrestment or poinding by a third party.'

A clause, numbered § 60, is added, relating to payment into Court in Scotland when breach of warranty is alleged :—

'In Scotland where a buyer elects to accept goods which he might have rejected, and to treat a breach of contract as only giving rise to a claim for damages, he may, in an action by the seller for the price, be required, in the discretion of the Court before which the action depends, to consign or pay into Court the price of the goods or part thereof, or to give other reasonable security for the due payment thereof.'

Lastly, by the interpretation clause, various Scots law terms are included under the corresponding English terms, *e.g.* pursuer, complainer, and claimant in a multiplepoinding are included under 'plaintiff.'

TABLE OF CASES.

	PAGE
Amaan v. Handyside, 1865, 3 Macp. 526,	119
Anderson, 1870, 9 Macp. 122,	80
Anderson v. Morice, 1875, L. R. 10 C. P. 609, and 1 App. Ca. 713,	78
Balfour v. Smith, 1877, 4 R. 454,	38
Barr v. Gibson, 1838, 3 M. & W. 390,	107
Bingham v. Bingham, 1 Ves. Sen. 126,	41
Black, 1867, 6 Macp. 136,	21
Booker & Co. v. Milne, 1870, 9 Macp. 314,	44
Brown v. Marr, 1880, 7 R. 427,	14
Bryan v. Lewis, 1826, Ry. & Moor. 386,	57
Buddle v. Green, 1857, 27 L. J. Ex. 24,	26
Campbell v. Mersey Docks Co., 1863, 14 C. B. n. s. 412,	79
City Bank v. Barrow, 1880, 5 App. Ca. 677,	55
Clark v. Spence, 1836, 4 A. & E. 466,	46
Cochrane v. Willis, 1865, 1 Ch. App. 58,	40
Coddington v. Paleologo, 1867, L. R. 2 Ex. 200,	49
Colonial Bank v. Whinney, 1886, 11 App. Ca. 435,	56
Cook v. Field, 1850, 15 Q. B. 460,	26
Cooper v. Phibbs, 1867, L. R. 2 H. L. 149,	37
Couturier v. Hastie, 1856, 5 H. L. Ca. 673,	37
Derry v. Peek, 1889, 14 App. Ca. 337,	54
Dobbie v. Duncanson, 1872, 10 Macp. 810,	119
Dunlop v. Higgins, 1848, 1 H. L. C. 381,	8, 141
Eichholz v. Bannister, 1864, 34 L. J. C. P. 105,	53
Elphick v. Barnes, 1880, 5 C. P. D. 321,	14
Freeth v. Burr, 1874, L. R. 9 C. P. 208,	18
Gompertz v. Bartlett, 1853, 2 E. & B. 849,	31
Grafton v. Armitage, 1845, 2 C. B. 336,	46
Graham v. Pollock, 1763, Mor. 14 198,	14
Grantham v. Hawley, Hob. 132	26

xiv   TABLE OF CASES.

	PAGE
Greaves v. Ashlin, 1813, 3 Camp. 425,	154
Hadley v. Baxendale, 1854, 9 Ex. 341,	140
Hale v. Rawson, 1858, 4 C. B. 85,	27
Hammond & Co. v. Bussey, 1887, 20 Q. B. Div. 86,	140
Hansen v. Craig & Rose, 1859, 21 D. 432,	79
Hargreave v. Spink, Q. B. Div., *Times'* L. R. Nov. 2, 1891,	64
Harrison v. Luke, 1845, 14 M. & W. 139,	6
Head v. Tattersall, 1871, 7 Ex. 7,	14
Hepburn v. Campbell, 1781, Mor. 14168,	87
Hibblethwaite v. M'Morine, 1839, 5 M. & W. 462,	57
Hitchcock v. Giddings, 4 Price 135,	26
Houldsworth v. Glasgow Bank, 1880, 5 App. Ca. 317,	119
Household Fire Insurance Co., 1879, 4 Ex. Div. 216,	8
Howe v. Smith, 1884, 27 Ch. D. 101,	68, 71
Jones v. Clifford, 1876, 3 Ch. Div. 779,	41
Jones v. Gordon, 1877, 2 App. Ca. 616,	54
Kelly v. Solari, 1841, 9 M. & W. 54,	38
Kemp v. Falk, 1882, 7 App. Ca. 573,	21
Kendal, 1883, 11 Q. B. Div. 368,	21
Kennedy v. Panama Mail Co., 1867, L. R. 2 Q. B. 580,	32
Lavaggi v. Pirie, 1872, 10 Macp. 312,	71
Lee v. Griffin, 1861, 1 B. & S. 272,	46
Life Association of Scotland v. Foster, 1873, 11 Macp. 351,	49
Lunn v. Thornton, 1845, 1 C. B. 379,	26
Macdonald, 1888, 15 R. 998,	14
Mackay v. Dick, 1881, 6 App. Ca. 251,	99
Macreth v. Simmons, 15 Ves. 344,	42
M'Bain v. Wallace, 1881, 6 App. Ca. 588,	48
Martindale v. Smith, 1841, 1 Q. B. 389,	20
Martineau v. Kitching, 1872, L. R. 7 Q. B. 454,	77
Maxwell v. Stevenson, 1831, 5 W. & S. 269,	126
Mersey Steel Co., 1874, 9 App. Ca. 434,	18
Montrose, Earl of, 1639, Mor. 14155,	71
Pirie v. Pirie, 1873, 11 Macp. 941,	98
Power v. Barham, 1836, 4 A. & E. 473,	93
Ragg v. Brown, 1708, Mor. 9492.	26
Richmond v. Railton, 1854, 16 D. 402,	44
Scrabster Harbour Trs. v. Sinclair, 1864, 2 Macp. 884,	41
Seath & Co. v. Moore, 1886, 11 App. Ca. 350,	47, 48
Sheldon v. Cox, 1824, 3 B. & C. 420,	6

Simpson *v.* Duncanson's Crs, 1786, Mor. 14 204,	47
Smith *v.* Hughes, 1871, L. R. 6 Q. B. 597,	33
Steven, 1760, Mor. 3158, ...	71
Stewart *v.* Kennedy, 1890, 15 App. Ca. 75, 108,	33, 142
Stoppel & Co. *v.* Stoddart, 1850, 13 D. 61,	21
Street *v.* Blay, 2 B. & Ad. 456, .	33
Strickland *v.* Turner, 1852, 7 Ex. 208,	37
Swan *v.* Martin, 1865, 3 Macp. 851, .	52
Taylor *v.* Caldwell, 1863, 3 B. & S. 826, .	107
Thacker *v.* Hardy, 1878, 4 Q. B. Div. 685,	27
Todd *v.* Armour, 1882, 9 R. 901, .	65
Turley v. Bates, 1863, 2 H. & C. 200,	79
Turnbull, 1874, 1 R. 730, . . .	18
Vickers *v.* Vickers, 1867, L. R. 4 Eq. 529,	11
Walker, 1873, 11 Macp. 906, .	80
Watt *v.* Findlay, 1846, 8 D. 529, . .	45
Watts *v.* Friend, 1830, 10 B. & C. 446, .	27
Webster *v.* Cramond Iron Co., 1875, 2 R. 752,	141
Wieler *v.* Schilizzi, 1856, 17 C. B. 619, . .	32
Wilks *v.* Atkinson, 1815, 1 Marshall 412.	173
Zagury *v.* Furnell, 1809, 2 Camp. 239, .	79

THE
DIGEST OF JUSTINIAN.

BOOK XVIII.

TITLE I.

DE CONTRAHENDA EMPTIONE.

LIBER DECIMUS OCTAVUS.

TIT. 1.

DE CONTRAHENDA EMPTIONE[1] ET DE PACTIS INTER EMPTOREM ET UENDITOREM COMPOSITIS[2] ET QUAE RES UENIRE NON POSSUNT.[3]

1. PAULUS libro XXXIII ad edictum.

ORIGO emendi uendendique a permutationibus coepit. olim enim non ita erat nummus, neque aliud merx aliud pretium uocabatur, sed unusquisque secundum necessitatem temporum ac rerum utilibus inutilia permutabat, quando plerumque euenit, ut quod alteri superest alteri desit. sed quia non semper nec facile concurrebat, ut, cum tu haberes quod ego desiderarem, inuicem haberem quod tu accipere uelles, electa materia est cuius publica ac perpetua aestimatio difficultatibus permutationum aequalitate quantitatis subueniret. eaque materia forma publica percussa usum dominiumque non tam ex substantia praebet quam ex quantitate, nec ultra merx utrumque sed alterum pretium uocatur.

1. Sed an sine nummis uenditio dici hodieque possit, dubitatur,

---

L. 1 pr.—The Greeks had already more fully analysed the advantages of money over a system of barter (see *e.g.* Arist., *Pol.* i. 9, *Ethic. Nic.* v. 6); but Paul's rapid sketch in the opening paragraph is sufficient for his purpose. Barter involved two inconveniences,—the trouble of finding a person who had the commodity you wanted, and at the same time wanted the commodity you had, and the difficulty of arranging an exchange in terms of commodities which were different on each occasion. Money meets both difficulties; it is a general medium of exchange, and so you find a ready buyer and seller at every step; it is also a common measure of values, and so you are spared the

[1] *Code* iv. 38. [2] *Code* iv. 54. [3] *Code* iv. 40.

BOOK XVIII.

TITLE I.

OF THE CONTRACT OF SALE AND OF SPECIAL COVENANTS BETWEEN BUYER AND SELLER, AND OF THINGS INCAPABLE OF SALE.

1. PAUL.

The practice of barter was the source from which buying and selling arose. In early times there was no money, and no distinction in language between 'wares' and 'price': a man simply exchanged things useless to him for things useful, as his needs and circumstances demanded, it being commonly the case that one man lacks something which his neighbour has in superabundance. But as it seldom came about quite naturally, that when you had what I required, I too had what you were willing to take, a substance was chosen to which a permanent value was attached by public authority, with the view of obviating the inconveniences of barter by means of its uniform value. When stamped by the state, this material serves as an instrument of exchange and of acquisition on account of its recognised value rather than its inherent qualities, and the word 'wares' is no longer used of both the articles exchanged, but one of them is called the 'price.'

1. It is a disputed point whether we can still speak of a sale

trouble of balancing the qualities of the two commodities against each other. The words '*aequalitate quantitatis*' refer to this second advantage of money—it is a constant quantity, a uniform standard with a value independent of its intrinsic worth. The introduction of a coinage marks the stage at which sale takes the place of exchange for all ordinary purposes.

§ 1. Barter having been the precursor of sale, it was natural that

ueluti si ego togam dedi, ut tunicam acciperem. Sabinus et Cassius esse emptionem et uenditionem putant: Nerua et Proculus permutationem, non emptionem hoc esse. Sabinus Homero teste utitur, qui exercitum Graecorum aere ferro hominibusque uinum emere refert, illis uersibus:

Ἔνθεν ἄρ' οἰνίζοντο καρηκομόωντες Ἀχαιοὶ
ἄλλοι μὲν χαλκῷ, ἄλλοι δ' αἴθωνι σιδήρῳ,
ἄλλοι δὲ ῥινοῖς, ἄλλοι δ' αὐτῇσι βόεσσι,
ἄλλοι δ' ἀνδραπόδεσσιν.[1]

sed hi uersus permutationem significare uidentur, non emptionem, sicut illi:

Ἔνθ' αὖτε Γλαύκῳ Κρονίδης φρένας ἐξέλετο Ζεύς,
ὃς πρὸς Τυδείδην Διομήδεα τεύχε' ἄμειβεν.[2]

---

some degree of confusion as to the legal relation between them should exist in later times. Gaius (iii. 141) gives a rather fuller account of the discussion between the two schools of jurists. The Sabinians maintained, on historical grounds, that a price in money was not essential to sale, and, therefore, that barter was a variety of sale. Their object probably was to bring cases of exchange within the idea and the remedies of sale, which had now won full recognition as a consensual contract enforcible by *bonae fidei* actions. The Proculians argued that in sale the ware and the price are essentially distinct, and the buyer and seller are plainly marked off from each other, whereas in the exchange of one *merx* for another you cannot tell which performs the function of price and which corresponds to the ware. Caelius Sabinus tried to meet this objection by showing that the distinction could be drawn in some cases of exchange, *e.g.* when the one party offered a thing for sale (*rem venalem habens*) and agreed to take another thing for it by way of price; and in such a case the emperor Gordian allowed an action analogous to the *actio empti* (C. iv. 64. 1). At best this was only a partial answer, and it failed to establish an objective test generally applicable. The view of Proculus, that the price must be in current money, is here approved by Paul and prevailed in the end, except in the case just mentioned, where one party marked out his 'res' as

[1] *Il.* vii. 472.   [2] *Il.* vi. 234.

without money; for instance, if I give a robe for a tunic, Sabinus and Cassius consider it purchase and sale, Nerva and Proculus regard it as barter. Sabinus cites the testimony of Homer, who tells, in the following lines, how the Greek army bought wine with bronze, iron, and slaves: 'then the long-haired Greeks got themselves wine—some with bronze, some with gleaming iron, some with hides, some with live oxen, and some with slaves.' But these lines seem to point not to sale, but to exchange; and so do those other lines: 'then Zeus, the son of Kronos, reft Glaucus of his wits, so that he exchanged arms with Diomede, son of Tydeus.' A better confirmation of his opinion would be

---

venalis; barter was classed with the innominate real contracts of the type *do ut des*, and as such was actionable as soon as one party had made his prestation. *Inst.* iii. 23. 2.

The main points of difference by Roman law were: (1) Sale was a consensual contract, barter a real contract, depending for its force on performance (*datio rei*) by one party. An agreement to sell gave rise to a binding obligation, an agreement to exchange did not, being regarded as *nudum pactum* (D. 19. 4. 1 pr.–2).

(2) In exchange the property in the thing must be passed, and so a good title is required on both sides (D. ib. § 3, *alienam rem dantem nullam contrahere permutationem*); the seller had only to warrant quiet possession.

(3) Delivery passed the property in things exchanged, but not in things sold, unless the price was paid or secured or credit given.

(4) A sale might be rescinded on the ground of *laesio enormis*, an exchange could not.

(5) The legal remedies were different: *e.g.* a seller who has given delivery on credit cannot demand his goods back in default of payment, he can only sue the buyer for the price; but the party who has made the first prestation in an exchange is entitled, if the counter prestation is refused, to get back his 'res' by the *condictio de causa data causa non secuta*.

The contract of exchange is, like sale, consensual in modern law, and its legal effects are generally the same. Cp. Pothier, *Vente*, §§ 620–630. In S. G. B. § 56, it is defined as a contract 'where the consideration for the transfer of the property in goods

magis autem pro hac sententia illud diceretur, quod alias idem poeta dicit:

πρίατο κτεάτεσσιν ἑοῖσιν.[1]

sed uerior est Nernae et Proculi sententia: nam ut aliud est uendere, aliud emere, alius emptor, alius uenditor, sic aliud est pretium, aliud merx: quod in permutatione discerni non potest, uter emptor, uter uenditor sit.

2. Est autem emptio iuris gentium, et ideo consensu per-

---

from one person to another consists of other goods;' but where it consists partly of other goods and partly of money (cp. L. 79 *infra*), the contract is deemed to be sale (*Sheldon* v. *Cox* (1824) 3 B. & C. 420): it is also proposed that the provisions relating to sales shall apply to exchange 'with any necessary modifications.' The proper remedy, where one of the exchanging parties has delivered goods and the other omits to send goods in return, is to bring an action for breach of the agreement, not for goods sold; a contract of barter cannot be changed into a contract to pay in money, unless the parties come to a fresh agreement to that effect, as by striking a balance in money (*Harrison* v. *Luke* (1845) 14 M. & W. 139). See further, Benjamin, *Sale*, p. 3, note (*e*).

In Scots law the two contracts are on the same footing as regards moveables, but there is an important distinction between a sale and an exchange ('excambion') of lands. In sale, warrandice is a personal obligation, unless there is an express agreement for real warrandice; but in excambion there is an *implied real* warrandice, in virtue of which the party suffering eviction from the subject he has received in exchange has a right of recourse upon his own lands in preference even to third parties who may have acquired rights. Ersk. ii. 3. 28.

§ 2. *Mancipatio*, which was to some extent the forerunner of contract of sale in the early law, required for its validity a solemn ceremonial to which aliens could not competently be parties. Informal sales by bare agreement were no doubt common, but the early law did not recognise them as grounds of action unless some solemnity of word or deed was superinduced upon them by oath, stipulation, nexum, or the like, for

[1] *Od.* i. 430.

the words used by the same poet in another place: 'he bought her with his wealth.' But the view of Nerva and Proculus is the truer one; for as we distinguish between buying and selling and between buyer and seller, so the wares and the price are different things; but in barter we cannot determine which is buyer and which is seller.

2. Sale is a contract *iuris gentium*, and is therefore completed which the presence of the parties was an indispensable requisite. The distinctive point about contract of sale is, that it depends on simple consent, which of itself creates mutual rights and duties such as delivery and payment. This effect is here ascribed to the *Jus Gentium*, a phrase vaguely denoting that body of institutions and rules which was originally adopted or worked out by the *praetor peregrinus* to regulate the dealings of aliens *inter se* or with citizens, and was gradually sanctioned by the authority of the urban praetors and the jurists as binding between citizen and citizen also, till it ultimately became a main department of the Roman law, parallel to the *jus civile*, but applicable to all freemen alike.

The consensual and real contracts were wholly institutions of this 'law of nations.' As regards sale, the all-important stage in its history was the recognition of a formless agreement to sell as actionable, and the conversion of the early form of the *actio empti*, which was based upon stipulations and express agreements, into a *bonae fidei* action, a change which probably took place in the last century of the Republic. One of the chief advantages of the new system was that parties in different places could now negotiate a sale, because it required no words of style as a stipulation did, and consent might be notified by letter or verbal message.

It may be remarked in this connection that the Roman texts throw no light on the difficult questions as to the time at which a contract by correspondence is to be held as completed, or within which a retractation of a proposal or an acceptance can be effectually made. The peculiar character attaching to the modern postal and telegraph services would in any case have altered the conditions of the problem. Still the theoretical discussions of the modern civil lawyers are interesting, *e.g.*

agitur et inter absentes contrahi potest et per nuntium et per litteras.

Vangerow, § 603; Windscheid, § 306: the extreme views are—(1) that there is no contract till the second party's acceptance of the first party's offer is brought to the knowledge of the latter; and on the other side (2) that a manifestation of will or intention to accept closes the bargain, even before it is communicated to the proposer: but there is great variety of opinion among the partisans of the second view as to how much must be done in order to bind the proposer and bar him from a revocation of his offer; some hold the writing of a letter of acceptance, some its despatch, some its arrival at the destination fixed, to be sufficient notice to make the bargain absolute.

By our law the contract is concluded by the posting of the acceptance within the prescribed or a seasonable time, no matter what becomes of the letter afterwards. *Dunlop* v. *Higgins* (1848) 1 H. L. C. 381; *Household Fire Insurance Co.* (1879) 4 Ex. Div. 216; cp. Pollock, *Contract*, p. 32 sq. and note B; Bell, *Princ.* § 78.

Terminology. The terms employed in connection with sale are of some interest. The bilateral contracts, especially sale and hiring, are frequently denoted by double expressions (*emptio-venditio, locatio-conductio*) corresponding to the twofold aspect of the transaction. But such precision of language is unnecessary, for the one term necessarily calls up the other by association, and would also be excessively cumbrous for ordinary purposes. Hence we find that where no emphasis is to be laid on the mutual relationship of the parties, the legal writers use either expression indifferently to designate the contract as a whole, *e.g.* Ulpian in L. 2, just as the French and we ourselves usually speak of 'vente' 'sale,' while the Germans from the opposite point of view call it 'kauf.' It is, perhaps, an indication of a certain liking for legal pedantry in the Roman mind, that we not uncommonly meet with tautologies of this kind in lay writers also.

Ihering makes too much of the double names sometimes applied to the bilateral contracts when he presses this usage into the service of his peculiar theory that the Romans never conceived

by consent, and may be concluded by messenger or letter, without the parties being present.

---

of bilateral obligation in our sense at all, and that these contracts really consisted of two unilateral agreements (originally two stipulations) placed side by side, and yet mutually independent. Cp. Mommsen, *Beiträge*, iii. 418.

Emere, as its compounds indicate, and as Festus remarks in three places, had in early Latin the same sense as *sumere* (take) or *accipere* (take of consent, *i.e.* receive), but there seems to be no example of this use in the classical authors; even in Plautus it means to buy, to acquire for an equivalent in money. There is no warrant for the assumption that the original meaning survived alongside of the specialised sense.

The verb and its derivatives (*emptio, emptus*) are used of two stages in a sale, sometimes of the conclusion (*perfectio*) of the contract, sometimes of its performance and the resulting acquisition of property rights.

Merx is used by Paul in this text as a technical term for the thing sold as opposed to the price, when he is pointing out the distinction between sale and exchange. He probably felt that *res* was too ambiguous for this purpose. It may be noted that *merx* does not occur in the definitions of sale given by Gaius (iii. 149, sq.), and in the *Institutes* (iii. tit. 23). Elsewhere it is used without special reference to sale, in the general sense of 'merchandise,' 'wares,' and it is said not to apply to immoveables nor to slaves (D. 50. 16. 66; ib. 207).

Mercari is merely a synonym for *emere*, as *distrahere* is for *vendere*.

Alienare includes, of course, many other forms of divesting oneself of property besides sale. It connotes nothing more than the parting with a thing; sometimes as opposed to sale it implies transfer of ownership (D. 50. 16. 67 pr.; ib. 28).

Lastly, *lex venditionis* is a phrase that frequently occurs to denote the terms which the parties have agreed on when making their bargain; any special condition, reservation, or obligation was incorporated in the *lex*, which apparently might be either written or oral. Compare the expressions *legem dare fundo*, *lex pignoris*, *lex censoria*, and the like, in the *Digest*, *passim*.

2. ULPIANUS libro I ad Sabinum.

Inter patrem et filium contrahi emptio non potest, sed de rebus castrensibus potest.

1. Sine pretio nulla uenditio est: non autem pretii numeratio, sed conuentio perficit sine scriptis habitam emptionem.

L. 2 pr.—So rigorously did the early law insist on the unity of the family, and its subordination to its one head, that no dependent member of it could hold property for himself; and it was a corollary of this, that there could be no civil obligation between a *filiusfamilias* and his *paterfamilias*, or any other person subject to the same *potestas* (D. 5. 1. 11; Gaius, iv. 78), though there might be natural obligation. In the early Empire this incapacity was removed, to a limited extent, both as regards property and obligation: a *filius* might have a separate estate belonging to him in full property, consisting of his acquisitions as a soldier on active service (*castrense peculium*), in respect of which he could contract even with his father on an equal footing: *filii familias in castrensi peculio uice patrum familiarum funguntur* (D. 14. 6. 2). The same doctrine was extended, under Constantine and his successors, to a son's earnings in the Civil Service and the Church (*peculium quasi-castrense*).

§ 1. It was a settled rule that a definite (*certum*) price was of the essence of sale, *Inst.* iii. 23. 1; and further, the price must be serious (L. 36), *i.e.* there must be intention to exact it; but it was sufficient for the validity of the contract that there had once been a price really incumbent upon the buyer to pay: nonpayment, or release from payment at a later date, did not nullify the sale. *Code* iv. 38. 9: *empti fides ac uenditi sine quantitate nulla est: placito autem pretio non numerato, sed solum tradita possessione istiusmodi contractus non habetur irritus, nec idcirco is qui comparauit minus recte possidet quod soluta summa quam dari conuenerat negatur.* Cp. Pothier, *Vente*, § 18.

The requirement of certainty did not mean that the price must of necessity be stated in the contract, but only that it should be determinable in the manner therein agreed on. In particular, it may here be noted that, according to a special decision of Justinian (*Code* iv. 38. 15; cp. *Inst.* iii. 23. 1), an agreement that the price should be fixed by the valuation of a third party named

2. ULPIAN.

There can be no contract of sale between a father and son, except with reference to what falls under the son's *peculium castrense*.

1. There can be no sale without a price; but it is not the payment of the price, but the agreement of parties, which completes a sale carried through without writing.

---

was effectual if he actually fixed a price; but if such party would not, or could not make a valuation, the sale was void, because no price had been settled. It was thus, in principle, a conditional sale. The decision was in accordance with the opinion of Proculus; Labeo had held such an agreement void (G. iii. 140). It follows from *Code l. c.* that the arbitrator must be named, (cp. D. 45. 1. 43); and that his valuation was binding, however capricious it might be, though such a result is contrary to the general principle that a reference to an arbitrator, in a *bonae fidei* contract, is to be taken as a reference to the *arbitrium boni viri* (D. 50. 17. 22, 1). But see Pothier, *Vente*, § 24.

If there was no agreement at all about the price, or the mode of ascertaining it,—*e.g.* if I order goods without asking the price, or give out a job without mentioning terms,—that was not contract of sale at all, but an innominate contract, under which a money equivalent for the goods delivered or work done could be recovered by *actio praescriptis verbis:* if the sum claimed was unreasonable, the judge had power to modify it. See *Inst.* iii. 24. 1; D. 19. 5. 22; 17. 2. 79; 18. 1. 35, 1.

The principles bearing on agreement to sell at a valuation have been adopted into English law (*Vickers* v. *Vickers* (1867) L. R. 4 Eq. 529, at p. 535). In that case one party, after appointing a valuer, refused to allow him to proceed with the valuation, and thus prevented the completion of the contract; *held*, that there was no existing contract which the Court could specifically enforce, and that it was impossible to substitute another arbitrator.

But in cases where the contract does not fix the price, or point out the mode of ascertaining it, our law has developed the idea of an implied understanding that the buyer shall pay a *reasonable* price. See S. G. B. §§ 8, 9; Benj. p. 88.

Proof of Sale. The general rule was, that none of the

3. ULPIANUS libro XXVIII ad Sabinum.

Si res ita distracta sit, ut si displicuisset inempta esset, constat non esse sub condicione distractam, sed resolui emptionem sub condicione.

consensual contracts required to be in writing (*Inst.* iii. tit. 22): hence, in countries which have followed the Roman law, all kinds of evidence, parole as well as written, are admitted in proof of the commercial contract for the sale of goods. The rules of evidence in England and America are peculiar, the famous Statute of Frauds (29 Chas. II. c. 3, sec. 17) having made a note or memorandum in writing indispensable for a valid contract ' for the sale of any goods, wares, and merchandise, for the price of £10 or upwards,' except the buyer has received part of the goods, or has given something in earnest or in part payment; see S. G. B. § 4. By the statutory law of most countries writing is indispensable for the sale of certain kinds of property not coming under the description of merchandise, *e.g.* lands, ships, patent rights, etc.; but it does not seem to have been essential in any case by Roman law.

The parties might, however, agree to reduce the contract to writing, and in that case Justinian enacted that its completion was suspended till the deed or record was duly executed; and in the meantime there was *locus poenitentiae*, so that either party might resile, subject to the penalty, if buyer, of forfeiting the arrha he had given (if any), or, if seller, of restoring double that which he had received. *Code* iv. 21. 17; *Inst.* iii. 23 pr. His object was to obviate disputes, which had previously occurred, as to the effect of such an agreement, writing having been employed sometimes with the intention of suspending the contract, sometimes merely to preserve evidence of its terms. Cp. Ersk. iii. 2. 2.

L. 3. A special agreement of this sort ' ut, si res displicuerit, inempta sit ' (hence known as *pactum displicentiae*) belongs to the class of adjected pacts which were in use to be made either at the time of the contract as subsidiary to it, or after an interval for the purpose of modifying the existing obligations. The party in whose favour this pact was made (usually the buyer) reserved power to himself to resile from the contract at his pleasure if he were dissatisfied. Sometimes the right was made conditional

3. ULPIAN.

When a thing is sold on the terms that, if disapproved by the buyer, it shall not be held as bought, it is settled that it is not the completion, but the recission of the sale that is made dependent upon the condition.

upon payment of a fine (*multa poenitentialis*); sometimes a period within which it must be exercised was agreed upon; if no period was fixed, disapproval might be intimated, and the thing returned within sixty days—this was the statutory rule, at all events, in sales of slaves (D 21. 1. 31, 22 and 23). If the party empowered did resile, it was held that there had been an effective sale which was now put an end to by a resolutive condition: *sed et illa emptio pura est, ubi convenit ut si displicuerit, intra diem certum inemptas it* (D. 41. 4. 2, 5; cp. C. iv. 58. 4; D. 18. 5. 6; 43. 24. 11, 13). It was, however, in the power of the parties to invert this agreement, so as to give it the character of a suspensive condition ('condition precedent') (D. 19. 5. 20 pr., 1; *Inst.* iii. 23. 4). The actions available for enforcing the pact were the *actio emti* (D. 19. 1. 11, 3) and the *actio redhibitoria*, under the edict of the aediles (C. iv. 58. 4). If the party resiling had in the meantime constituted any real rights over the subject, they stood; *e.g.* if the buyer had hypothecated the thing, the seller could demand that before rescinding the contract he should clear off the hypothec (D. 20. 6. 3). Where the condition is resolutive, the most important effect is that the ownership of the thing sold passes by delivery to the vendee, who can divest himself of it by giving timeous notice of dissatisfaction. Suppose the thing has been injured or totally destroyed without the fault of the vendee, is he still entitled to disapprove and have the sale cancelled? There seems to be no direct authority on the point, since Julian's statement in D. 18. 2. 2, 1, that the risk passes with the property under a resolutive condition, may be meant to apply only to *in diem addictio* and such other conditions as are not dependent on the mere will of the party seeking to cancel the contract. Some civilians think that the vendor bore all risks; others hold that the sale could not be cancelled if the thing had ceased to exist, *i.e.* that the risk of total destruction lay upon the vendee according to the maxim *res perit domino*, whereas the risk of deterioration remained with the vendor.

4. Pomponius libro ix ad Sabinum.

Et liberi hominis et loci sacri et religiosi, qui haberi non potest, emptio intellegitur, si ab ignorante emitur,

5. Paulus libro v ad Sabinum.

quia difficile dinosci potest liber homo a seruo.

The corresponding bargain in our law is 'sale on trial,' or 'on approbation.' As to the passing of the property in goods sold on approval, see S. G. B., § 20, rule 4. *Head* v. *Tattersall* (1871) 7 Ex. 7, is an example of such a provision operating as a *resolutive* condition ('condition subsequent'). A bought a horse of B, warranted to have been hunted with the Bicester hounds, under the condition that he was to be at liberty to return it, if it did not answer its description, up to the following Wednesday. While in A's possession, the horse took fright and sustained injuries, though not through any neglect or default on his part. A returned the horse within the time, as not corresponding to the warrantry, and sued B for the price he had paid. *Held*, that A's right to return was unaffected by the accident that happened to the horse while in his possession; and observed, that the effect of the contract was to vest the property in the buyer, subject to a right of rescission in a particular event, when it would revest on the seller, who as eventual owner should bear the risk of depreciation. As a general rule, however, where goods are sent on trial or 'on sale or return,' the condition, while unfulfilled, *suspends* the contract, and there is no completed sale 'until the approval is given either expressly, or by implication resulting from keeping the goods beyond the time allowed for trial.' See *Elphick* v. *Barnes* (1880), 5 C. P. D. 321, for circumstances in which the sale of a horse, under a condition of eight days' trial, was held not to be absolute, so long as the vendee had an option to return; the horse having died on the third day without fault of either party, the maxim *res perit domino* was applied, and the vendor held not entitled to recover the price.

In the Scotch case, *Graham* v. *Pollock* (1763) M. 14198, effect was given to a *pactum displicentiae*. *Brown* v. *Marr* (1880) 7 R. 427, and *Macdonald* (1888) 15 R. 998, may be consulted for divergent opinions on the question whether the condition implied in a bargain of 'sale or return' is resolutive or suspensive.

4. POMPONIUS.

The purchase of a free man and of sacred and religious ground, which is incapable of appropriation, is considered valid, provided the buyer is ignorant of their true character,

5. PAUL.

because it is difficult to distinguish a free man from a slave.

LL. 4, 5.—When an agreement was impossible of performance because it stipulated for something either physically impossible or, which was held equivalent (D 45. 1. 137, 6), inconsistent with legal principle, the agreement was void according to the general rule '*imposibilium nulla obligatio*,' and the obligor got off his engagement scot free. But an exception was made in favour of one who bought a freeman under the impression that he was a slave, probably for the practical reason stated in L. 5 that such a mistake was highly excusable. Some of the conditions under which the 'peculiar institution' existed at Rome subjected the purchaser, no matter how careful, to a serious risk of error; for, in addition to the ordinary abuses of the slave trade, such as kidnapping, substitution, and the like, with which readers of Plautus are familiar, it was common for free men to let themselves be sold as slaves in order to share in the price—a practice so rife under the Empire that the fraud had to be repressed by refusing such persons the right to assert their freedom (D. 40. tit. 13); and, further, it was only to a limited extent that the slave population was distinguishable by marked characteristics of race or colour. The sale of a supposed slave was, therefore, treated as the sale of a thing not belonging to the seller; the *bonâ fide* purchaser was protected against the risk of the putative slave proving his free status, just as he was in the other case against eviction at the hands of the true owner, by the *stipulatio duplae*. See *infra* L. 34, 2; 70 (which proves that fraud on the seller's part was not an essential condition of his responsibility, as might be inferred from *Inst.* iii. 23. 5); D. 21. 2. 39, 3.

But Pomponius does not treat the sale of a free person as the only exceptional case; he appears to hold generally that, if the buyer is in good faith, every sale of a *res extra commercium* is valid to the same effect, *i.e.* it subjects the seller to liability as

6. Pomponius libro ix ad Sabinum.

Sed Celsus filius ait hominem liberum scientem te emere non posse nec cuiuscumque rei si scias alienationem [prohibitam] esse: ut sacra et religiosa loca aut quorum commercium non sit, ut publica, quae non in pecunia populi, sed in publico usu habeantur, ut est campus Martius.

1. Si fundus annua bima trima die ea lege uenisset, ut, si in diem statutum pecunia soluta non esset, fundus inemptus foret et

---

for eviction: and the passage in the *Institutes* (iii. 23. 5), is to be read in the same sense. Ulpian, Paul, and Modestine, on the other hand, appear to indicate the contrary opinion (LL. 22–24; 34, 1; 62, 1 *infra*, and notes). Savigny (*Obl.* ii. § 81), with many able commentators, denies that there is any contradiction in the passages cited; but even among those who agree in denying that there is an 'antinomy,' there is no consensus of opinion as to the meaning of the authorities; some hold that the validity of the sale is generally recognised, others find the opposite doctrine in all the texts.

L. 6 pr.—Some inferior MSS. insert '*prohibitam*' before *esse*: 'if you know that the law declares them incapable of alienation.' Some editors get the same sense by inserting '*non*.' A construction for the genitive '*cuiuscumque rei*' may be got either by supplying '*emptionem esse*' from what precedes, or by repeating '*alienationem*.'

Res sacrae and *religiosae* are defined in *Inst.* ii. 1. 7–9; Gaius, ii. §§ 6, 9. *Res publicae* are of two kinds: (1) some belong to the people in the same sense as things belong to a private owner (*e.g.* the *ager publicus*—'crown lands,' as we say), and these were said to be *in patrimonio seu pecunia populi*—they were capable of alienation, and were the subject of contract quite commonly; (2) others are *in usu publico, i.e.* owing to their nature or destination no private person can own them, but all may use them—they cannot be alienated so long as they retain their character.

§ 1. This is an example of the pact known as *lex commissoria*, which entitles one party to a contract to treat it as a nullity in case the other party fails to fulfil his engagements at the proper time (D. 18. tit. 3. *passim*). In practice it was imposed on the buyer,

6. POMPONIUS.

But Celsus the younger says that you cannot knowingly purchase a free man, nor anything whatever which you know to be inalienable; for example, sacred and religious spots, or those which are withdrawn from commerce, as public places, which are not held to belong patrimonially to the community, but to be dedicated to the public use, *e.g.* the Campus Martius.

1. If lands are sold to be paid for by instalments in one, two, and three years, under the condition that, if the price be not paid

in the interest of the seller, as a security for payment of the price in credit sales, and it could not be enforced by the buyer against the will of the seller. As soon as the price was due and unpaid, the seller could, without making a formal demand for payment, cancel the sale, or at his option hold the buyer to it, and sue him for the price and damages; but when he had once declared his choice in any way he could not go back upon it. In case of doubt, this agreement was treated as a resolutive condition.

Where the price was payable by instalments, the right to resile generally arose as soon as one of the instalments was in arrear, so here and D. 4. 4. 38 pr.; but it was quite permissible to make the agreement inoperative till the date of the last instalment had passed without payment. Cp. D. 13. 7. 8, 3, which exemplifies the different ways of conferring on the pledgee the right to sell a pledge given in security of an annual payment, and supplies two forms of such a clause (1) *si qua pecunia sua die soluta non erit*, the effect of which was to give a power of sale after default of the first payment, and (2) *nisi sua quaque die pecunia soluta esset*, which suspended the power of sale till the last instalment was due and unpaid.

This point may be illustrated by the class of questions arising in our Courts upon contracts for the sale of goods to be delivered and paid for by instalments. It is not settled whether default in making delivery of the first or any subsequent instalment goes to the root of the consideration and justifies the buyer in cancelling the contract, apart from any special evidence of the intention of parties; but the failure of the buyer to pay the first, or any subsequent instalment of the price, is not regarded as enough

ut, si interim emptor fundum coluerit fructusque ex eo perceperit, inempto eo facto restituerentur, et ut, quanti minoris postea alii uenisset, ut id emptor uenditori praestaret: ad diem pecunia non soluta, placet uenditori ex uendito eo nomine actionem esse. nec conturbari debemus, quod inempto fundo facto dicatur

---

per se to entitle the seller to rescind the contract. *Freeth* v. *Burr* (1874) L. R. 9 C. P. 208 was the case of a contract to deliver pig-iron in two parcels, half in two weeks, the remainder in four: payment, net cash fourteen days after delivery of each parcel. Owing to delay of six months in delivering the first parcel, the buyers refused to pay for it, claiming a right to set off the loss that they had sustained through being obliged to procure other iron; but they still urged the delivery of the second parcel. The seller treated the refusal to pay as a breach and an abandonment of the contract, and declined to deliver any more. *Held* he was wrong and liable in damages for the non-delivery; and observed that 'in cases of this sort, where the question is whether the one party is set free by the action of the other, the real matter for consideration is, whether the acts or conduct of the one do, or do not, amount to an intimation of an intention to abandon the contract.' Cp. *Mersey Steel Co.* (1874) 9 App. Ca. 434; S. G. B. § 33; *Turnbull* (1874) 1 R. 730; Bell, *Prin.* § 108.

The *lex c.* had certain penal consequences, for the buyer is (by implication of law, where not by express agreement) bound to forfeit what he has given as earnest, and what he has paid to account of the price, but is allowed to retain, as compensation for his loss, the fruits he has meantime gathered (D. 18. 3. 6; ib. 4, 1; ib. 8).

The seller might even go so far as to stipulate by a special covenant that the vendee should be responsible to him for any loss sustained on a re-sale of the goods, and for the produce or fruits that had accrued from the subject *pendente conditione:* as in the case here figured, and in D. 18. 3. 4, 3.

The *actio venditi* was the proper action for enforcing restoration of the subject and its accessions, and all other claims arising under the pact; for the action on a *bonae fidei* contract extended to all matters embraced in any adjected pact, and was competent even where it had been agreed that the contract should be off in

by the term fixed, the sale shall be held cancelled; and if the purchaser in the interval crops the lands, he shall account for the value upon the rescission of the sale, and shall make up to the vendor any loss he may subsequently sustain by reselling for a less price,—it is settled that, if the price be not paid by the term appointed, the vendor can bring an action on the sale. The statement that an action on sale will lie, although the sale is declared to be off, need not occasion any difficulty; for in all cases of sale the intention is more important than the language:

---

a certain event—this was the opinion of Sabinus; but Proculus, considering it absurd that an action intended to secure the execution of a contract should be used to annul it, held that an *actio praescriptis verbis* was the proper procedure (D. 19. 5. 12). The Sabinian view, followed with some hesitation by Paul (D. 18. 5. 6), and adopted here with more confidence by Pomponius, prevailed in the end./ Cp. D. 18. 3. 4 pr.; 19. 1. 11, 3.; ib. 6. The pact (he argues) was intended simply to release the vendor from his contractual engagements on the expiry of a certain period, and to invest him again with the free disposal of his property, but not to have retroactive effect so as to annul all that had gone before, as if the contract had never been made. The continued efficacy of the contract is plain, both from the penal consequences which followed, and from the consideration that, if it had been avoided to all intents, the *lex commissoria* as an adjected pact would have been equally void.

It is a disputed question whether the seller was entitled to bring a *rei vindicatio, i.e.* to claim the thing sold as his, on the ground that the property in it (which passed to the buyer upon delivery where credit was given) had been revested in him as the direct result of his exercising his right to rescind the sale. The main authorities on the point are the Rescripts in C. iv. 54. 1–4, and they seem to yield a negative answer. Of course where the agreement was to operate as a *suspensive* condition, the seller as undivested owner could maintain a real action against the person in possession.

The tendency of modern law is more favourable to the transfer of property and the security of commerce; it rejects the idea of any implied condition or hypothec for security of the price after

actionem ex uendito futuram esse : in emptis enim et uenditis potius id quod actum, quam id quod dictum sit sequendum est, et cum lege id dictum sit, apparet hoc dumtaxat actum esse, ne uenditor emptori pecunia ad diem non soluta obligatus esset, non ut omnis obligatio empti et uenditi utrique solueretur.

2. Condicio, quae initio contractus dicta est, postea alia pactione immutari potest, sicuti etiam abiri a tota emptione potest, si nondum impleta sunt quae utrimque praestari debuerunt.

7. ULPIANUS libro XXVIII ad Sabinum.

Haec uenditio serui 'si rationes domini computasset arbitrio'

---

actual delivery; and even express conditions, of the nature of the *lex commissoria*, to enable the seller to rescind a completed sale and reclaim the goods after they have been delivered into the actual or constructive possession of the buyer, in the event of his failure to pay the price by an appointed day, are jealously interpreted. A *resolutive* condition of this kind is treated in Scots law as a personal obligation only, effectual between the vendor and vendee, but of no avail against third persons, *e.g.* the creditors of the vendee or *bonâ fide* purchasers from him; but if the condition as to payment be so conceived as to be truly *suspensive* of the sale, the property does not pass till the condition is purified, and therefore it cannot be attached by the buyer's creditors (Bell, *Com.* i. 260). In England, the vendor's sole remedy against the vendee who has got possession of his goods, and wrongfully neglects or refuses to pay for them, is, like that of other creditors, by personal action for the price: he cannot treat the contract as rescinded, because the vendee makes default in paying at the appointed time (*Martindale* v. *Smith* (1841) 1 Q. B. 389), a stipulation as to the time of payment not being deemed by English law to be of the essence of the contract (S. G. B. § 11). Similarly, by the civil law, the *actio venditi* was the only competent process for a vendor who had sold on credit, and given delivery without securing himself by the *lex commissoria*. C. iv. 30. 8; C. iv. 44. 14; Pothier, *Vente*, § 475.

But as regards the earlier stages of sale, before the buyer is in actual possession, our law studies the interest of the unpaid seller by giving him certain *rights against the goods:* (1) if the seller is

now here, notwithstanding the terms used in the contract, it is plain that the parties intended simply that the vendor should not continue under obligation to the vendee in the event of the money not being punctually paid, and not that both sides should be released from every obligation incident to a sale.

2. A term made at the inception of the contract may be varied by a subsequent agreement, just as the sale can be abandoned altogether, so long as the parties have not fulfilled their mutual obligations.

7. ULPIAN.

The sale of a slave on these terms, ' if he give in satisfactory

---

still in possession of the goods, and the buyer, whether solvent or insolvent, makes default in payment of the price, the seller has by English law a 'lien,' by Scots law a 'right of retention,' differing in principle but similar in practical effect (see *Black* (1867) 6 Macp. 136); (2) if the goods have passed out of the hands of the seller into the possession of a neutral carrier or middleman in the course of transit to the buyer, the seller has, by the common law of both countries, the right of 'stoppage *in transitu*,' *i.e.* of intercepting the goods, if he can, and resuming possession, provided the buyer is insolvent; and (3) a right of re-sale under certain circumstances. See generally, S. G. B. §§. 40-49, and remarks of Bowen, L. J., on stoppage *in transitu*, in *Kendal* (1883) 11 Q. B. Div. at p. 368. It is now admitted that the seller, by merely exercising the right of stoppage, does not rescind the contract of sale, but is still a creditor for the price. *Stoppel & Co.* v. *Stoddart* (1850), 13 D. 61 (Scotch), and *Kemp* v. *Falk* (1882) 7 App. Ca. 573.

§ 2. '*Condicio*' has not its technical sense here; it means simply any term of a sale. Sale, like all contracts, can be revoked by *contrarius consensus* or *contraria voluntas* of the parties *re integra*, so long as nothing has followed upon the conclusion of the contract. Matters are not entire if, *e.g.*, the seller is freed by accidental destruction of the thing sold. C. iv. 45. 2.

L. 7 pr.—The case put is that of the sale of a slave by his owner, subject to the condition 'if he renders accounts to my satisfaction,' and the question is, what is the import of the con-

condicionalis est: condicionales autem uenditiones tunc perficiuntur, cum impleta fuerit condicio. sed utrum haec est uenditionis condicio, si ipse dominus putasset suo arbitrio, an uero si arbitrio uiri boni? nam si arbitrium domini accipiamus, uenditio nulla est, quemadmodum si quis ita uendiderit, si uoluerit, uel stipulanti sic spondeat ' si uoluero, decem dabo ': neque enim debet in arbitrium rei conferri, an sit obstrictus. placuit itaque ueteribus magis in uiri boni arbitrium id collatum uideri quam in domini. si igitur rationes potuit accipere nec accepit, uel accepit, fingit autem se non accepisse, impleta condicio emptionis est et ex empto uenditor conueniri potest.

1. Huiusmodi emptio ' quanti tu eum emisti,' ' quantum pretii in arca habeo,' ualet: nec enim incertum est pretium tam euidenti uenditione: magis enim ignoratur quanti emptus sit, quam in rei ueritate incertum est.

2. Si quis ita emerit: 'est mihi fundus emptus centum et quanto pluris eum uendidero,' ualet uenditio et statim impletur:

---

dition? If it means that the accounts are to be submitted absolutely to the discretionary judgment of the seller, the sale is a nullity; it falls under that class of conditional dispositions where the condition depends on the mere will of the person to be bound ('the obligor'), which therefore, as a rule, create no obligation, no 'vinculum juris quo *necessitate* adstringimur.' D. 44. 7. 8: *sub hac condicione 'si uolam' nulla fit obligatio: pro non dicto enim est quod dare nisi uelis cogi non possis:* so in D. 45. 1. 17, *et saepe*, of stipulations: and as the engagements in a contract of sale are reciprocal, neither party is bound, C. iv. 38. 13: *In uendentis uel ementis uoluntatem collata condicione comparandi, quia non adstringit necessitate contrahentes, obligatio nulla est: idcirco dominus inuitus ex huiusmodi conuentione rem propriam uel quilibet alius distrahere non compellitur.* (Sale on approval, 'si res emtori placuerit,' must be treated as an exception from this general principle: Savigny, *Syst.* iii. § 117. 2). But the condition admits of an interpretation which will support the sale, for Ulpian lays it down (in the same book of his Commentary on Sabinus, from which this text is taken) as a general rule of construction, that a condition qualifying a *bonae fidei* contract whereby

accounts to his master,' is a conditional sale; and such sales are complete when the condition is fulfilled. But does the condition here mean, that the slave's accounts shall be submitted to the judgment of his master, or of a fair-minded person? If we take it as referring to the master's opinion, the sale is void—it is just like selling on condition that one chooses, or like answering the question in a stipulation thus, 'If I please, I will give ten aurei,' for it must not be left to the debtor to decide whether he is bound or not. And so the old jurists adopted the view that this condition imported a reference to the judgment of a fair person other than the master. If, therefore, the master might have had accounts stated but declined to take them, or if he has received them but gives out the contrary, the condition is purified, and the action on purchase can be brought against the vendor.

1. A purchase on such terms as 'for what you gave for him,' 'for the money I have in my coffer,' is good; for the price is not uncertain, where the terms are so plain: the parties, indeed, may be ignorant of the amount of the price, but it is not really indeterminate.

2. If a purchaser makes these terms, 'I buy the lands for 100 aurei and whatever more I shall sell them for,' the sale is valid

---

any matter is referred to the opinion of the owner or his agent is to be taken as a reference to the judgment of a *vir bonus* (D. 50. 17. 22, 1). The jurists, applying this principle to the present case, made the condition dependent on a rational, instead of an arbitrary, judgment. The *bonus vir* is a sort of standard embodiment of honesty and fair dealing, and aptitude for the equitable settlement of disputes, just as the respectable householder (*bonus paterfamilias*) serves as a criterion of his distinctive qualities, ordinary and reasonable care and prudence.

§ 1. The contract is incomplete if the price is left open; but it is sufficiently fixed, if it is defined by some objective fact, past or present, at the time the contract is made. It is, in fact, certain, and all that remains is to ascertain it. Cp. D. 45. 1. 75.

§ 2. If a part of the price is fixed within the contract, it is enough; the rest may be left to depend on a future and uncertain

habet enim certum pretium centum, augebitur autem pretium, si pluris emptor fundum uendiderit.

8. Pomponius libro IX ad Sabinum.

Nec emptio nec uenditio sine re quae ueneat potest intellegi. et tamen fructus et partus futuri recte ementur, ut, cum editus esset partus, iam tunc, cum contractum esset negotium, uenditio facta intellegatur: sed si id egerit uenditor, ne nascatur aut fiant, ex empto agi posse.

---

event. Cp. D. 19. 1. 13, 24. It may be inferred that a sale would not be complete if the whole price were fixed by reference to a future contingency, *e.g.* I agree to sell you a house for the same price as may be got for the adjoining one; that is a conditional sale. Cp. Pothier, § 28.

L. 8.—It is essential to the idea of sale that there should be an object (*res*) to which the contract may attach. But the law allowed things not yet in existence, things which might never exist to be sold; how is this to be reconciled with the rule that there can be no sale *sine re*? Two cases of the sale of future and uncertain things must be distinguished: (i.) A sale of what might be expected in the ordinary course of nature to exist, as a future crop or the young of animals, called by the civilians '*emptio rei speratae*,' was conditional upon the thing coming into existence; if it never existed, there was no claim on either side apart from fault (*e.g.* interference to prevent the land or the animals yielding their increase, cp. D. 50. 17. 161); if it did, the buyer must pay the price, no matter whether the quality came up to his expectations or not. See pr. *supra*; 39, § 1 (price in proportion to the quantity of crop); D. 45. 1. 73 (where a stipulation for a future crop, etc., is treated as *pura*, but not exigible till performance becomes possible). Pomponius seeks to harmonise such a sale with the general rule by the fiction that, as soon as the thing actually exists, the contract draws back to the date of the completed agreement. (ii.) The sale of an expectation dependent on a mere chance was sale pure and simple ('*emptio spei*' or '*aleae*'); here the contract is to stand under all circumstances, and the price

and is immediately complete; for the seller gets a fixed price of 100 aurei, which will be increased if the purchaser gets more for the lands.

8. POMPONIUS.

There cannot possibly be a purchase or sale without a thing for sale; and yet future produce and young unborn may lawfully be purchased, with the result that, on the occurrence of the birth, the sale is regarded as completed at the time when the bargain was made; but if the seller tries to prevent the subject coming into existence, the action on purchase is competent.

---

must be paid in any event, whether much, or little, or nothing comes of the chance. The contract is absolute for the buyer, but the obligation of the seller is conditional upon the existence of the thing. Pomponius treats it as an exceptional case of a sale *sine re;* but that is a misconception, the true subject of the sale being the prospect or chance of getting the thing, and not the thing itself, just as in the sale of a lottery ticket, or of a horse's chance of winning a race, the equivalent for the price is a chance, which is very likely to prove worthless, but in the meantime possesses a money value. Such a chance is a '*res*,' in the wide jural sense of the word, quite as much as a claim of debt or other incorporeal is. For examples of '*emptio spei*,' see also D. 19. 1. 12; ib. 18; 17. 4. 7; ib. 11. The usual example, a cast of a fisherman's net, is rather a case of hire of materials and labour than of sale, at least as regards fish in the sea, which are not the property of the fisherman till he catches them.

It was a question of construction in each case whether the parties intended the one kind of bargain or the other. It is not clear, as is often asserted, that there was a presumption in case of doubt that a conditional sale (*emptio rei speratae*) was meant.

Missilia means things thrown as largess to the mob: it was held to be the intention of the owner to transfer the property to an uncertain person, and so each individual in the crowd becomes owner of what he gets (*Inst.* ii. 1. 46; D. 41. 1. 9, 7); the present text implies that the appropriation is not complete till the scramble is over, the seller in the case figured not being

1. Aliquando tamen et sine re uenditio intellegitur, ueluti cum quasi alea emitur. quod fit, cum captum piscium uel auium uel missilium emitur: emptio enim contrahitur etiam si nihil inciderit, quia spei emptio est: et quod missilium nomine eo casu captum est si euictum fuerit, nulla eo nomine ex empto obligatio contrahitur, quia id actum intellegitur.

9. ULPIANUS libro XXVIII ad Sabinum.

In uenditionibus et emptionibus consensum debere intercedere palam est: ceterum siue in ipsa emptione dissentient siue in

---

answerable for what he picks up, and then has wrested from him (*evictum*), but only for what he gets and can keep.

For the sale of *future* things in the sense of goods to be made to order, to be manufactured, see *Inst.* iii. 24. 4; D. 19. 2. 2, 1; h. t. 20 and 65; Windscheid, § 401. 3.

It is mostly in this sense that we now use the term: '"future goods" means goods to be manufactured, or acquired by the seller after the making of the contract of sale,' S. G. B. § 62: they may be the subject of an agreement to sell, but not of an actual sale so as to pass the property and the risk, § 5, cp. §§ 18–20; *Lunn* v. *Thornton* (1845) 1 C. B. 379 ('goods which should at any time thereafter remain and be in the dwelling-house'). This distinction is quite foreign to the Roman law.

The sale of a *spes* is recognised by our chief modern authorities —Pothier, § 6; Erskine, 3. 3. 3.; Benj. p. 87; but there seem to be no decided cases quite in point. See, however, *dicta* per Martin, B., 'No doubt a man *may* buy a chance of obtaining goods, but here the plaintiff bought the *slates*' (*Buddle* v. *Green* (1857) 27 L. J. Ex. 24); and per Richards, C. B., 'If a man will make a purchase of a chance, he must abide by the consequences' (*Hitchcock* v. *Giddings*, 4 Price 135). The sale of an expected inheritance (which is not illegal by our law, *Ragg* v. *Brown* (1708) Mor. 9492; *Cook* v. *Field* (1850) 15 Q. B. 460) and of a goodwill (at least in the sense of Lord Eldon's definition, 'the chance that the old customers will resort to the old place') are perhaps the nearest analogies to the *emptio spei*.

Several illustrations of the *emptio rei speratae* occur. Thus it was held in the old case of *Grantham* v. *Hawley* (quoted by

1. In some instances, however, we can conceive of sale even without a thing sold, as when one buys a 'chance.' Such is the case when you buy the haul of a fisherman's or fowler's net, or all the largess one can pick up, for there is a valid sale even if nothing should be got, because you bought an expectation; and, as regards the sale of largess, the seller incurs no obligation in respect of anything that is wrested from him after he has caught it, for that is presumed to have been the intention of the parties.

9. ULPIAN.

Consent is of course a necessary element in every contract of sale; and if the parties are not agreed,—whether about the

---

Benj. p. 82.) that there could be a valid sale of future goods which had a *potential existence, i.e.* were the natural growth or increase of something already belonging to the seller. So Pothier (§ 5) recognises the sale of the expected produce of a vineyard, just as 'futures' are sold on our Cotton Exchanges. Cp. *dicta* as to the sale of next year's crop of apples in a specified orchard (*Thacker* v. *Hardy* (1878) 4 Q. B. Div. 685, an action for indemnity and commission on Stock Exchange contracts made by a broker for a client who was speculating on 'differences'); *Watts* v. *Friend* (1830) 10 B. & C. 446 (contract for sale of a crop of turnip seed not yet sown); *Hale* v. *Rawson* (1858) 4 C. B. 85, where a contract for the sale of tallow to be delivered on the safe arrival of a certain vessel, was held to be conditional on the single contingency contemplated, viz. the arrival of the vessel, and, the vessel having arrived with no tallow on board, the seller was found liable in damages for non-delivery.

LL. 9–11.—These three leges may be taken together, as they all deal with certain cases of mistake (*error*). Other passages on the same topic are LL. 14; 15; 34 pr.; 41, 1; 44; 45; 57; 58; 62, 1; and 19. 1. 21, 1.

Ulpian starts by laying down the general principle in L. 9 pr. that one of the essentials of a contract of sale is consent of the parties; but there is no real consent if the parties are not at one upon the following particulars—the legal category to which the bargain belongs, the price, or any other point (such as the person

pretio siue in quo alio, emptio imperfecta est. si igitur ego me fundum emere putarem Cornelianum, tu mihi te uendere Sempronianum putasti, quia in corpore dissensimus, emptio nulla est. idem est, si ego me Stichum, tu Pamphilum absentem uendere putasti: nam cum in corpore dissentiatur, apparet nullam esse emptionem.

1. Plane si in nomine dissentiamus, uerum de corpore constet, nulla dubitatio est, quin ualeat emptio et uenditio: nihil enim facit error nominis, cum de corpore constat.

2. Inde quaeritur, si in ipso corpore non erratur, sed in substantia error sit, ut puta si acetum pro uino ueneat, aes pro auro uel plumbum pro argento uel quid aliud argento simile, an emptio et uenditio sit. Marcellus scribsit libro sexto digestorum emptionem esse et uenditionem, quia in corpus consensum est, etsi in materia sit erratum. ego in uino quidem consentio, quia eadem prope οὐσία est, si modo uinum acuit: ceterum si uinum non acuit, sed ab initio acetum fuit, ut embamma, aliud pro alio uenisse uidetur. in ceteris autem nullam esse uenditionem puto, quotiens in materia erratur.

---

contracted with, or the subject-matter of the contract). Now, one source of misunderstanding or want of agreement is the absence of true ideas (ignorance), another is the presence of false ideas (error); but as these differ only in so far as the one is negative and the other positive, they are generally discussed together under the same head of Mistake. That subject belongs to the general doctrine of contract, so that it may be assumed here that error *as such* has in general no legal effects at all, and it is only in exceptional cases of what is called essential or fundamental error, or *error in substantialibus*, that it operates to avoid an agreement. The question dealt with here is, what kind of error is inconsistent with the mutual assent required for a contract of sale?

The first case taken up is *error in corpore*, mistake as to the identity of the thing to be sold: if the buyer and seller had different things in view, that is fatal to the contract. It is the same in other bilateral contracts (D. 44. 7. 57), and in stipulations (D. 45. 1. 83, 1; ib. 137, 1). Even delivery will not

nature of the transaction, or about the price, or on some other point,—there is no completed contract. Hence if I supposed I was buying the Cornelian estate while you meant to sell me the Sempronian, the sale is a nullity, because we are not at one as to the subject-matter. It is just the same if I believed I was buying Stichus and you intended to sell me Pamphilus, the slave not being present: we have different individuals in view, and so the sale is plainly void.

1. If we are agreed upon the subject-matter and differ only about its name, there is of course no doubt about the validity of the sale; for a mistake about the name is immaterial, if the identity is not in dispute.

2. A further question is, Whether there is a sale in cases where there is no mistake about the specific thing, but only about its nature?—for instance, if vinegar is sold for wine, bronze for gold, lead or anything else resembling silver for silver. According to Marcellus (*Digest*, book vi.), the sale is valid, because the parties were agreed as to the subject sold, though mistaken about its composition. In the case of the wine I agree with him, if it has merely turned sour, for its substance is almost unchanged; but if the stuff is not wine turned, but was always real vinegar, such as we use at table, it would appear that one commodity has been sold for another. The sale is void, in my opinion, in the other cases, there being a mistake about the kind of material.

---

pass the property or confer possession *ad usucapionem* in face of such an error (D. 41. 2. 34). As to mistake about the identity of an accessory, see *infra* L. 34 pr. But the parties may intend the same specific thing, and give it a wrong name: that has no effect (L. 9, 1; cp. D. 45. 1. 32). Similarly, a misdescription of a person or thing in a testamentary writing is immaterial, if the identity is not in dispute, *falsa demonstratio non nocet dummodo constet de persona*. The mistake being in the expression merely and not in the intention, a court of law will correct it by the context, or by proper extrinsic evidence.

Again (L. 9, 2), though the parties have the same thing in

30   XVIII. I. *DE CONTRAHENDA EMPTIONE*. [L. 10

10. PAULUS libro V ad Sabinum.

Aliter atque si aurum quidem fuerit, deterius autem quam emptor existimaret: tunc enim emptio ualet.

---

view, there may be a mistake as to what is here called its *substantia*, and elsewhere (LL. 11 and 14) its *materia*,—that is, error as to its quality or material attributes. The name *error in substantia* has often been inappropriately applied to this kind of mistake, as if it always concerned the material or substance of which the thing is made, and were always to be regarded as essential; whereas an error as to the qualities of the material, its goodness, etc., was called *error in bonitate*, and was held, as a rule, to be non-essential. But Savigny has shown that this distinction is irrelevant, though logically correct: for instance, if a buyer thinks a female slave is a male slave, the sale is void, yet the idea of a difference of *materia* or *substantia* between the sexes is out of the question. Similarly, in all the examples put by the jurists of a sale being rescinded on account of a mistake about the *materia*, Savigny finds that the rule rests on something else than the abstract idea of substance (οὐσία); and he lays down a principle, which has been generally approved in spite of the difficulties presented by one or two of the texts referred to above, viz. that an error of this kind is essential when a quality is wrongly attributed to the subject-matter of the agreement, in virtue of which the thing would, according to the ordinary ideas and language of trade, fall under a different category of merchandise from what it actually belongs to. In other words, a sale is not void unless the difference between the thing sold, as it is, and as it is mistakenly supposed to be, amounts to a difference in kind, according to the ordinary classification of commodities; for then, as Ulpian puts it, *aliud pro alio uenisse uidetur*. Sav. *Syst.* iii. §§ 137, 138.

In the examples here given, the words *aurum aes*, etc., probably mean vessels of gold, bronze, etc., and not the unwrought metal, which could not so readily be mistaken. Cp. L. 14. The mistake of a base metal for a precious metal avoids the contract, even though the article be plated (L. 41, 1), because gold and silver articles are a special class of goods, of high intrinsic value apart from the workmanship, and the workers in these metals form a class quite distinct from coppersmiths or plumbers. Appar-

10. PAUL.

It is different when the thing sold is really gold, but of poorer quality than the buyer thought; in that case the sale stands.

ently Marcellus (like Labeo, quoted by Marcian in L. 45) held the view that error *in materia* did not rescind the contract—an opinion superseded by that of Ulpian; indeed they are not really in agreement even to the extent stated in the text, for Ulpian distinguishes bad wine from stuff that is not wine at all, and upholds the sale of the former for the same reason as Paul upholds the sale of inferior gold (L. 10), whereas the sale would stand in both cases according to Marcellus, but for a different reason.

A mistake about the fineness of gold is not essential, because gold may be more or less alloyed without ceasing to be gold in the ordinary trade sense (L. 10).

Savigny explains the case put in L. 11, 1 (cp. 19. 1. 11, 5) in the same way: mistake about the sex of a slave is essential, because male and female slaves were looked on as different kinds of merchandise. It is not the distinction of sex, but the difference of employment that is material: female slaves were employed in household work, male slaves in trades and agriculture.

For mistake as to other particulars,—the nature of the transaction, the price, etc.,—see Vangerow, § 604.

A good selection of English cases on Mistake will be found in Finch's Select Cases, pp. 466 sq.: one or two may be cited here in which analogies drawn from the civil law were employed. In *Gompertz* v. *Bartlett* (1853) 2 E. & B. 849, the purchaser of what purported to be a foreign bill of exchange, but was really a domestic bill and worthless because unstamped, was held entitled to recover the price from the vendor on the ground that the article did not answer the description of that which was sold, viz. a foreign bill. 'The case is precisely as if a bar was sold as gold, but was in fact brass, the vendor being innocent. In such a case the purchaser may recover.' This statement is scarcely definite enough: what is implied in *pro auro*, 'as gold,' is (1) a mistake common to the buyer and seller, each believing that the subject-matter is gold, and (2) a mutual intention to contract about *gold* and nothing else. Cp. L. 14 *infra*. But the ground of judgment in the case cited was not so much mistake, as failure to deliver a genuine article marketable by the name used in describing it;

11. Ulpianus libro xxviii ad Sabinum.

Alioquin quid dicemus, si caecus emptor fuit uel si in materia erratur uel in minus perito discernendarum materiarum? in corpus eos consensisse dicemus? et quemadmodum consensit, qui non uidit?

1. Quod si ego me uirginem emere putarem, cum esset iam mulier, emptio ualebit: in sexu enim non est erratum. ceterum si ego mulierem uenderem, tu puerum emere existimasti, quia in sexu error est, nulla emptio, nulla uenditio est.

---

for it is well settled that a sale under a particular description is equivalent to a condition precedent to the vendor's right of action, and, if something else is delivered instead of the described article, the buyer may reject, and recover the price if paid. Cp. S. G. B. § 15: 'Where there is a contract for the sale of goods by description, there is an implied condition that the goods shall correspond with the description.' Where, however, the article tendered answers the description, the buyer must, in the absence of fraud and warranty, take it with all faults. In *Wieler* v. *Schilizzi* (1856) 17 C. B. 619, there was a contract for the sale of Calcutta linseed, and it was held the buyer had a right to expect an article saleable in the market as such. ' If a man buys an article as gold, which everyone knows requires a certain amount of alloy, he cannot be said to get " gold " if he gets an article so depreciated in quality as to consist of gold only to the extent of one carat.'

The rule governing all questions of mistake as to the subject-matter of the contract is fully explained in *Kennedy* v. *Panama Mail Co.* (1867) L. R. 2 Q. B. 580. 'An innocent misrepresentation or misapprehension does not authorise a rescission unless it is such as to show that there is a complete difference in substance between what was supposed to be and what was taken, so as to constitute a failure of consideration.' After referring to LL. 9–11, Lord Blackburn proceeds: 'The principle of our law is the same as that of the civil law; and the difficulty in every case is to determine whether the mistake or misapprehension is as to the substance of the whole consideration, going, as it were, to the root of the matter, or only to some point, even though a material point, an error as to which does not affect the substance of the whole consideration.'

11. ULPIAN.

But what if the buyer was blind, or if he mistook the material, or lacked experience in discriminating between materials? Can we say that the parties are agreed upon a specific thing? But how can there be assent by one who has not seen the thing?

1. If I buy a female slave supposing her to be a virgin, when she is not so, the sale will stand; for there was no mistake about the sex. But if I sell you a woman, and you suppose you are buying a slave boy there is no contract, because there is a mistake about the sex.

With Ulpian's example of a female slave thought to be a virgin when she was not, he compares *Street* v. *Blay*, 2 B. & Ad. 456, where it was held, in the case of a horse supposed to be sound but not really so, that if the belief was induced by an honest misrepresentation as to its soundness, though it may be clear that both vendor and purchaser thought that they were dealing about a sound horse and were mistaken, yet the purchaser must pay the whole price, unless there was a warranty. If the misapprehension relates only to some quality or accident, even though that may have been the actuating motive to the purchaser, yet the contract remains binding.

It should be noted that by English law a sale will not be avoided by the mistake of one side alone as to a material attribute, unless produced by the other party. The same law seems laid down for Scotland in *Stewart* v. *Kennedy* (1890) 15 App. Ca. at p. 121, 'in the case of onerous contracts reduced to writing, the erroneous belief of one of the contracting parties, in regard to the nature of the obligations which he has undertaken, will not be sufficient to give him the right to rescind, unless such belief has been induced by the representations, fraudulent or not, of the other party to the contract;' and in *Smith* v. *Hughes* (1871) L. R. 6 Q. B. 597, it was observed that passive acquiescence of the seller in the self-deception of the buyer does not entitle the latter to avoid the contract. In the civil law, on the contrary, the sale was always avoided by the buyer's essential error, no matter whether the seller shared in it or not, and in the latter case, whether he was passively acquiescent in or actively furthered the misconception. See further, Pollock, *Contract*, p. 464 sq.

12. Pomponius libro xxxi ad Quintum Mucium.

In huiusmodi autem quaestionibus personae ementium et uendentium spectari debent, non eorum quibus adquiritur ex eo contractu actio: nam si seruus meus uel filius qui in mea potestate est me praesente suo nomine emat, non est quaerendum, quid ego existimem, sed quid ille qui contrahit.

13. Pomponius libro ix ad Sabinum.

Sed si seruo meo, uel ei cui mandauero, uendas sciens fugitiuum, illo ignorante, me sciente, non teneri te ex empto uerum est.

14. Ulpianus libro xxviii ad Sabinum.

Quid tamen dicemus, si in materia et qualitate ambo errarent? ut puta si et ego me uendere aurum putarem et tu emere, cum aes esset? ut puta coheredes uiriolam, quae aurea dicebatur, pretio exquisito uni heredi uendidissent eaque inuenta esset magna ex parte aenea? uenditionem esse constat ideo quia auri aliquid habuit. nam si inauratum aliquid sit, licet ego aureum putem, ualet uenditio: si autem aes pro auro ueneat, non ualet.

LL. 12, 13.—See for details as to the contractual capacity of a slave or *filiusfamilias*, *Inst.* ii. tit. 9; iii. tit. 17 and 28; and as to the liabilities arising from their contracts, iv. tit. 7. Though the owner or father took all benefit and got the title to sue on the contract, yet if any question affecting its validity arose, it was only the actual contractor's intention and information that were relevant. Of course, if the slave acted merely as a 'nuntius' or intermediary between his owner and the other party, the contract is in reality the owner's, and he can sue or be sued directly. The case contemplated in L. 12 is where the son or slave contracts in his own name with the knowledge of his *pater* or *dominus*, but without express authority (*jussus*).

In L. 13 the case is one of authorised agency; a slave or an '*extranea persona*' buys a slave for his principal in virtue of a mandate, and a question arises as to a *vitium* affecting the slave. Here the knowledge of the contracting party is plainly the material fact. (*a*) If the mandatary knows the slave to be a runaway, it matters not whether the mandant knows or not; no action is

12. POMPONIUS.

In such questions, however, the persons we must look to are the actual parties to the contract, not those who may be entitled to sue under it: when my slave, or a son under my power, buys in his own name in my presence, the question is not what is in my mind, but what is in the mind of the contracting party.

13. POMPONIUS.

But if you knowingly sell to my slave or mandatary a slave whom I know to be a runaway, though he does not know it, undoubtedly no action on purchase is maintainable against you.

14. ULPIAN.

But what if both parties were mistaken about the nature and quality of the thing; for example, if I thought I was selling and you thought you were buying gold, when it was bronze? or suppose that an heir bought from his co-heirs at a very high price a bracelet, described as being of gold but afterwards found to consist in great part of alloy. It is certain that the sale is good because there is some gold in it. For if a thing, which I took to be pure gold, contains an admixture of gold, that will support a sale: but if bronze be sold as gold, the sale is void.

---

competent at the instance of either (D. 21. 1. 51, 1). (*b*) If the mandatary is unaware but the mandant knows, the former can maintain the *actio redhibitoria*, and cannot be met by the plea that his principal knew all the while (D. *loc. cit.*); but if, as is figured here, the mandant sues the action, he can be effectually met by the plea of fraud. See as to fugitive slaves, L. 35, 3 *infra*.

L. 14.—Savigny thinks that we are to understand from the words *ambo errarent* that the vendor in the examples put in LL. 9–11 *supra* was under no mistake himself, and from the phrase *aes pro auro veneat* that he was cognisant of the vendee's mistake, and was guilty of a fraud or deceit upon him. If so, the fraud would entail other consequences besides the reduction of the sale, *e.g.* obligation to indemnify the vendee for any prejudice he may have sustained.

15. Paulus libro v ad Sabinum.

Et si consensum fuerit in corpus, id tamen in rerum natura ante uenditionem esse desierit, nulla emptio est.

1. Ignorantia emptori prodest, quae non in supinum hominem cadit.

Materia and *qualitas* are perhaps not synonyms; they may refer to distinct cases, (1) error as to the stuff or material, (2) error as to its quality or goodness.

Inauratum probably means that the thing is made of a mixture of gold and alloy, not that it is gilded or plated: the latter is expressed by '*cooperta auro*' in L. 41, 1. Cujas harmonises the two texts in this way.

It seems that in a stipulation a mistake as to the material properties did not make the transaction void, if parties were agreed as to the specific subject (*corpus*). D. 45. 1. 22; cp. *Inst.* iii. 19. 23; D. 13. 7. 1, 2 (pledge). The reason for this difference (according to Ihering, *Geist*, ii. 428) is that the formal contracts reflect the materialism of the old *strictum jus* from which they emanated, while sale looks to the intention more than the external fact in the spirit of the later jurisprudence to which it belongs. Even in sale we trace a development of opinion: for Marcellus (9, 2 *supra*) argued that, when a buyer mistook a bronze vase for gold and paid for it as such, it was *this* vase he wanted after all, and the sale must stand *quia in corpus consensum est;* but Ulpian answered No; the sale is void, for his *will* was directed not to the external appearance of the vase, but to the essential qualities he assumed it possessed—fitness for its purpose, genuineness, and the like: the latter is the accepted doctrine of the *Pandects*.

L. 15 pr.—If the subject sold had perished or been totally destroyed before the contract was complete, the sale was absolutely void; and the knowledge or other state of mind of the parties made no difference to the rule, which, as Savigny remarks (*Syst*. iii. 303), is an argument against mistake being considered the ground of nullity in these cases. It should also be noticed that a stipulation was void in such a case (D. 44. 7. 1, 9), while it was valid in spite of essential error, other than

15. Paul.

Though the specific subject has been agreed upon, yet if it has ceased to exist absolutely before the completion of the contract, the sale is void.

1. It is only such ignorance as does not bespeak a careless man that will avail the purchaser.

---

error *in corpore*. The jurists seem to have based the rule rather on the ground of impossibility of performance owing to the non-existence of the subject. Cp. h. t. L. 8 pr. (no sale *sine re*); ib. 44; D. 18. 4. 7. As to *partial* destruction, see *infra* LL. 57, 58.

The proposed rule in S. G. B. § 6—'Where there is a contract for the sale of specific goods, and the goods unknown to the seller have ceased to exist at the time of the contract, the contract is void,' is based on *Couturier* v. *Hastie* (1856) 5 H. L. Ca. 673 (sale of a specific cargo previously lost), a case which proceeded on the view that, the parties having contemplated something as existing which was really non-existent, the agreement failed for want of any real contents. It was unsuccessfully argued for the defence that the expectation (*spes*) of a cargo, subject to whatever might have happened after it was shipped, was what the parties meant to contract about. Cp. *Strickland* v. *Turner* (1852) 7 Ex. 208, where the sale of an annuity dependent on a life that had, unknown to either, already expired at the date of the contract was held void, and the purchaser obtained return of the price.

§ 1. For the rule that ignorance of *fact* due to gross carelessness is not a ground of relief, see D. 22. 6. 6, *nec supina ignorantia ferenda est factum ignorantis*: D. 21. 1. 55, *non . . . dissolutam ignorationem emptoris excusari oportebit*. The prejudicial effects that seem to be due to ignorance are really attributable to the negligence which causes it. Ignorance of *law* was in general no excuse; it was presumed to be culpable, for law is limited while fact is infinitely various and difficult to interpret (D. 22. 6. 2; ib. 9, 2: D. 17. 1. 29, 1). It was observed in *Cooper* v. *Phibbs*, L. R. 2 H. L. 149, that in the maxim *ignorantia juris neminem excusat* 'the word *jus* is used in the sense of denoting general law, the ordinary law of the country. But when the word *jus* is used in the sense of denoting a private

2. Si rem meam mihi ignoranti uendideris et iussu meo alii tradideris, non putat Pomponius dominium meum transire, quoniam non hoc mihi propositum fuit, sed quasi tuum dominium ad eum transire : et ideo etiam si donaturus mihi rem meam iussu meo alii tradas, idem dicendum erit.

16. Pomponius libro IX ad Sabinum.

Suae rei emptio non ualet, siue sciens siue ignorans emi : sed si ignorans emi, quod soluero repetere potero, quia nulla obligatio fuit.

1. Nec tamen emptioni obstat, si in ea re usus fructus dumtaxat ementis sit :

17. Paulus libro XXXIII ad edictum.

officio tamen iudicis pretium minuetur.

---

right, that maxim has no application. Private right of ownership is a matter of fact; it may be the result also of matter of law; but if parties contract under a mutual mistake and misapprehension as to their relative and respective rights, the result is that that agreement is liable to be set aside as having proceeded upon a common mistake.'

The English cases on recovering back money paid under a mistake of fact do not harmonise with the civil law, for negligence is not held to bar the right: the possession of the means of knowledge has no force except as evidence going to show that in fact the party was not mistaken. *Kelly* v. *Solari* (1841) 9 M. & W. 54; *Balfour* v. *Smith* (1877) 4 R. 454; Bell, *Prin.* § 534.

§ 2. Mistake as to the ownership of a thing (*error in dominio*) was in general not fatal to a contract about the thing, but it prevented transfer of the property by delivery if it was such as to be inconsistent with the intention to alienate. Cp. D. 41. 1. 35 : *si procurator meus uel tutor pupilli rem suam quasi meam uel pupilli alii tradiderint, non recessit ab eis dominium et nulla est alienatio, quia nemo errans rem suam amittit :* which is not irreconcileable with D. 17. 1. 49 ; see Vangerow, i. § 311.

LL. 16–18.—An agreement to buy one's own property was void, whether the buyer was under a mistake as to the fact or

2. If I buy a thing from you, not knowing that it belongs to me already, and by my direction you deliver it to a third person, Pomponius holds that my right of property is not transferred, because that was not my intention, but that your supposed ownership should pass to him; and the same result follows when you intend to make me a gift of something already mine, and at my request you hand it over to some other person.

16. Pomponius.

The owner of a thing cannot validly purchase it, whether he knows it is his or not: but if he bought it by mistake, he can recover what he paid for it, because no obligation ever existed.

1. But a man is not barred from purchasing a thing by having merely the usufruct of it:

17. Paul.

but it will be the duty of the judge to make a deduction from the price in such a case.

---

not: in the latter case, however, he could not recover the price by *condictio indebiti*, for he had paid what he knew he did not owe. The ground of the nullity was not the mistake, but the fact that an essential element of contract was wanting, for *neque pignus, neque depositum, neque precarium, neque emptio, neque locatio rei suae consistere potest* (D. 50. 17. 45 pr.; cp. C. iv. 38. 4. 10; L. 39 pr. *infra;* D. 19. 2. 9, 6). The principle was stated in this way, according to Ihering, in order to enable an owner, who had bought a thing in ignorance of his right of property, to make it effectual against the seller suing for the price. In the older system of pleading the plea of ownership could not be stated directly as a defence to an action on contract; it had to be put in the form of a denial of the ground of action: the sale is void, because its subject is my property. If the owner bought in the knowledge of his right, the law construed his intention so as to make it consistent with the fact; thus it substituted the idea of purchase of possession for purchase of property in such a case (L. 34, 4). A *conditional* purchase of a thing, in which one had a right of property defeasible in a certain

18. Pomponius libro IX ad Sabinum.

Sed si communis ea res emptori cum alio sit, dici debet scisso pretio pro portione pro parte emptionem ualere, pro parte non ualere.

1. Si seruus domini iussu in demonstrandis finibus agri uenditi uel errore uel dolo plus demonstrauerit, id tamen demonstratum accipi oportet quod dominus senserit: et idem Alfenus scripsit de uacua possessione per seruum tradita.

19. Pomponius libro XXXI ad Quintum Mucium.

Quod uendidi non aliter fit accipientis, quam si aut pretium

---

event, was quite permissible, for the contract was legally possible, and would be capable of execution if and when the event contemplated should occur (L. 61). Cp. Pothier, *Vente*, §§ 8, 9.

A stipulation for a *res sua* made under a mistake was also void '*naturali ratione*,' like one for a non-existent object or a *res extra commercium* (D. 44. 7. 1, 10).

Though usufruct included very extensive rights over the subject, amounting to what we call the beneficial use and enjoyment, it was in law only a personal servitude, a *jus in re aliena*: it was quite competent, therefore, for the usufructuary to acquire the fee (*nuda proprietas*), whereupon the servitude and the bare property were consolidated in the full *dominium*. If he bought in ignorance of his right of usufruct, the sale was valid, but the price would be abated by the judge making an allowance for the value of the usufruct (L. 17; cp. *Inst.* ii. 20. 9).

If the subject sold already belonged in part to the purchaser, the sale was good for the part which did not belong to him, and a deduction was made from the price corresponding to the value of the part belonging to him (L. 18 pr.).

The following were substantially cases of parties purchasing their own property, not knowing it was theirs; and the ground of judgment seems to have been that they had contracted under an implied condition that the subject-matter was in existence, which totally failed. In *Cochrane* v. *Willis* (1865) 1 Ch. App. 58 a reversioner agreed with the assignee in bankruptcy of the tenant for life for the sale of the timber on the estate, and it turned out that, unknown to both, the tenant for life was dead

18. POMPONIUS.

If the purchaser and another are co-owners of the subject bought, the price should be apportioned according to their shares, and the purchase declared valid for the one part and void for the other.

1. Although a slave, in pointing out by his master's orders the boundaries of a field he had sold, has, whether by mistake or fraudulently, pointed out more than it contains, nevertheless it must not be taken that any more was pointed out than his master meant to be shown: and the same rule is laid down by Alfenus about the delivery of free possession by the hands of a slave.

19. POMPONIUS.

The property in a thing sold does not pass to the vendee till at the date of the agreement. *Held*, that the agreement was founded on a mistake, and was without consideration, and the Court refused to enforce it. Cp. *Jones* v. *Clifford* (1876) 3 Ch. Div. 779, and *Bingham* v. *Bingham*, there cited and explained; *Scrabster Harbour Trs.* v. *Sinclair* (1864) 2 Macp. 884.

The examples of mistake by a slave, given in L. 18, § 1, may be compared with the case of a servant who, misapprehending his orders, gives delivery of goods without receiving the price,— the agreement being for cash on delivery: the property does not pass, and the seller can sue for restoration of the goods. Bell, *Com.* i. 258; Benj. p. 287.

L. 19.—The meaning of this text is that sale and delivery did not pass the property in the thing sold unless (1) the price had been paid, or (2) the seller had received personal or real security by guarantee or pledge, L. 53 *infra*, or (3) had relied on the buyer's credit: the satisfaction of the seller in one of these three ways was treated as an *implied* condition precedent to the transference of his ownership in spite of the delivery of possession. So long as the seller remained in possession of the thing sold, he had a right of retention over it in security of the unpaid price (*quasi pignus retinere potest*, D. 19. 1. 13, 8); but after he had parted with the possession, the above rule was applied in his favour, giving him a sort of privilege over the property not only

nobis solutum sit aut satis eo nomine factum uel etiam fidem habuerimus emptori sine ulla satisfactione.

---

against the vendee but against his creditors and purchasers from him as well. The rule held equally of moveable and immoveable property. [But it is only as regards immoveables that there is any survival of it, for the English equity doctrine of the vendor's lien on land sold for the purchase-money has been ascribed to this source (per Lord Eldon, *Mackreth* v. *Symmons*, 15 Ves. 344).] It was in effect a rule of construction: the intention to aliene was to be inferred only from one of the above facts, and not from the mere agreement to sell. If the seller handed over the subject without giving credit and without receiving the price or security, it was presumed that he meant not to divest himself but to retain the *dominium*, so as to be in a position, if necessary, to make good his claim by a real action (*vindicatio*) against the buyer or other person into whose hands the subject had passed. Delivery following upon sale, donation, or other *justa causa dominii transferendi*, regularly operated a transfer of ownership (D. 41. 1. 31 pr.); but the legal presumption just mentioned barred or at least suspended the normal effect of a *traditio* in virtue of sale. We may say that, in sales without credit, it was only sale *plus* payment or security that formed a sufficient *causa*.

Sometimes an *express* agreement was made reserving the property until the price was paid, called *pactum reservati dominii* (D. 41. 2. 38, 1; 43. 26. 20). This presupposes an intention not to exact instant payment, and therefore implies a tacit credit. It operated generally as a suspensive condition. See further, Vangerow, § 311, A. 2.

The practical effect of the rule is exemplified in D. 14. 4. 5, 18: its *rationale* may be inferred from an important passage in the *Institutes* (ii. 1. 41), where it is said to have been laid down in the Twelve Tables. Critics are agreed that this statement cannot be taken as literally true. See Ihering, *Geist*, ii. 568; Exner, *Tradition*, p. 338. Voigt (Die xii. Tafeln, ii. p. 142) suggests that Tribonian derived his information not from the Tables directly, but through a jurist of the middle Empire, and that the Tables contained some provision of the kind applicable to sales by mancipation (*res venditae et mancipatae*, etc.), which was in course of time extended to ordinary contracts of sale by the

the vendor has been paid or has got security for the price, or else has given credit without security.

interpretatio of the jurists, whereupon the word *traditae* was substituted for *mancipatae* in the wording of the rule.

Probably *pignus* and *expromissor* are also accretions on the original rule, for they presuppose a legally enforceable obligation, and neither mancipation nor such informal sale as was in daily use at the time of the Twelve Tables created such a bond; besides, the only security we know of as existing at that date is *vadimonium*. When coined money came into use, the necessity for some statutory protection for the vendor would begin to be felt, in order to prevent the Quiritary ownership passing by mancipation (which soon became a mere form of conveyance), while the seller might not have received the price at the time of the actual sale: in which case, as he had no remedy by personal action against the purchaser to enforce payment, the law declared him to be undivested owner notwithstanding the mancipation.[1] This principle once established was maintained during all the stages in the history of sale; but, as it would in its strict form have proved a serious hindrance to commerce, the classical jurists may have sought to render it more elastic by adding a clause (which appears in the *Institutes* as a separate statement)—that the giving of credit was to be held equivalent to payment of the price as regards the effect upon the property.

This important principle of the civil law found at one time considerable acceptance in many Continental states: thus Pothier (*Vente*, § 322) lays it down that delivery on the title of sale is subject to an implied condition which suspends the transference of the property till the price is paid or secured, unless credit is given expressly, or by implication as by fixing a term of payment or by allowing a considerable time to elapse without a demand —otherwise credit is not to be presumed from delivery alone (§ 324). In fact, 'a kind of secondary contract' had to be entered into at the time of delivery, by which the seller agreed to give credit and to renounce his hypothec. The result of this was, that not only fraud, going to the root of the original contract of sale, but also a slighter degree of fraud, practised at the time of delivery to induce credit, was a sufficient ground for restitution.

[1] Cp. Muirhead, *Roman Law*, p. 135.

20. POMPONIUS libro IX ad Sabinum.

Sabinus respondit, si quam rem nobis fieri uelimus etiam, ueluti statuam uel uas aliquod seu uestem, ut nihil aliud quam

But in Great Britain this principle has not been followed in the *mercantile* contract of sale. As indicated in the note to L. 6 *supra*, the unpaid seller has certain rights against the goods, so long as they are in his possession or in course of transit to the buyer; but as soon as they come into the possession of the buyer by the vendor's authority, the transference is completed and the price is matter of personal credit merely. 'Sale being perfected, and the thing delivered, the property therefore becomes the buyer's, if it was the seller's; and there is no dependence of it till the price be paid or secured, as was in the civil law; neither hypothecation of it for the price' (Stair, i. 14. 2). Like many of the legal hypothecs known to the civil law, it has been swept away 'that commerce might be more sure, and everyone may more easily know his condition with whom he contracts.' But express conditions annexed to the transference will receive effect: thus, in *Richmond* v. *Railton* (1854) 16 D. 402, Lord Justice-Clerk Hope observed: 'The right of property passed by the voluntary act of the sellers in giving delivery without any arrangement or stipulation as to the price. If parties furnishing goods meant to enforce the condition of a ready-money sale, and prevent the legal results of delivery voluntarily made according to the law of Scotland, they ought as they effectually can to protect themselves by insisting on payment or proper arrangements for payment before they give delivery.'

To complete this review of the seller's securities, it is necessary to mention the buyer's right of rejection on insolvency, and the seller's claim for restitution on the ground of fraud. (1) A purchaser, knowing his insolvency but not yet a bankrupt, may and ought to reject goods proferred for delivery at any time before they have come into his actual possession, the effect being to rescind the contract and restore the property, if the seller does not dissent. *Booker & Co.* v. *Milne* (1870) 9 Macp. 314; Bell, *Prin.* § 1310. In England this is treated as part of the doctrine of stoppage *in transitu*, and it is held that after bankruptcy the buyer cannot reject (Benj. 493-5, 881).

(2) Fraud in procuring delivery, in particular fraudulent con-

20. Pomponius.

According to another opinion of Sabinus, if a man orders an article, such as a statue, a particular vessel, or a coat, to be made

---

cealment of insolvency, undermines the consent given to a contract of sale, and entitles the seller to recover the goods after delivery. In *Watt* v. *Findlay* (1846) 8 D. 529, a positive pledge was given at the time of delivery to pay two days after, while the party was at the moment preparing a petition and affidavit for sequestration. *Held*, that the property of the goods, although delivered, did not pass owing to deceit practised in order to induce the delivery.

L. 20.—Sale and location resembled each other so closely that it was often found difficult to draw a clear line between them. In both it was necessary that something should be delivered in return for a consideration, which must be in current money, and must be definite. Where the contract was for permission to use a subject without a time being fixed for its return, as in grants of *emphyteusis* (*Inst.* iii. 24. 3; Gaius, iii. 145, cp. our 'feu-contract') and *superficies* (L. 32 *infra*), there was much doubt to which head the contract belonged. Again, there was a question as to the case here put, where you ordered an article to be made for you for a fixed price, the workman supplying the materials: the opinion of Cassius was that the transaction was a mixture of both contracts, a sale of the material by the workman to you, accompanied by a *brevi manu* delivery of it back to him, and a hire of his labour (Gaius, iii. 147; *Inst.* iii. 24. 4); but the view of Sabinus was ultimately adopted, that the contract was a unity (*unum esse negotium* D. 19. 2. 2, 1), and that, when the workman supplied the material, it was simply sale, and, when you found the material, it was location. The criterion is stated by Javolen in L. 65 *infra* in this way: in sale there is a transfer of the property in the material from the vendor to the vendee; in location there is not (*non solet locatio dominium mutare*, D. 19. 2. 39). Location, however, does in some cases import a transmutation of property as an incidental result, *e.g.* D. 19. 2. 22, 2: *cum insulam aedificandam loco, ut sua impensa conductor omnia faciat, proprietatem quidem corum ad me transfert et tamen locatio est: locat enim artifex operam suam, id est faciendi necessitatem.* Here the '*corpus ipsum*' is my site, not his materials. Cp. ib. L. 31.

pecuniam daremus, emptionem uideri nec posse ullam locationem esse, ubi corpus ipsum non detur ab eo cui id fieret: aliter atque si aream darem, ubi insulam aedificares, quoniam tunc a me substantia profiscitur.

In Scots law hiring is held to be strictly 'an engagement to do certain work upon materials furnished to the workman'; but when the workman contributes the materials as well as the labour, as in the general case of manufactures, it is sale, 'though, properly speaking, there are combined with the contract of sale other contracts — as *locatio operis*, mandate, etc.' (Bell, *Prin.* §§ 90, 147). This recalls the opinion of Cassius, that the contract is a complex one of a peculiar nature.

The question has been more canvassed in English law, partly on account of the former strict rules of pleading which made it necessary to sue under different counts, according as the contract was for the sale of goods or for work and labour, and still more on account of the 17th section of the Statute of Frauds, which has repeatedly raised the question, What is a contract for the sale of goods within the meaning of the Statute? It was at one time thought to be a sufficient test to ask, Who furnishes the materials? If it is the employer, the contract is for work and labour; if it is the workman, it is sale: but this is not quite correct—*e.g.* if I damage a bicycle which I have hired from the maker, and employ him to repair it, he can sue me for work done and materials furnished by himself to repair his own machine; *Grafton* v. *Armitage* (1845) 2 C. B. 336. The criterion now approved is thus stated in *Lee* v. *Griffin* (1861) 1 B. & S. 272: 'If the contract be such that when carried out it will *result in the sale of a chattel*, the party cannot sue for work and labour; but, if the result of the contract is that the party has done work and labour which ends in nothing that can become the subject of a sale, the party cannot sue for goods sold and delivered.' The contract is sale, 'if it contemplates the ultimate delivery of a chattel.' See discussion in Benj. pp. 94-110, and *Law Quarterly Review*, vol. i. p. 1 (Sir J. F. Stephen and Sir F. Pollock).

When does the property in a special article to be made for the buyer vest in him? The general rule of English law is stated in *Clark* v. *Spence* (1836) 4 A. & E. 466 thus: 'Under

for him, agreeing simply to pay the price of it, that falls under sale, for it is essential to the contract of hire that the materials be furnished by the person for whom the thing is to be made: but the case is different when I give a site for you to build a block of houses on, for there I provide the material.

a contract for building a vessel, or making any other thing not existing in specie at the time of the contract, no property vests in the purchaser during the progress of the work, nor until the vessel or thing is finished and delivered, or at least ready for delivery and approved by the purchaser. The builder or maker is not bound to deliver to the purchaser the identical vessel or thing which is in progress, but may, if he please, dispose of that to some other person, and deliver to the purchaser another vessel or thing, provided it answers to the specification contained in the contract.' See S. G. B. § 20, rules 2 and 5. But 'if it appears to be the intention of the parties to a contract for building a ship that, at a particular stage of its construction, the vessel, so far as then finished, shall be appropriated to the contract of sale, the property of the vessel, as soon as it has reached that stage of completion, will pass to the purchaser, and subsequent additions made to the chattel thus vested will *accessione* become his property'; and such an intention is to be inferred where the contract is to pay for the ship by instalments according to the progress of the work, and where the purchaser or some one appointed by him regularly inspects the work; and there is no difference in principle between the sale of a ship and any other *corpus manufactum* in course of construction. See per Lord Watson in *Seath & Co.* v. *Moore* (1886) 11 App. Ca. 350, 380.

In Scotland 'when a manufacture in the workman's hand unfinished is purchased, and the price paid; or when, by periodical payments, it is appropriated as it advances, the law holds it as delivered' (Bell, *Prin.* § 1303), on the principle of specification, the maker holding thereafter for the true owner. This proposition rests on the leading case, *Simpson* v. *Duncanson's Crs.* (1786) M. 14,204; Bell, *Com.* i. 189 note, who refers to the opinion of Julian (in D. G. 1. 61, 1) that, where a ship is built with another's materials, *proprietas totius navis carinae causam sequitur*. The principle of *Simpson's* case, as recognising in this special class of contracts an equitable exception from the

21. PAULUS libro V ad Sabinum.

Labeo scripsit obscuritatem pacti nocere potius debere uenditori qui id dixerit quam emptori, quia potuit re integra apertius dicere.

22. ULPIANUS libro XXVIII ad Sabinum.

Hanc legem uenditionis ' si quid sacri uel religiosi est, eius uenit nihil' superuacuam non esse, sed ad modica loca pertinere. ceterum si omne religiosum uel sacrum uel publicum uenierit, nullam esse emptionem,

23. PAULUS libro V ad Sabinum.

(et quod soluerit eo nomine, emptor condicere potest)

24. ULPIANUS libro XXVIII ad Sabinum

in modicis autem ex empto esse actionem, quia non specialiter locus sacer uel religiosus uenit, sed emptioni maioris partis accessit.

---

strict rule that delivery is essential to pass the property, is thought to be still good law, though its authority in the case of a ship on the stocks paid for by stated instalments was doubted in *M'Bain* v. *Wallace* (1881) 6 App. Ca. 588, where the same result was reached by a wide construction of the first section of the Mercantile Law Amendment Act. See also *Seath & Co., supra,* where it was held that marine engines which were in course of construction belonged, on the bankruptcy of the engineer, to his trustee, and not to the shipbuilder who had ordered them and made advances on them; in that case there was no express stipulation, and no evidence of an intention that the property in the completed portions of the work should pass to the purchaser on payment of a proportionate instalment of the price. These two decisions seem to a considerable extent to assimilate the law of both countries as to the property in unfinished ships or machinery paid for by instalments during the progress of the work.

L. 21.—For this rule of construction, compare D. 50. 17. 172 pr.: *in contrahenda uenditione ambiguum pactum contra uenditorem interpretandum est.* Cp. D. 2. 14. 39 and 45. 1. 99.

21. PAUL.

Labeo has laid down that an ambiguity in the terms of the contract ought to be construed against the seller who framed them, for he might have expressed himself more clearly while matters were still entire.

22. ULPIAN.

A term of sale to this effect, 'if any of the ground be sacred or religious, it is excepted from the sale,' is not superfluous; it applies to plots of moderate size. But if the whole of the ground sold be religious, sacred, or public, the sale is void.

23. PAUL.

(and the buyer can bring a *condictio* to recover his money);

24. ULPIAN.

in respect of small plots, however, [without such clause], an action on purchase will lie, because the sacred or religious ground is not sold specifically, but as an accessory to the bulk of the lands.

The decisions in D. 8. 3. 30 and 8. 2. 17, 3 illustrate its strict application. It is adopted in the French Code, art. 1602, but not in English law, though some effect is given to the maxim that an ambiguous clause in a contract or writ is to be construed against the person founding on it, *verba sunt interpretanda contra proferentem*. See remarks on the construction of written contracts by Kelly, C.-B., in *Coddington* v. *Palæologo* (1867) L. R. 2 Ex. 200. Erskine says, 'Doubtful clauses in obligations are to be interpreted against the granter' (*Inst.* iii. 3. 87). *Life Ass$^{n.}$ of Scotland* v. *Foster* (1873) 11 Macp. 351.

LL. 22-24.—The clause *si quid*, etc., amounts to a notice by the seller that he does not warrant that some part of the lands is not *divini iuris*, and so exempt from commerce. It may turn out that small portions are *extra commercium*, in which case the sale as a whole is valid, and the clause is essential to protect the seller from a claim of damages for eviction from such parcels, which the buyer could enforce by action on the contract but for this agreement (L. 24): it may be found, however, that the whole

50 XVIII. 1. *DE CONTRAHENDA EMPTIONE.* [L. 25.

25. ULPIANUS libro XXXIV ad Sabinum.

Si ita distrahatur 'illa aut illa res,' utram eliget uenditor, haec erit empta.

1. Qui uendidit necesse non habet fundum emptoris facere, ut cogitur fundum stipulanti spopondit.

---

subject (or the major portion of it) is *extra commercium*, in which case the clause is superfluous, for the sale is void on the general ground of impossibility of performance. Ulpian plainly holds a contract to sell what is wholly or mainly withdrawn from commerce to be a nullity in all cases, even where the buyer is ignorant of the true nature of the subject-matter; that is the case contemplated in L. 22, otherwise there could be no question of suing for damages, and, moreover, the *condictio indebiti* for return of the price (L. 23) would be inadmissible, because it presupposes the buyer's ignorance of the circumstance which renders the contract void. Paul and Modestine are of the same opinion, and probably the compilers of the *Digest* meant to adopt this doctrine, but they inadvertently admitted an excerpt from the earlier jurist Pomponius, to the effect that the sale of a *res extra commercium*, like that of a free man, is valid in the sense that a *bona fide* purchaser may sue the vendor for double the price in lieu of the prestation which is impossible (L. 4 *supra*).

Observe that, though religious ground was *extra commercium*, there might be a special property in it, viz. the exclusive right to use it as a burial-place. Where such a right was attached to the ownership of lands, it was transmissible to purchasers as an accessory of the 'profane' lands, though incapable of sale by itself. See Ersk. ii. 1. 8; Pothier, *Vente*, § 10.

L. 25 pr.—For the effects of an alternative sale, see L. 34. 6 *infra*.

§ 1. The obligation on the vendor was to hand over and warrant to the buyer the lawful and undisturbed possession of subject (*praestare emptori rem habere licere*), not to make him owner (*dare*): so long as the buyer was enabled by delivery to enter on the full and uncontested possession (*vacua possessio*, D. 19. 1. 2, 1), and to enjoy it as matter of fact, he could not complain of any defect in the legal title, *uenditori sufficit ob euictionem*

25. ULPIAN.

If there be a sale of 'this or that thing,' the seller is entitled to choose which shall be held as sold.

1. The seller of land is not obliged to make it the property of the purchaser, as one who promises it by a stipulation is bound to do.

---

se obligare, possessionem tradere et purgari dolo malo: itaque, si evicta res non sit, nihil debet (D. 19. 4. 1). Cp. D. 50. 16. 188 pr.: *habere duobus modis dicitur, altero iure dominii, altero obtinere sine interpellatione id quod quis emerit.* The reason is possibly a historical one, reaching back to the time when there was only one kind of property at Rome, *dominium ex iure Quiritium*. Sale was a product of the *ius gentium*, and was therefore accommodated to the legal position of aliens, who would have been incapacitated from buying a *res mancipi* from a citizen, and from selling him anything whatever, if the undertaking required of the seller had been *dare* in the technical sense. The seller was merely bound to transfer all his right and title, and if that was defective the buyer was left to complete his title by usucapion: in the meantime he had an ample guarantee in the stipulation by which the seller warranted him against eviction at the suit of the true owner, so that he was quite safe except the seller became insolvent. Cp. D. 19. 1. 11, 2; ib. 30, 1: Pothier, §§ 1, 48, 82. See L. 41 pr. *infra* for a purchase under the special condition that the seller shall purge the subject of incumbrances by a certain date. Celsus holds that if there be an express engagement to transfer the property (*dedi tibi pecuniam ut mihi Stichum dares*, D. 12. 4. 16), the contract is not a sale at all, but an innominate contract *do ut des;* hence the risk does not pass, and if there is default in passing the property in Stichus, the money is recoverable at once by a *condictio causa data causa non secuta*. In the strict verbal contract of stipulation, on the other hand, the obligation *dare* was appropriate: *haec stipulatio 'fundum Tusculanum dari?' ostendit se certi esse, continetque ut dominium omnimodo efficiatur stipulatoris quoquo modo* (D. 45. 1. 75, 10).

This leading principle of the Roman law as to the effect of sale in passing title resulted in the rule stated in L. 28, that the sale of a *res aliena* was permissible. This doctrine was received

26. Pomponius libro XVII ad Sabinum.

Si sciens emam ab eo cui bonis interdictum sit uel cui tempus ad deliberandum de hereditate ita datum sit, ut ei deminuendi potestas non sit, dominus non ero: dissimiliter atque si a debitore sciens creditorem fraudari emero.

27. Paulus libro VIII ad Sabinum.

Qui a quolibet rem emit, quam putat ipsius esse, bona fide

---

into the early law of the continent through the influence of such jurists as Dumoulin and Pothier; but the principle and the rule would both seem to have been swept away by art. 1599 of the French Code, '*La vente de la chose d'autrui est nulle.*' This implies a principle directly the reverse of the civil law, viz. that the nature and purpose of sale is to transfer the property in a thing from the seller to the buyer, and the modern definitions of sale are generally framed in accordance with this idea. Cp. S. G. B., § 1. Curiously enough, however, the definitions in the French Code follow so closely the language of the Roman law as to throw some doubt on the intention of its authors to abandon the position that a sale merely transfers the right of possession; but it is now quite settled, both from its general scope and on authority, that the code was intended to give effect to the modern view which attaches to sale the obligation to transfer the actual ownership. Troplong, *Vente*, Nos. 4, 230.

Lord Stair adopted the civil law, as was customary in his day. ' Delivery of the goods or things bought, with the obligation of warrandice in case of eviction, which is implied in sale, though not expressed, is the implement of it on the seller's part; and even though the buyer know and make it appear that it were not the seller's, yet he could demand no more but delivery and warrandice' (*Inst.* i. 14. 1). It rather appears as if this were still the law of Scotland as regards corporeal moveables (cp. *Swan v. Martin* (1865) 3 Macp. 851); but it has long been fixed that, in sales of heritage, the property must be passed, and a good title given, before the vendee can be called upon to pay the price, unless he has agreed to waive his right and to take the title of the vendor as it stands.

In England the buyer of goods has a double protection: (1) it

26. Pomponius.

If I buy from a person whom I know to be interdicted from managing his estate, or to have been granted time to deliberate about taking up an inheritance without any power of alienation, I do not acquire ownership thereby; but it is different if I buy from a debtor with the knowledge that he is defrauding his creditor.

27. Paul.

If you buy a thing from a person whom you believe to be the

---

has been settled law since *Eichholz* v. *Bannister* (1864) 34 L. J. C. P. 105 that, in a contract of sale, there is an implied condition on the part of the seller that he has a right to sell the goods, unless the circumstances are such as to show a different intention. This is usually called 'implied warranty of title,' and rests really on the principle of representation or estoppel. (2) There is an implied covenant for quiet possession, which is analogous to the implied guarantee against eviction of the Roman law. See S. G. B., § 14.

L. 26.—The result in the two cases first mentioned would not have been different although the purchaser had been unaware of the incapacity of the seller; the *sciens* is inserted to complete the comparison with the case of a purchaser who knows that the seller is making an alienation in fraud of creditors, and is therefore in *malâ fide* (Pothier). Cp. D. 42. tit 8, *Quae in fraudem creditorum facta sunt ut restituantur.* Though the owner alienated in fraud of creditors, yet the delivery with his consent carried the property; but we must hold that the transaction was reducible by the *actio Pauliana*, for it lay even against a purchaser for value if he was cognisant of the insolvency of the seller.

In Scotland the effect of interdiction is not to annul acts or deeds, but only to reduce them so far as prejudicial; and the incapacity of persons interdicted is confined to their heritable estate. Bell, *Prin.* § 2123 sq.

L. 27.—*Bonâ fides* in a purchaser, which was one of the conditions requisite for acquisition by *usucapio*, is defined in D. 50. 16. 109 : '*Bonae fidei emptor*' *esse uidetur, qui ignorauit eam rem*

emit: at qui sine tutoris auctoritate a pupillo emit, uel falso tutore auctore, quem scit tutorem non esse, non uidetur bona fide emere, ut et Sabinus scripsit.

28. ULPIANUS libro XLI ad Sabinum.

Rem alienam distrahere quem posse nulla dubitatio est: nam emptio est et uenditio: sed res emptori auferri potest.

---

alienam esse, aut putauit cum qui uendidit ius uendendi habere, puta procuratorem aut tutorem esse. It implied honest belief in the goodness of one's title, and excusable ignorance of any flaw in it.

According to the Bills of Exchange Act (1882) § 90, 'a thing is deemed to be done " in good faith," when it is in fact done honestly, whether it be done negligently or not.' In *Jones* v. *Gordon* (1877) 2 App. Ca. 616, a bill had been taken at considerable undervalue; *held*, that, though that fact was not of itself sufficient to affect the title of the holder, it was an important element in considering whether the man who gave the undervalue was acting *bonâ fide*, in ignorance and error, or was assisting in committing a fraud, and avoided making enquiries because they might be injurious to him. The House of Lords, in *Derry* v. *Peek* (1889) 14 App. Ca. 337, has negatived the idea of 'legal fraud' as a category intermediate between *bona fides* on the one hand and *mala fides* (fraud) on the other. 'Fraud is proved when it is shown that a false representation has been made knowingly, or without belief in its truth, or recklessly, without caring whether it be true or false. A false statement, made through carelessness and without reasonable ground for believing it to be true, may be evidence of fraud, but does not necessarily amount to fraud.'

L. 28.—The unqualified assertion that one can validly sell what belongs to another is rather surprising to a modern lawyer. It is, however, the proper corollary of the principle that sale is not a transfer of property but of guaranteed possession (L. 25, and note). As the vendor was not bound *ad dandum* but only *ad tradendum*, the obligation could not be said to be *absolutely* impossible, though it might be so *relatively, i.e.* for that particular vendor; hence the law held there was an effectual contract, binding the seller to acquire the property and secure the buyer in

owner, that is buying in good faith; but if you buy from a pupil without the concurrence of his tutor, or with the concurrence of a pretended tutor whom you know not to be the tutor, you cannot be considered as buying in good faith; and that is the opinion of Sabinus also.

28. ULPIAN.

It is undoubted that one may sell what belongs to another, for there is here a complete contract of sale; only the purchaser may be evicted.

---

possession according to the contract, or to pay damages for his failure. Cp. Pothier, §§ 7, 325. The purchaser, on the other hand, was not at liberty to refuse to accept delivery or to pay the price on the ground that he could show that the title offered was bad; he had no claim so long as he was not dispossessed by the sentence of a competent court. If the buyer believed that the seller had power to alienate, he was in the position of a *bonâ fide possessor*, and his possession *pro emptore* when continued for the prescriptive period made him owner in the fullest sense, whereupon the original owner's right was extinguished, and he had only an action against the seller for damages. This idea was consistently applied; thus, if the thing perished accidentally before any question of eviction was mooted, the buyer was bound to pay the price, the risk having passed just as if the seller had been owner (D. 21. 2. 21 pr.). The *bonâ fides* of the vendor was, of course, presupposed; for, if he knew he was not owner and sold to one who was ignorant of the fact, so as intentionally to expose the latter to the risk of eviction, he was held to have acted fraudulently, and the buyer could maintain an adapted action on the contract without waiting for actual eviction (D. 19. 1. 30, 1). It was theft to sell and deliver a corporeal moveable, knowing it to belong to another. *Inst.* ii. 6. 3.

A modern code would state the reverse of this proposition as the general rule of law, and would explain the peculiar cases in which the sale of a thing which does not belong to the seller is valid as exceptions from the rule. Lord Blackburn observed in *City Bank* v. *Barrow* (1880) 5 App. Ca., at p. 677: 'The rule not merely of English common law, but I take it of Roman civil law, and I apprehend of all the old laws of Europe, by which I mean the

29. ULPIANUS libro XLIII ad Sabinum.

Quotiens seruus uenit, non cum peculio distrahitur: et ideo siue non sit exceptum, siue exceptum sit, ne cum peculio ueneat,

laws existing before the *Code Napoléon*, that no man could confer a greater title than he himself had, has been found in modern practice to be inconvenient to its full extent in commercial transactions, especially since the practice of advancing money upon the security of goods and merchandise came to be so important as it is; and I quite agree that there have therefore been modifications of that principle introduced into the law of this country, and I dare say into the laws of other countries.' The following passage, approved as a statement of English law by the House of Lords in *Colonial Bank* v. *Whinney* (1886) 11 App. Ca., at p. 435, indicates the exceptional cases where there may be a good sale by a person not the owner: 'At common law, a person in possession of goods could not confer on another, either by sale or pledge, any better title to the goods than he had himself. To this general rule there was an exception of sales in market overt, and an apparent exception where the person in possession had a title defeasible on account of fraud. But the general rule was that, to make either a sale or a pledge valid against the owner of the goods sold or pledged, it must be shown that the seller or pledger had authority from the owner to sell or pledge, as the case might be. If the owner of the goods had so acted as to clothe the seller or pledger with apparent authority to sell or pledge, he was at common law precluded, as against those who were induced *bonâ fide* to act on the faith of that apparent authority, from denying that he had given such an authority, and the result as to them was the same as if he had really given it. But there was no such preclusion as against those who had notice that the real authority was limited.' See further, S. G. B., §§ 24-28; Story, *Sale*, § 188 sq.

In Scotland there is no privilege in favour of a *bonâ fide* purchaser in public market; but otherwise the law is similar to that of England. Many cases turn on the principle of 'reputed ownership,' the legal presumption that the possessor of moveables is the owner; for example, when goods are sold and left in the vendor's possession without any substantial change of his title, and dealt with by him as if they were his own in such a way as

29. ULPIAN.

The sale of a slave does not include his *peculium*, and so it is not regarded as an accessory of the sale, whether specially reserved to accredit him, the vendee cannot have any claim to obtain delivery in a question with the onerous creditors of the vendor. Again, by the Factors Act (1890), which reproduces the common law of Scotland, a mercantile agent, who is with consent of the owner in possession of goods or of the documents of title to goods (such as a bill of lading or delivery order), may effectually sell the goods to a *bonâ fide* purchaser without notice of his lack of authority.

It was at one time held (*Bryan* v. *Lewis* (1826) Ry. & Moor. 386), apparently on grounds of public policy, that an executory contract for the sale of goods not yet belonging to the vendor, but which he intends to purchase in the market against the time of delivery, is not a valid contract, but a mere wager on the price of the commodity. But this case was expressly overruled in *Hibblethwaite* v. *McMorine* (1839) 5 M. & W. 462, where it was observed that such a doctrine had no principle in its favour, it being immaterial, in the case of a contract which may be performed by the delivery of any goods of the kind bargained for, whether the vendor has the goods in his possession at the time of the contract or not, provided he has them ready for delivery at the time when the contract is to be fulfilled; moreover, it would put an end to half the contracts made in the course of trade, such as those for army and navy supplies. But if contracts for the sale of shares not belonging to the vendor are not really meant to be executed, but are merely devices to cover speculations in the rise or fall of prices, they are truly wagers and are void under the Statute against gaming (8 & 9 Vict. c. 109).

L. 29.—This rule, that when a slave was sold his *peculium* was not included as a pertinent (cp. D. 21. 2. 3), and the provision of the edict of the aediles that the trappings (*ornamenta*) with which an animal was decked at the time of sale must be handed over to the buyer (D. 21. 1. 38 pr.), are almost the only decisions in the *Digest* referring to accessories in the sale of moveable property. It was extremely common to bargain that the *peculium* should go to the buyer; such a term of the sale was generally expressed thus—'*accessurum dico* (D. 21. 1. 44 pr.).

non cum peculio distractus uidetur. unde si qua res fuerit peculiaris a seruo subrepta, condici potest uidelicet quasi furtiua: hoc ita si res ad emptorem peruenit.

30. ULPIANUS libro XXXII ad edictum.

Sed ad exhibendum agi posse nihilo minus et ex uendito puto.

31. POMPONIUS libro XXII ad Sabinum.

Sed et si quid postea accessit peculio, reddendum est uenditori, ueluti partus et quod ex operis uicarii perceptum est.

32. ULPIANUS libro XLIV ad Sabinum.

Qui tabernas argentarias uel ceteras quae in solo publico sunt uendit, non solum, sed ius uendit, cum istae tabernae publicae sunt, quarum usus ad priuatos pertinet.

33. POMPONIUS libro XXXIII ad Sabinum.

Cum in lege uenditionis ita sit scriptum: 'flumina stillicidia uti nunc sunt, ut ita sint,' nec additur, quae flumina uel stillicidia, primum spectari oportet, quid acti sit: si non id appareat, tunc id accipitur quod uenditori nocet: ambigua enim oratio est.

L. 31.—A *seruus ordinarius* might employ his *peculium* in buying slaves for himself, who were called *servi vicarii*. The latter belonged *de facto* to the *seruus ordinarius*, though in strict law they formed part of his *peculium*, and therefore belonged to his owner. Cp. *Inst.* iv. 7. 4.

L. 32.—The idea that A could have a real right, capable of alienation, in respect of buildings on B's *solum*, was foreign to the strict civil law (the maxim of which was *semper superficies solo cedit*), but it gradually won recognition by the aid of the praetor. For some time the notion prevailed that there was a peculiar kind of lease or sale of the ground in such a case (see tit. *de superficibus*, D. 43. 18); but Ulpian reached the true conception —that the subject of the sale is not the ground, but the right to use the surface. In the case here contemplated the *solum* is public property, and could not be sold on that account: what is sold is the right to use the *solum*, that right having vested in a

or not. Hence if the slave purloins any part of it, a *condictio* is maintainable just as for anything stolen, that is, supposing it has come into the buyer's hands.

30. ULPIAN.

In my opinion an action *ad exhibendum* and an action on the sale are equally competent.

31. POMPONIUS.

Moreover any subsequent addition to the *peculium* must be restored to the vendor, *e.g.* any young that may be born, or any profits made out of the labour of a slave owned by the slave who was sold.

32. ULPIAN.

The seller of a banker's or other booth erected on public ground does not sell the *solum* but only a right in it, for these booths are public property though the use of them belongs to private persons.

33. POMPONIUS.

When the articles of sale contain a clause that 'the flow of the rain-water and the eaves-drop shall remain as at present,' without giving any further specification, the first thing to look to is what was the arrangement actually meant; if that is not clear, the construction which is prejudicial to the seller is to be adopted, because there is an ambiguity in the terms used.

---

private person. So if a person drove in piles in the sea-shore and built on it, he acquired a real right in the structure, so long as it stood, though not in the soil. *Inst.* ii. 1. 5.

The bankers (*argentarii*) were under the supervision of the *praefectus urbi*, and carried on their business in booths round the forum; hence '*foro cedere*' is to become bankrupt. The booths were public property, built by the censors, who sold the use of them to the bankers. Livy, xxxix. 44; xl. 51; *Digest*, 2. 13. 4–13.

L. 33.—The rain-water that drops from the roof of a house was called *stillicidium*; if collected and passed on by a roue or

34. PAULUS libro XXXIII ad edictum.

Si in emptione fundi dictum sit accedere Stichum seruum neque intellegatur, quis ex pluribus accesserit, cum de alio emptor, de alio uenditor senserit, nihilo minus fundi uenditionem ualere constat: sed Labeo ait eum Stichum deberi quem uenditor intellexerit. nec refert, quanti sit accessio, siue plus in ea sit quam in ipsa re cui accedat an minus: plerasque enim res aliquando propter accessiones emimus, sicuti cum domus propter marmora et statuas et tabulas pictas ematur.

1. Omnium rerum quas quis habere uel possidere uel persequi potest uenditio recte fit: quas uero natura uel gentium ius uel mores ciuitatis commercio exuerunt, earum nulla uenditio est.

2. Liberum hominem scientes emere non possumus. sed nec talis emptio aut stipulatio admittenda est: 'cum seruus erit,'

---

spout, it was called *flumen*. For the nature of these urban servitudes regarding water from the roof, see D. 8. 2. 20 and 21. In D. 8. 2. 17, 3 the same clause occurs as here, and it is explained as amounting to an undertaking by the seller that the adjoining tenement is bound to receive the water from the house for sale, and that the latter is burdened with no servitude of this kind; the result being that the owner of the servient land is prohibited from building anything that might interfere with the flow of the rain-water off the purchaser's house.

A proprietor who had no servitude of eavesdrop was required by Roman law to build two and a half feet within his own march. In many Scotch burghs custom prescribes a free margin of nine inches; failing custom, the Dean of Guild has power to fix the distance. Ersk. *Inst.* ii. 9. 9.

L. 34 pr.—This text establishes that mistake touching an accessory, if there be agreement as to the principal subject of the sale, does not amount to essential error. Cujas thinks that *emptor* should be read in place of *uenditor*, both on account of the context (*plerasque enim res*, etc.), and because, as matter of construction, the presumption is against the seller where there is any ambiguity: but the conjecture is unnecessary, for the decision may quite well be put on the ground that the seller is debtor for

34. Paul.

It was a condition in a sale of lands that the slave Stichus was to pass with the lands, but it is not clear which of several slaves (of that name) was meant, the buyer and the seller having had different individuals in view; it is settled that the sale of the lands is good notwithstanding: and Labeo holds that the Stichus whom the seller meant is due. It is immaterial what the value of the accessory is, whether greater or less than that of the principal thing: for it is true of most things that they are occasionally bought for the sake of their accessories, a house for example on account of its marble ornaments, statues, and frescoes.

1. Whatever can be held as private property, or possessed, or sued for may lawfully be sold; but things which are withdrawn from commerce, by the law of nature or of nations or by public policy, are incapable of sale.

2. A free man cannot be purchased by one who knows his condition: neither is it permissible to purchase or stipulate for him 'in the event of his becoming a slave,' although a future

---

the delivery of an indeterminate subject (a *genus*), and therefore the choice of the individual rests with him.

§ 1. This is the most general definition given of the subject-matter of the contract, and it is adopted by the Scotch institutional writers, as indeed is the case with most of the general statements of law in this title. *Habere* has here its narrower sense implying ownership; the wider meaning which it often has is here conveyed by *possidere*; and *persequi* covers incorporeals, such as a claim of debt (*nomen*). Examples of sales held to be void on grounds of public policy (*mores civitatis*) will be found in L. 46 (no person holding an office of trust to buy goods under his care), and L. 62 (no civil servant to buy real property in his province): for statement of the principle see *Digest*, 2. 14. 27, 4; 28. 7. 15. Similar principles are recognised in all civilised states; thus contracts contrary to public policy or morality are void at common law in this country, and are often struck at by special statutes besides, *e.g.* sales of offices of trust or of the salaries attached to them.

§ 2. After stating generally in § 1 that the sale of things

quamuis dixerimus futuras res emi posse : nec enim fas est eiusmodi casus exspectare.

3. Item si et emptor et uenditor scit furtiuum esse quod uenit, a neutra parte obligatio contrahitur: si emptor solus scit, non obligabitur uenditor nec tamen ex uendito quicquam consequitur, nisi ultro quod conuenerit praestet : quod si uenditor scit, emptor ignorauit, utrinque obligatio contrahitur, et ita Pomponius quoque scribit.

---

which are not subjects of commerce is null, Paul here declares the sale of a free man void if the buyer knew his condition, implying apparently that the sale was valid if the buyer did not know, for he passes on in § 3 with the word '*item*' to deal with the sale of a *res furtiva*, which was not void unless the buyer knew the thing to be stolen. Cp. L. 4 *supra*. For the ethical grounds on which the sale of a free man under the condition *cum servus esse coeperit* was held to be inadmissible, cp. D. 45. 1. 83, 5, *casum aduersamque fortunam spectari hominis liberi neque ciuile neque naturale est.*

§ 3. There are four possible cases of the sale of stolen property : (1) Both parties know of the *vitium :* the sale is null, and neither party can demand performance of the contract because of his bad faith—*dolus dolo compensatur*. (2) Only the buyer knows : the seller is free from his obligation, but he must take the necessary steps to perform it if he prefers to maintain an action for the price ; the buyer cannot sue, being in bad faith. (3) Only the seller knows : the innocent buyer can bring the *actio empti*, and so compel the seller either to deliver or pay damages for his failure ; the buyer is bound simply to pay the price. (4) Neither party knows : the sale is effectual.

The words *quod conuenerit* (case 2) mean just *rem venditam ;* the seller can sue for the price only on condition that he implements his part of the bargain by making arrangements with the owner to purge the *vitium* and deliver the article to the buyer. This case is an example of what the Germans call '*das kinkende geschäft*' (*negotium claudicans*), *i.e.* a bilateral agreement, binding on the one party, but not on the other, owing to incapacity to contract, or on account of some external defect (cp. D. 19. 1. 13, 29)—if a pupil sells without the active con-

thing may, as already stated, be bought, because it is an improper thing to anticipate such a catastrophe.

3. Again, if both buyer and seller know that the thing for sale has been stolen, neither of them undertakes any obligation: if only the buyer knows, the seller will not be bound, and on the other hand he can have no claim arising out of the sale unless he voluntarily performs his part of the bargain; whereas, if the seller knows and the buyer does not, both parties are bound. Pomponius concurs in this view.

---

currence of his tutor, the purchaser is bound but the pupil is not. It is in the option of the pupil to hold to or reject the bargain, irrespective of the will of the other party; but he cannot maintain the transaction without recognising and validating the obligation undertaken by himself—the contract is valid as a whole or not at all. A *negotium* of this kind is 'relatively void' (Savigny, *Syst.* iv. 541); its existence depends on the decision of the party interested, and the other party is bound to await that decision. For another view, see note to L. 13, 29 *cit.*

These rules are based on plain grounds of morality and public policy. Thus if the seller alone is aware of the taint, the contract is valid, and the innocent purchaser is protected by his claim for indemnity, which is in this case independent of eviction; but if both are in bad faith, the contract is completely null, because the law regards both the seller, who alienates a moveable which he knows to be another's without the consent of the owner, and the buyer, who accepts the property knowing it to be stolen, as guilty of or accessory to an act of theft (C. vi. 2. 6; ib. 12; Gaius, ii. 50).

No contract between third parties regarding a *res furtiva* could prejudice the rights of the owner. In addition to the actions he could bring for recovery of the thing stolen, or its value, or a penalty for the theft, he was protected against the risk of a *bona fide* acquirer from the thief completing a title by usucapion unknown to him. By a rule as old as the Twelve Tables '*rei furtivae aeterna auctoritas esto*,' and by the *lex Atinia* some three centuries later, stolen property was excepted from the law of prescription. The *vitium furti* which tainted the property could only be purged by its return into the hands of the owner,

4. Rei suae emptio tunc ualet, cum ab initio id agatur, ut possessionem emat, quam forte uenditor habuit, et in iudicio possessionis potior esset.

---

or at least by his coming to know where it was, so that he could bring his real action for recovery. See generally, *Inst.* ii. tit. 6; Pothier, *Vente*, § 269 sq.

In England the rules of *market overt* (that is open), which have grown up by ancient custom in the supposed interest of commerce, give a protection to the *bonâ fide* purchaser in a question with the true owner, which he did not enjoy by the civil law. 'The general rule of law is, that all sales, and contracts of anything vendible in fairs or markets overt, shall not only be good between the parties, but also be binding on all those that have any right or property therein' (2 Blackstone, *Com.* 449; cp. S. G. B., § 24). In the country, the only market overt is that which is held in the market-place set apart by custom for the sale of particular goods, and on the special days fixed for particular towns by charter or prescription; but in the city of London, every shop in which goods are publicly exposed for sale is market overt 'for such things as the owner professes to trade in,' and that on every day except Sunday. The recent case as to stolen jewels sold to City jewellers (*Hargreave* v. *Spink*, Q. B. Div., Nov. 2, 1891) decides that a show-room above a shop is not market overt, but leaves the question open whether sales *to* the shopkeeper, or only sales *by* him, of such goods as he deals in, are privileged. But though the property in stolen goods, when sold in market overt, passes to the buyer, yet it revests in the person who was the owner when the offender is prosecuted to conviction (24 & 25 Vict. c. 96, a statutory rule dating back to Henry VIII.). It should be observed that there are other situations in which the privileges attached to a sale in open market make the buyer secure in his purchase: the sale is good, for instance, although the seller should have received the goods on loan or deposit, or have previously sold them to another, retaining the possession.

The English rules as to market overt have no place in the law of Scotland or America. Scots law, following closely the civil law, regards stolen property as affected with an inherent vice (*vitium reale*, or *labes realis*), which is not purged to any extent

4. You can validly purchase a thing that is already yours, provided your intention has all along been to acquire the possession of it which happens to be with the vendor, and so to improve your position in a possessory action.

by a sale in open market, and cannot be removed except by the return of the property to its original owner. The owner can follow it into the hands of a purchaser in spite of the most perfect good faith. There is an exception as regards bills of exchange, and bills of lading acquired *bonâ fide* in the course of trade. Bell, *Prin.* § 527 sq. In *Todd* v. *Armour* (1882) 9 R. 901, where the Scotch Court upheld the sale in open market in Ireland of a stolen horse, a well-grounded preference was expressed for the Scotch system. The principle applies not only where the goods sold have been stolen from the owner, where the seller therefore had no title at all, but also in other cases of purchase in good faith *a non domino;* thus, if a person has lawful possession of goods on a title of loan or pledge, and fraudulently sells them, the lender or pledgor can demand restitution of them from a *bonâ fide* purchaser. Brown, *Sale*, p. 417 sq.; and note to Bell, *Com.* i. 305.

In comparing the civil and the modern law, it must be borne in mind that, under the Roman system, theft fell under the law of Obligations; it was simply a violation of the rights of property (*delictum*), which subjected the thief and any person aiding and abetting him to civil action at the instance of the party wronged: in modern jurisprudence, on the contrary, theft is part of the criminal code, and the law regarding it has been developed mainly from this point of view.

§ 4. Suppose the ownership and the possession of a thing have been severed, it might happen that the owner prefers to pay the possessor—even if a thief—to hand over the thing to him rather than go to the trouble and expense of asserting his right as *dominus* by legal process. Hence the law recognised the idea of '*emptio possessionis,*' provided (1) the buyer was proprietor and aware of the fact (*ab initio id agatur*), and (2) the seller was in a position to convey the legal title to possession which an ordinary seller had to give (*possessio ad interdicta*)—if he was merely a *detentor* holding for another, he had no independent right that could form the subject of a sale, and he could not

5. Alia causa est degustandi, alia metiendi: gustus enim ad hoc proficit, ut improbare liceat, mensura uero non eo proficit, ut aut plus aut minus ueneat, sed ut appareat, quantum ematur.

6. Si emptio ita facta fuerit: 'est mihi emptus Stichus aut Pamphilus,' in potestate est uenditoris, quem uelit dare, sicut in stipulationibus, sed uno mortuo qui superest dandus est: et ideo prioris periculum ad uenditorem, posterioris ad emptorem respicit. sed et si pariter decesserunt, pretium debebitur: unus enim utique periculo emptoris uixit. idem dicendum est etiam, si emptoris fuit arbitrium quem uellet habere, si modo hoc solum arbitrio eius commissum sit, ut quem uoluisset emptum haberet, non et illud, an emptum haberet.

7. Tutor rem pupilli emere non potest: idemque porrigendum est ad similia, id est ad curatores procuratores et qui negotia aliena gerunt.

---

make the buyer *superior in interdicto*. Cp. note to L. 16 *supra*, and *Digest*, 41. 2. 8.

Faber thinks the words *et in iudicio*, etc., refer to the seller, and mean that he must have the jural possession as a condition of selling; but they apply more naturally to the buyer, for it is his aim to be enabled to use the interdicts with effect. The latter view is supported by the *Basilika*; they also confirm the MS. reading '*et*,' which some editors propose to replace by *ut* or *ita ut*.

§ 5. It was very common in the wine trade, especially in large transactions ('*in doliis*,' '*auersione*'), for the buyer to stipulate that he should be afforded an opportunity of tasting the wine ('*degustatio*,' '*emptio ad gustum*'), though there seems to be no text which says that such a condition was always *implied* (cp. Cato, *De Re Rust.* c. 148; D. 18. 6. 1 pr.; ib. 4, 1; ib. 15). The trial must be made within the term fixed, or, if no term is fixed, upon delivery without undue delay: default is held to be a renunciation of the condition. The import of the condition was, that the buyer could reject the wine only if it proved to be sour or mouldy (*propter acorem vel mucorem*); but if it was of merchantable quality, as we say, it appears he was bound to accept it, though it was not to his taste. This proviso, in fact, operated

5. Tasting has quite a different function from measuring; the right to taste implies a power of rejection, whereas the measuring of the commodity does not serve to increase or diminish the quantity sold, but only to show how much there is of it.

6. If the purchase is made in these terms, 'Stichus or Pamphilus is mine by purchase,' it is in the power of the vendor to give whichever he likes, just as in similar stipulations; but if one die, the survivor must be given, so that the vendor bears the risk of the former, the vendee the risk of the latter: but though both have died at the same time, the price remains due, for one at least lived at the risk of the vendee. The same is true where it was left to the purchaser to choose which he would have, provided the only thing left to his option was which he preferred to buy, and not whether he should buy at all.

7. A tutor cannot purchase anything belonging to his ward: a principle which must be extended to all similar cases, as curators, agents, and all who manage other people's business.

---

as a resolutive condition; accordingly the risk of the wine perishing (*periculum interitus*) passed to the buyer immediately, while the risk of deterioration in the respects above mentioned remained with the seller till the trial was made. The framers of the French Civil Code, however, wrongly regarding it as a suspensive condition, laid down the rule that the sale of wine, oil, etc., shall not be complete until the buyer has tasted and accepted (art. 1587), a rule which has proved most inconvenient in practice.

The condition in a sale *ad mensuram* has quite different effects: till the measuring takes place, there is no completed sale for want of determination of the thing sold.

§ 6. The first slave dies for the seller, for he is still debtor for the delivery, and must perform his obligation by delivering the other; the second dies for the buyer, for he must pay the purchase-price, though he gets nothing in exchange, the obligation of the seller being now impossible of performance. This is an example of the ordinary rule as to risk, where neither party is in fault. *Inst.* iii. 23. 3; *Digest*, 18. 6. 8 pr., etc.

Compare, for the seller's option in an alternative sale, L. 25 pr., and for the buyer's option, L. 7 pr.

35. GAIUS libro X ad edictum prouinciale.

Quod saepe arrae nomine pro emptione datur, non eo pertinet, quasi sine arra conuentio nihil proficiat, sed ut euidentius probari possit conuenisse de pretio.

L. 35 pr.—Phoenician traders carried the custom and the Hebrew name of earnest ('*érávón*, a pledge) into Greece and Italy; the word took the form ἀρραβὼν in Greek, and this is copied in early Latin, but in the jurists the form is always *arra*: the resemblance of our word 'earnest' (in Welsh 'ernes,' in Scotch 'arles') may be accidental (Skeat).[1] It might be either a sum of money or a token of some value (often a ring, D. 14. 3. 5, 15; 19. 1. 11, 6), given by the one contracting party to the other when the bargain was struck, as a sign of its completion and also as a pledge of its fulfilment. The point mainly insisted on in the texts is that earnest, though often given, was not a necessary condition; it was really a means of facilitating proof of the contract. *Inst.* iii. 23 pr.: *emptio et uenditio contrahitur simulatque de pretio conuenerit, quamuis nondum pretium numeratum sit ac ne arra quidem data sit: nam quod arrae nomine datur, argumentum est emptionis et uenditionis contractae.* Cp. Gaius, iii. § 139. Some have thought, from the emphasis with which it is laid down that earnest was not a requisite of sale, that it may have played a more important part in the earlier law. If sale was originally a conveyance,—an immediate exchange of the wares for the price,—in the next stage of its development there might be a relaxation of the necessity for instant payment, and the giving of a trifle as earnest of the price might be held sufficient to make out *rei interventus* and ground an action. The symbolical act of giving earnest would thus serve as a bridge between the purely formal and the purely consensual modes of sale. However this may be, it was not an essential part of a valid contract by the law of the classical period, although it was a common accessory. Neither was there any idea at this time of either party getting off his engagements by forfeiting the *arra*; it simply marked off the concluded contract and, in particular, the assent as to the price, from the preliminary negotiations. It was thus distinct from part-payment, which properly followed at the time of delivery, consisted of money, and indicated that credit was

[1] Cp. *Howe* v. *Smith*, 27 Ch. D. at p. 102.

35. Gaius.

It is common in making a purchase to give something by way of earnest, not because the agreement would be ineffectual without earnest, but to serve as a positive proof that the parties are at one as to the price.

given for the balance (C. iv. 45. 2): although if earnest was given in money, it might, when the contract came to be executed, be imputed to the price (D. 18. 3. 6, 2 ; ib. 8); if the earnest was something other than money, an action on the contract or a *condictio sine causa* would lie to enforce its return (D. 19. 1. 11, 6). It was forfeited to the seller if he put in force the *lex commissoria*. See p. 18.

The above seems to be the only form of earnest recognised in the *Pandects*; and it has received from the commentators the name *arra confirmatoria*. But Justinian, while leaving the classical practice in force, sanctioned by his later legislation a quite distinct, and possibly foreign, institution, to which the name *arra contractu imperfecto data* has been given, because it creates a certain tie between the negotiating parties who are in treaty with a view to effecting a sale. Hieronymus refers to it as *arrabo futurae emptionis quasi quoddam testimonium*. The novelty was that this earnest was given not upon the completion of the contract but during the preliminaries, and was held to be merely evidence of willingness to complete the contract. Either party was at liberty to draw back from the projected sale if he chose to incur a penalty, and the law, in that event, made the earnest the measure of damages to be paid by the party refusing to go on,—if it was the giver of the earnest, he forfeited what he had given ; if it was the receiver, he had to restore the *arra* and as much more (C. iv. 21. 17, 1 ; cp. *Inst.* iii. 23 pr.). Unfortunately it is impossible to harmonise these passages in all points (see Bechmann, *Kauf*, ii. p. 422). Many think that the passage in the *Inst.* (*hoc enim subsecuto*, etc.) refers to *completed* sales and the penalties for non-execution. If so, the change introduced by Justinian came to this: either (1) that a sacrifice of the *arra*, whether given before or after the contract, and whether the contract was oral or written, entitled either party to refuse performance,—a serious innovation in the doctrine of Obligation, which, however, has never wanted champions in France,—or (2) that

1. Illud constat imperfectum esse negotium, cum emere uolenti sic uenditor dicit: 'quanti uelis, quanti aequum putaueris, quanti aestimaueris, habebis emptum.'

2. Ueneni mali quidam putant non contrahi emptionem, quia nec societas aut mandatum flagitiosae rei ullas uires habet: quae sententia potest sane uera uideri de his quae nullo modo adiectione alterius materiae usu nobis esse possunt: de his uero quae mixta aliis materiis adeo nocendi naturam deponunt, ut ex

---

forfeiture of the *arra* given upon the completion of the contract was now made a cumulative penalty upon a party who refused voluntary performance, additional to the action which (it is said) lay against him to enforce specific performance or damages in lieu of it,—an opinion which has the balance of authority in its favour. Cp. Pothier, *Vente*, § 507 sq.; Savigny, *Obl.* ii. p. 276, who says that the change was that the *arra confirmatoria* received the further character of an accessory penal sum.

There is no controversy as to the other innovation introduced by Justinian (*Inst. loc. cit.*, cp. p. 12), whereby a contract which the parties had agreed to reduce to writing was not to be held complete and final till the document (*instrumentum*) had been drawn up with all proper formalities; before that, it was open to either party to recede *sine poena*, however far matters had advanced, unless earnest had been given, in which case the amount of the earnest formed the measure of the damages to be paid by the party withdrawing from the bargain.

Curiously enough, art. 1590 in the French Code: '*Si la promesse de vente a été faite avec des arrhes, chacun des contractans est maître de s'en départir, celui qui les a données en les perdant, et celui qui les a reçues en restituant le double,*' has been as fruitful of controversy as Justinian's legislation on this subject. Obviously it puts a promise to sell in suspense if earnest be given; but the Code says nothing as to the effect of earnest accompanying a concluded sale, and so the old discussion has been revived in the Courts and among the commentators whether either party is allowed to abandon the sale on sacrificing the earnest.

In England earnest is still of some importance, because either earnest or part payment (which are distinct, earnest being a coin or anything of value actually given, ' to bind the bargain,' and not

XVIII. 1. DE CONTRAHENDA EMPTIONE.

1. It is quite settled that the transaction is incomplete, when the seller says to the intending purchaser: 'you shall have the thing for what you please,' 'for what you think fair,' 'for what you think it worth.'

2. Some are of opinion that a contract to buy poison will not stand any more than a partnership or a mandate for an improper purpose: this opinion may no doubt be considered sound with respect to poisons which do not admit of being compounded with another substance into something useful to man; but the contrary is true of those which lose their hurtful qualities by mixture

---

as part of the price) validates a parol contract for the sale of goods worth £10 or more (*Statute of Frauds*, § 17). On forfeiture of earnest, see *Howe* v. *Smith* (1884) 27 Ch. D. 101; and on the question whether the giving of earnest can alter the property, Benj. p. 314, who holds its true legal effect to be evidentiary only, the property passing in virtue of the bargain and sale which it completes.

The Scotch text-writers assign the same function to earnest as the classical jurists did. Stair, i. 14. 3; Erskine, iii. 3. 5. It is in use in certain localities in the hiring of servants as the test of engagement; but it is not essential, unless prescribed by local usage, when there is *locus poenitentiae* till it has been given. The return of the earnest never dissolves an engagement by Scots law. Bell, *Prin.* § 173.

§ 1. The general opinion is that a sale in which the fixing of the price is referred to the buyer is null (see p. 22, note, and Pothier, § 23); but Windscheid (§ 386) thinks the bargain is not invalid, though it is incomplete (*imperfectum*) till the price is actually named, which must be done *pro viri boni arbitrio*,—an unjust estimate can be set aside.

By Scots law the price may be referred to the award of one of the parties, subject to equitable modification by the judge. Ersk. iii. 3. 4; Bell, *Prin.* § 92; *Earl of Montrose* (1639) M. 14, 155; *Steven* (1760) M. 3158; *Lavaggi* v. *Pirie* (1872) 10 Macp. 312.

§ 2. The law as to the sale of poisons is stated at length in *Digest*, 48, tit. 8, *Ad legem Corneliam de sicariis et veneficis*, esp. L. 3. *Venenum* itself was a word of neutral meaning, including

his antidoti et alia quaedam salubria medicamenta conficiantur, aliud dici potest.

3. Si quis amico peregre eunti mandauerit, ut fugitiuum suum quaerat et si inuenerit uendat, nec ipse contra senatus consultum committit, quia non uendidit, neque amicus eius, quia praesentem uendit: emptor quoque, qui praesentem emit, recte negotium gerere intellegitur.

4. Si res uendita per furtum perierit, prius animaduertendum erit, quid inter eos de custodia rei conuenerat: si nihil appareat conuenisse, talis custodia desideranda est a uenditore, qualem bonus pater familias suis rebus adhibet: quam si praestiterit et tamen rem perdidit, securus esse debet, ut tamen scilicet uindicationem rei et condictionem exhibeat emptori. unde uidebimus in personam eius qui alienam rem uendiderit: cum is nullam uindicationem aut condictionem habere possit, ob id ipsum damnandus est, quia, si suam rem uendidisset, potuisset eas actiones ad emptorem transferre.

---

medicines and love-philtres (*amatorium*); the statute only struck at the preparation, sale, and possession of noxious drugs (*venena mala*) *necandi hominis causa*. Apart from the statutory provisions in that behalf, contracts which had for their object anything contrary to morals and public policy were void at common law, as they are with us: *si maleficii societas coita sit, constat nullam esse societatem* (D. 17. 2. 57).

§ 3. The reference is to a SC. mentioned in D. 48. 15. 2. That title deals at length with the *lex Fabia de plagiariis* (under which it was a criminal offence to buy or sell a free person with the knowledge that he was so) and with the sale of slaves *in fuga*. The SC. forbade what was called *emptio fugae*, i.e. a sale of a runaway slave by his owner under which the buyer took the risk of his capture, as the buyer of a *spes* took the risk of the expectation being realised. A mandate, however, to search for and sell the runaway, and a sale conditional upon his being caught, were not illegal transactions, because the sale is postponed till the slave has ceased to be *in fuga*. Cp. *Inst.* ii. 6. 1.

§ 4. Though *periculum rei venditae nondum traditae est emptoris*, yet there was an accessory obligation on the seller to be guilty

with other substances, so that antidotes and other health-giving medicines are prepared from them.

3. A man who gives a friend who is about to travel a mandate to search for his runaway slave and sell him if he finds him, does not himself contravene the senatus-consult, for he has not sold him, neither does his friend because he sells a slave who is present; and it is quite a legal transaction on the buyer's part also, for he buys a slave who is present.

4. In the event of the thing sold being lost by theft, the first point to be looked to is, What agreement was made about the custody of the thing? If it appears there was none, the same degree of watchfulness is to be required of the seller as a careful man bestows upon his own affairs: if he comes up to that standard, and has notwithstanding lost the thing, he should incur no liability, provided of course he cedes to the purchaser his real action and his personal action. This will explain the rule applicable to the case of one who sells what belongs to another: he is liable in damages just because these actions are not competent to him; for, had he sold what belonged to him, he would have been in a position to cede the right to these actions to the buyer.

---

of no default in taking care of the thing until delivery, to exercise the care of a *bonus paterfamilias*: *custodiam autem uenditor talem praestare debet quam praestant hi quibus res commodata est, ut diligentiam praestet exactiorem quam in suis rebus adhiberet* (D. 18. 6. 3). He was answerable for fault absolutely, (*culpa leuis in abstracto* as the modern civilians call it, *i.e.* fault measured by the care bestowed on their own property by careful men generally), according to the maxim, *in contractibus in quibus utriusque contrahentis utilitas uersatur, leuis culpa, non etiam leuissima praestatur* (cp. *Inst.* iii. 23. 3), *quidquid enim sine dolo et culpa uenditoris accidit, in eo uenditor securus est*; and he was excused only by *damnum fatale uel uis magna* (D. 18. 6. 2, 1). But the seller might by express undertaking become responsible for *casus* as well; he was then said *custodiam suscipere*, and was bound to show the utmost possible vigilance, and to answer even for accident, unless at all events he could show that no human

5. In his quae pondere numero mensuraue constant, ueluti frumento uino oleo argento, modo ea seruantur quae in ceteris, ut simul atque de pretio conuenerit, uideatur perfecta uenditio, modo ut, etiamsi de pretio conuenerit, non tamen aliter uideatur perfecta uenditio, quam si admensa adpensa adnumerataue sint. nam si omne uinum uel oleum uel frumentum uel argentum quantumcumque esset uno pretio uenierit, idem iuris est quod in ceteris rebus. quod si uinum ita uenierit, ut in singulas amphoras, item oleum, ut in singulos metretas, item frumentum, ut in singulos medios, item argentum, ut in singulas libras certum pretium diceretur, quaeritur, quando uideatur emptio perfici. quod similiter scilicet quaeritur et de his quae numero constant, si pro numero corporum pretium fuerit statutum. Sabinus et Cassius tunc perfici emptionem existimant, cum adnumerata admensa adpensaue sint, quia uenditio quasi sub hac condicione uidetur fieri, ut* in singulos metretas aut in singulos modios quos quasue admensus eris, aut in singulas libras quas adpenderis, aut in singula corpora quae adnumeraueris.

---

foresight could have guarded against it. Such, for instance, was the obligation of shipmasters, etc., under the Edict; they were held *omnium recipere custodiam quae in nauem illata sunt*, and were responsible *etiamsi sine culpa res periit uel damnum datum est, nisi si quid damno fatali contingit* (D. 4. 9. 1, 8; ib. 3, 1; cp. *Juridical Review* (Oct. 1891), iii. p. 316).

As to the seller's duty of transferring his rights of action, see *Inst. loc. cit.;* D. 19. 1. 31 pr. The vendee could not bring the *actio furti* in his own name before delivery (D. 47. 2. 14 pr.; ib. 81 pr.).

Pothier (*Vente*, § 55) holds that, when the vendee is *in mora* by delaying or refusing to take away the goods, the vendor's obligation is narrowed down to liability for malicious conduct or gross neglect, according to the rule *cum moram emptor adhibere coepit, iam non culpam, sed dolum malum tantum praestandum a uenditore* (D. 18. 6. 18).

The vendor is, by Scots law also, under a similar obligation to attend to the vendee's interest in the interval between sale and delivery. Ersk. iii. 3. 7. The cases have mainly been with reference to the precautions proper to be taken where goods are to be

5. With regard to things which are weighed, counted, or measured, as grain, wine, oil, silver, sometimes the same principle holds for them as for other things—a sale is considered complete as soon as the price is settled; sometimes the rule is that, although the price is settled, yet the sale is not held to be complete until a process of measuring, weighing, or counting has followed. Thus when a whole lot of wine, oil, grain, or silver is sold for a slump sum, however much there may be of it, the law is the same as for other things. But when wine is sold at so much a jar, oil at so much a measure, wheat at so much a bushel, silver at so much a pound, the question arises, When is the sale complete? The same question, of course, arises about things which pass by number, when a price is fixed at so much a head. Sabinus and Cassius think the sale is completed only when the counting, measuring, or weighing has been done, because the sale would seem to be made subject to this condition, so to speak, that the contract is to have reference to the separate measures or bushels to be measured, the separate pounds to be weighed, or the separate units to be counted out of the mass.

---

delivered at a distant place and have to be transmitted through a carrier. Cp. S. G. B. §§ 34, 35; Bell, *Prin.* §§ 116–118.

Lord Blackburn (*Sale*, p. 260) seems to hold that where the seller remains in possession of goods after the property in them has passed to the buyer—as it does in England in virtue of the contract, if the goods are specific and no contrary intention appears—the seller is a bailee for the buyer, and is subject to the same responsibility for careful keeping as the Roman law imposed upon the seller before the property had passed by delivery. 'But there appears to be no decision defining the nature of such bailment' (Chalmers, *Sale*, p. 36).

§§ 5–7. On the question of *periculum* generally, see Vangerow, § 591. The rule of Roman law is quite distinct that, as soon as the contract is complete, the goods are at the risk of the purchaser, and, if they perish accidentally, the seller is absolutely free, but the buyer is bound to pay the price, although the goods have not been delivered and the property in them has not been transferred. The all-important matter, therefore, is to ascertain *when* a sale is

6. Ergo et si grex uenierit, si quidem uniuersaliter uno pretio, perfecta uidetur, postquam de pretio conuenerit: si uero in singula corpora certo pretio, eadem erunt, quae proxime tractauimus.

---

complete to the effect of passing the risk: *necessario sciendum est quando perfecta sit emptio: tunc enim sciemus, cuius periculum sit, nam perfecta emptione periculum ad emptorem respiciet* (D. 18. 6. 8 pr.). The sequel to that passage states very tersely what is requisite to perfect the contract: *et si id quod uenierit appareat quid quale quantum sit, et pretium, et pure uenit, perfecta est emptio.* Cp. *Inst.* iii. 23. 3.

§§ 5 and 6 take up the question when a contract for the sale of things which pass by weight, number, or measure ('fungibles') is complete. The answer is that they may be sold in two ways: (*a*) they may be specifically ascertained as a separate lot, and a gross price be fixed for the whole, as in a sale *en bloc* of all the corn in a granary (the exact quantity being unknown) or of a whole flock of sheep for a slump price (sale *per aversionem* (L. 62, 2) or *universaliter uno pretio*); it is on exactly the same footing as an ordinary sale, and the risk is changed as soon as the parties are *ad idem* on the subject sold and the price. Cp. D. 18. 6. 1, 1; C. iv. 48. 1, 1; ib. 2: (*β*) Though the quantity or lot is specifically distinguished, yet the price may be fixed at so much per unit: here the amount of the price depends upon an operation of weighing, counting, or measuring, and it could never be liquidated if some *casus fortuitus* made it impossible to ascertain the number of units; it is like a sale where the fixing of the price is referred to a third party (p. 10, note) and is therefore held to be conditional, and the risk remains on the seller until the act necessary for the purpose of ascertaining the price is performed. Some civilians think that in this case also the sale is perfect, because the subject is identified and the price agreed on, and nothing is unascertained except its money value; but this view, though plausible on general grounds, cannot be maintained in face of §§ 5, 6 above.

Some words seem to have dropped out after *ut* * (§ 5 *fin.*): Mommsen suggests *in singulas amphoras contrahatur aut;* another conjecture is *pretium constituatur.*

In §§ 5, 6, a whole quantity was sold. In § 7 only a part of a

6. So in the case of a flock, if it is sold for a slump price, the sale is held to be complete, immediately the price is fixed; but if it is sold at so much a head, the rule we have just explained will apply.

---

larger whole (say ten dozen of wine out of a large cellar) is sold; and the same rule applies, whether the price be so much a dozen or so much for the lot. Here the contract is not complete (*nondum apparet quid uenierit*) till the necessary separation of the quantity sold has been made, till specific goods are appropriated to the contract as we say; meanwhile the seller bears the whole risk (*omne periculum, i.e.* both the risk of deterioration and of total destruction). C. iv. 48. 2 ; D. 18. 6. 5 ; Vat. Fr. 16. The civilians discuss under what conditions the setting apart of individual *corpora* to which the contract is to attach must be carried out so as to alter the risk (Windscheid, § 390), but there is a lack of authority in the texts. It has been suggested that the same principle should have been applied here as in the case of an alternative obligation (L. 34, 6), so that, if the seller's obligation became imprestable owing to the accidental destruction of the whole mass or bulk out of which the *res vendita* was to be taken under the contract, the buyer would still be liable for the price; the non-separation of his specific goods, it may be said, is an irrelevant fact, seeing that his portion (whichever it might have been) has perished with the rest. But the buyer, whose only hold upon the seller is that the latter is bound to separate and deliver say ten sheep out of a large flock, where the number of possible combinations of ten may be endless, has not the right to a specific thing in any ordinary sense. Hence the *obligatio generis* was looked upon as practically a conditional sale, and therefore imperfect in the sense here appropriate, till the condition of weighing, measuring, or counting was purified. Cp. Pothier, *Vente*, § 308 sq.

The incidence of the risk is practically the same in modern law. But English law reaches this result by a different road: the theory is that 'the risk of the loss is *prima facie* in the person in whom the property is' (Lord Blackburn in *Martineau* v. *Kitching* (1872) L. R. 7 Q. B. p. 454; cp. S. G. B. § 22), and the maxim *res perit domino* applies to sales (which it did not by the Roman law). The law of Scotland adopts the maxim

7. Sed et si ex dolcario pars uini uenierit, ueluti metretae centum, uerissimum est (quod et constare uidetur) antequam admetiatur, omne periculum ad uenditorem pertinere: nec interest, unum pretium omnium centum metretarum in semel dictum sit an in singulos eos.

---

of the civil law *periculum rei uenditae nondum traditae est emptoris*, the theory being that accidental destruction of the thing sold extinguishes the buyer's *jus ad rem specificam* by making the seller's obligation to deliver it imprestable, while the buyer's obligation to pay the price subsists unaffected (Pothier, *Vente*, §§ 56, 307; Brodie's Stair, p. 854 sq.; Bell, *Prin.* § 87). It follows from this that in Roman and Scots law the doctrine of risk forms no criterion by which the question of property can be decided; while in English law if it can be shown that the risk attached to one person or the other, that is an argument for showing that the property was meant to be in him. But though the risk usually attaches to the ownership, they are not inseparable. The expression *res perit domino* is ambiguous: 'the distinction must be borne in mind between being the loser of the property and the loser by the contract; for if the parties have agreed, as they certainly may, that although the property is to be in one party, yet if the goods are lost, the other party is to pay for them, it is clear that the risk is no test of property in that case' (Blackburn, *Sale*, p. 245; cp. Bell, *Com.* i. 180). Thus risk is always in the end a question of intention; if the terms of the contract are express, they receive effect; if not, the Courts have adopted certain rules of construction for arriving at the presumed intention both as to the property, and the risk as an incident of it. See S. G. B. § 20. The question usually is: (1) Where the goods are specific, whether the seller is bound to do something to them to put them into a deliverable state, meaning a state in which the buyer is bound to accept them; and (2) where the goods are specific and in a deliverable state, whether anything remains to be done to them (such as measuring, counting, weighing, or testing) by the seller or by the parties jointly for the purpose of ascertaining the price: if so, the doing of such act or thing is presumed to be intended as a condition precedent to the passing of the property and the risk. *Anderson* v. *Morice* (1875) L. R. 10 C. P. 609 and 1 App. Ca. 713, and *Turley* v.

7. When part of the wine in a cellar is sold, say 100 measures, it is quite fixed (as seems to be admitted on all hands) that all the risk lies on the vendor until the quantity is measured off, and it makes no difference whether the price named was a slump sum for the whole hundred or so much a measure.

Bates (1863) 2 H. & C. 200 (where the earlier cases are reviewed) may be taken as typical cases under these heads.

It will be observed that the second of these principles is just the rule stated in §§ 5, 6 of this lex, regarding the necessity of ascertaining the money value of the price where it depends on number, weight, etc., before the contract is complete to the effect of passing the risk. This rule is said to have been arbitrarily adopted from the Roman law within the present century[1]: thus in *Zagury* v. *Furnell* (1809) 2 Camp. 239, where several bales each containing five dozen goat-skins were sold at so much a dozen and all burnt before counting (which was proved to be the duty of the seller by usage), Lord Ellenborough was of opinion that 'as the enumeration of the skins was necessary to ascertain the price, this was an act for the benefit of the seller; and as this act remained to be done by him when the fire happened, there was not a complete transfer to the purchaser, and the skins continued at the seller's risk.' As the law of England does not require the price to be fixed in money before a sale is complete, it is hard to see why the risk and property should not have passed. But the rule is now well established, and the only question is whether its operation should be confined to acts to be done by the seller.

The sale of an undivided or unseparated portion of a specific mass or bulk (as in § 7 of the text) may be compared with *Campbell* v. *Mersey Docks Co.* (1863) 14 C. B. n. s. 412, and other cases in Benj., p. 295 sq., where it was held that neither property nor risk could pass unless, and until, the goods were ascertained by separation or division.

In the Scotch case, *Hansen* v. *Craig & Rose* (1859) 21 D. 432, a cargo of oil, the actual weight of which was stated in the contract, along with particulars from which the gross price could be readily calculated, was destroyed by fire when ready for delivery; *held*, that the contract was complete and the risk had

---
[1] See Blackburn, *Sale*, p. 174 sq.

8. Si quis in uendendo praedio confinem celauerit, quem emptor si audisset, empturus non esset, teneri uenditorem.

36. ULPIANUS libro XLIII ad edictum.

Cum in uenditione quis pretium rei ponit donationis causa non exacturus, non uidetur uendere.

37. ULPIANUS libro III disputationum.

Si quis fundum iure hereditario sibi delatum ita uendidisset: 'erit tibi emptus tanti, quanti a testatore emptus est,' mox inueniatur non emptus, sed donatus testatori, uidetur quasi sine pretio facta uenditio, ideoque similis erit sub condicione factae uenditioni, quae nulla est, si condicio defecerit.

38. ULPIANUS libro VII disputationum.

Si quis donationis causa minoris uendat, uenditio ualet:

passed to the buyer, although he had not checked the weight and quality of the oil, which he was entitled by usage to do. Lord J.-C. Inglis there expressed an opinion that where a mass of fungibles, certain and known by general description but of unascertained extent, has been sold at a price according to measure, the contract is not complete so as to transfer the risk to the buyer until the mass has been measured and the price thus ascertained. Though there seems to be no express decision on that point, nor on the case where the quantity sold is still an undivided part of a larger mass, Bell pronounces in favour of the same practical result as has been reached in England (*Com.* i. 473; where the learned editor of the 7th ed. dissents). See also *Anderson* (1870) 9 Macp. 122, and *Walker* (1873) 11 Macp. 906.

§ 8. Pothier adopts this decision and puts it among the engagements to which good faith binds the vendor, *au moins dans le for de la conscience* (§ 236). It could hardly be maintained now *dans le for extérieur* that the seller of lands has a duty to inform the buyer that he will have a troublesome neighbour. The modern conscience is content with *caveat emptor* in a matter of this kind.

L. 36.—This text is one of the foundations for the familiar rule that the price must be '*verum*'—the agreement that the

8. The seller of a piece of land is responsible for having concealed the name of an adjoining proprietor, if the knowledge of it would have kept the purchaser from buying.

36. ULPIAN.

When a person sells a thing, putting a price on it which he does not mean to exact, his purpose being to make a gift of it, that is not held to be a sale.

37. ULPIAN.

When a man sells an estate to which he has succeeded under a will on these terms, 'you shall have it for what the testator paid for it,' and it afterwards transpires that the testator got it in gift and not by purchase, the sale is regarded as one in which no price has been fixed, and so it is in the same position as a conditional sale, which is void if the condition fails.

38. ULPIAN.

If a person sells for a small price meaning to make a gift, the seller is to get the price and the buyer is to get the thing must be seriously meant (L. 2. 1, note). If the mention of a price is a mere sham, tacked on for the look of the thing, the disposition is invalid as a sale, but valid as a donation according to the maxim *plus valet quod agitur quam quod simulate concipitur*. So *Code* iv. 38. 3: *Si donationis causa uenditionis simulatus contractus est, emptio sui deficit substantia:* ib. 9, *donationis gratia praedii facta uenditione si traditio sequatur, actione pretii nulla competente perficitur donatio.* Under Justinian no special form was required for a donation of less than 500 *solidi;* so that a gift under cloak of a sale would be good up to that amount. Pothier, § 18.

L. 37.—There is here only the appearance of a price, and so no sale: on the other hand there was no intention to make a gift, and so no donation. Donation would be inferred, if the heir had known that the testator got a gift of the lands. Pothier, § 16.

L. 38.—If a thing is purposely sold under value out of regard for the buyer, such a disposition ('*venditio gratiosa*') is quite

totiens enim dicimus in totum uenditionem non ualere, quotiens uniuersa uenditio donationis causa facta est: quotiens uero uiliore pretio res donationis causa distrahitur, dubium non est uenditionem ualere. hoc inter ceteros: inter uirum uero et uxorem donationis causa uenditio facta pretio uiliore nullius momenti est.

39. Iulianus libro xv digestorum.

Si debitor rem pigneratam a creditore redemerit, quasi suae rei emptor actione ex uendito non tenetur et omnia in integro sunt creditori.

1. Uerisimile est eum qui fructum oliuae pendentis uendidisset, et stipulatus est decem pondo olei quod natum esset, pretium constituisse ex eo quod natum esset usque ad decem pondo olei: idcirco solis quinque collectis non amplius emptor* petere potest quam quinque pondo olei, quae collecta essent, a plerisque responsum est.

---

valid as a sale, because in this case there is a price, though a low one; at the same time it has the character of donation *pro tanto*. The price, however, must not be nugatory, or so disproportionate to the value of the thing as to suggest that it is not seriously meant: *si quis conduxerit nummo uno, conductio nulla est, quia et hoc donationis instar inducit* (D. 19. 2. 46; cp. D. 41. 2. 10, 2).

Sale at a low price by one spouse to the other was invalid owing to the prohibition of *donatio inter virum et uxorem*. See D. 24. 1. 5, 5 for further developments of the principle. Pothier, §§ 19–21, 39.

Observe that the above texts do not involve the condition that the price shall be *iustum* or adequate to the true worth of the thing.

L. 39 pr.—*In integro sunt* means that the creditor has the same right over the pledge as before the attempted purchase. So also L. 16 pr. *supra*, and D. 13. 7. 40 pr.: *debitor a creditore pignus quod dedit frustra emit, cum rei suae nulla emptio sit*. The proprietor is still *dominus* of his pledge, and the only thing he can do is to pay the debt and thus relieve the *res pignerata* from the *nexus* under which it lies. From D. 17. 1. 22, 3 it seems that the owner could give a mandate to a friend to buy in his pledges

sale is valid; for it is only when donation is the sole consideration moving the sale that we hold it absolutely void; but when a thing is sold at a reduced price as a mode of donation, there is no doubt that the sale is good. This is true of all parties except husband and wife; a sale at a low price by one spouse to the other, intended to operate as a donation, has no force whatever.

39. JULIAN.

A debtor, who buys from his creditor a thing he has pledged, cannot be sued by the action on sale, the principle being that he is buying his own property, and the creditor's rights remain unaffected.

1. Where a man has sold the crop of olives on a tree and stipulated for ten pounds of the oil to be obtained, it appears to me that he has fixed a price out of the oil that may be produced not exceeding ten pounds: accordingly, if the yield of oil is only five pounds, the buyer cannot claim anything more than the five pounds actually obtained; such is the opinion of most of the jurists.

---

when exposed for sale; the friend acquired the property for himself in the first instance according to the Roman idea of agency. Though the owner could purchase an adverse right of possession (p. 65), apparently he was not regarded as purchasing at all when he discharged a personal or real burden affecting his property; but in the case of a servitude, in particular, this must be held to be doubtful in the absence of distinct authority, for there are traces of the practical extinction of a servitude being accomplished by the grant of a counter-servitude in favour of the hitherto servient tenement, in which case there would be a quite intelligible *res vendita*.

Some of the dispositions which the civil law held to be sales we should now treat as assignments, *e.g.* claims of debt.

§ 1. The circumstances supposed are that a man has sold an expected olive-crop (an *emptio rei speratae*, L. 8 *supra*), and has stipulated for 10 lbs. of the oil that may be produced (words which are held to be *taxative*), the buyer to be at the expense of pressing the oil. *Held*, that the buyer cannot demand from the

40. PAULUS libro IV epitomarum Alfendi digestorum.

Qui fundum uendebat, in lege ita dixerat, ut emptor in diebus triginta proximis fundum metiretur et de modo renuntiaret, et si ante eam diem non renuntiasset, ut uenditoris fides soluta esset: emptor intra diem mensurae quo minorem modum esse credidit renuntiauit et pecuniam pro eo accepit: postea eum fundum uendidit et cum ipse emptori suo admetiretur, multo minorem modum agri quam putauerat inuenit: quaerebat, an id quod minor is esset consequi a suo uenditore posset. respondit interesse, quemadmodum lex diceretur: nam si ita dictum esset, ut emptor diebus triginta proximis fundum metiatur et domino renuntiet, quanto modus agri minor sit, quod * post diem trigensimum renuntiasset, nihil ei profuturum: sed si ita pactum esset, ut emptor in diebus proximis fundum metiatur et de modo agri renuntiet, etsi * in diebus triginta [non] renuntiasset minorem modum agri esse, quamuis multis post annis posse eum quo minor is modus agri fuisset repetere.

---

seller more than 5 lbs., if that is the whole yield of oil. When pounds of oil are mentioned in lieu of price, we must suppose Julian to mean their money value; otherwise the bargain would not be sale. The point decided is that the seller is responsible for no more than the actual yield; he could not be sued by the buyer for damages for the other 5 lbs. Cp. *Basil.* xix. 1. 37 : *uendidi tibi fructum pendentis oliuae uel promisi decem pondo, et solu quinque pondo nasci contigit: non amplius quam quinque pondo a me exigentur.*

That is quite an intelligible decision, but what the context leads us to expect is a determination not as to the seller's liability for the deficient yield, but whether the buyer is liable to pay anything more than the value of 5 lbs. Hence many editors suspect that an error has crept into the report; the sense desired may be got by reading *ab emptore* for *emptor*, or better, *cum petere posse* (Mommsen) for *emptor petere potest*. The main point would then be that the price fixed is simply a *limit;* the buyer of the crop is to pay the seller nothing if there is no crop, for such a sale is conditional (p. 24); if there is a crop, the price

40. PAUL.

The seller of a piece of ground had made it a term of the sale that the purchaser should measure the land within the next month and give him notice as to the measurement, and that failing notice before the expiry of the month the seller should be relieved of his obligation: the purchaser timeously intimated what the shortage was according to his belief, and was repaid a proportionate sum: some time after he sold the land, and, on remeasuring it for the purchaser, he found its area was much less than he had supposed: he asked whether he could recover the value of the deficiency from the man who sold it to him. The answer was that it depended upon the language used in the contract: if its terms were, 'the purchaser shall measure the land within a month from this date and shall intimate to the owner what shortage he discovers,' any notice given after the expiry of the month would be of no avail; but if the contract ran thus, 'the buyer is to measure the land within the next few days and make a statement as to the extent,' if he notified within a month that it fell short of the measurement stated, he can sue for compensation for the short measure, no matter how many years after.

---

will be proportionate to the yield, up to but not exceeding 10 lbs., and the surplus will go to the buyer as profit.

L. 40 pr.—Various questions of interpretation are taken up in this and the succeeding sections. It may be noted with reference to the opinions of 'patented' counsel which form so large a part of the *Digest*, that we often find the case stated, and the answer to it put in the third person (*quaerebat, respondit, ait*) from which we may infer that the writer is reporting or quoting the opinion of some other counsel.

The opinion on the circumstances here submitted seems to admit of no doubt. The clause in the *lex venditionis* specified a month as the time within which the buyer was to check the measurement of the lands, and give notice to the seller if he had any claim to make for shortage. He had the lands measured timeously, and recovered the price of the deficiency from the

1. In lege fundi aquam accessuram dixit: quaerebatur, an etiam iter aquae accessisset. respondit sibi uideri id actum esse, et ideo iter quoque uenditorem tradere oportere.

2. Qui agrum uendebat, dixit fundi iugera decem et octo esse, et quod eius admensum erit, ad singula iugera certum pretium stipulatus erat: uiginti inuenta sunt: pro uiginti deberi pecuniam respondit.

3. Fundi uenditor frumenta manu sata receperat: in eo fundo

---

seller. On a re-sale after the thirty days, he discovered that he had overstated the contents on the occasion of the first measurement, and he wished to make a further claim. Counsel simply refers him to the clause in the contract fixing a definite term of thirty days, and adds that, if the term had been indefinite (as *in diebus proximis*), it would be construed more liberally, and he could have brought the action at any interval of time, although he had not given notice within thirty days: that is the meaning, if the MS. reading *et si* is retained, and *non* is inserted before *renuntiasset* as seems to be necessary. Mommsen suggests *si* for *et si*, which gives a good sense: if the buyer gives notice of his challenge within a reasonable period, such as thirty days, he can bring his action at any future time. Even the indefinite term *dies proximi* must have meant a short period.

The reading *quod** has less authority but is more intelligible than *quo*.

In the time of Justinian actions generally had to be brought within thirty years (C. vii. 39. 3).

If in the above case the purchaser had employed a surveyor on the first occasion, he would have had an action against him if he had fraudulently misstated the extent of the lands. See *Digest*, 11, tit. 6 : *Si mensor falsum modum dixerit*.

§ 1. The seller in this case evidently owned an adjoining piece of ground where there was a spring, and bound himself to give the purchaser of the lands he was selling a right to draw water from it. *Qui habet haustum, iter quoque habere uidetur ad hauriendum* (D. 8. 3. 3, 3). For implied grant of necessary ways, see Bell, *Prin.* §§ 739, 992.

§ 2. Here certain lands were sold as containing eighteen acres, and the price was fixed at so much an acre, so that the sale was

1. In the conditions of sale a right to draw water was promised as an accessory of the lands sold : the question was asked whether the right to the water carried with it a right to access as well. The answer was that that seemed to have been within the view of the parties and therefore the seller must provide an access also.

2. The seller of a plot of ground stated that it contained eighteen acres, and stipulated for a certain price for each acre it should be found to contain ; the number proved to be twenty ; an opinion was given that the buyer must pay for twenty.

3. The seller of a farm reserved for himself the sown crops:

ad mensuram. In such a case, if it turns out that there are more or fewer acres than was stated, the price will be raised or lowered in proportion. But if the lands had been sold *en bloc* for a slump sum, a mistake of either party as to the acreage would have made no difference to the price.

An error as to the quantity merely of the *res vendita* was not essential error by Roman law; but it let in a claim for augmentation or diminution of the price, as the case might be, (*a*) where the subject of the contract was a fixed *quantum* of a thing, and more or less was delivered by mistake (D. 19. 1. 2 pr.; D. 4. 3. 18, 3 ; D. 12. 6. 26, 4–6); and (β) when a specific thing was sold at a price fixed according to its separate units, which is the case here put. See, for details, Pothier, §§ 250–258 ; Vangerow, § 604, (3). It may be added that a specification of quantity may be made at the completion of a sale as a promise or engagement collateral to the contract, and not as the true subject of it ; the effect is, that if less be given than was guaranteed, the buyer can sue for a proportionate reduction of the price (D. 21. 2. 69, 6).

The law of Scotland is materially different both as to the nature and effect of an error in extent. 'A description by measurement entitles the purchaser to insist for the quantity described, and no more ; any valid objection on account of error entitling him to the option of giving up the purchase, if it amount to error *in substantialibus*' (Bell, *Prin.* § 893). *Hepburn* v. *Campbell* (1781) M. 14,168, was a case very like that in § 2, and the decision was the same, except that it was further held that the purchaser might throw up the bargain if he thought fit.

§ 3. Sown crops went to the buyer, unless reserved (D. 19.

ex stipula seges erat enata: quaesitum est, an pacto contineretur. respondit maxime referre, quid est actum: ceterum secundum uerba non esse actum,* quod ex stipula nasceretur, non magis quam si quid ex sacco saccarii cecidisset aut ex eo quod auibus ex aere cecidisset natum esset.

4. Cum fundum quis uendiderat et omnem fructum receperat, et arundinem et siluam caeduam in fructu esse respondit.

5. Dolia, quae in fundo domini essent, accessura dixit: etiam ea quae seruus qui fundum coluerat emisset peculiaria, emptori cessura respondit.

6. Rota quoque, per quam aqua traheretur, nihilo minus aedificii est quam situla.

41. IULIANUS libro III ad Urseium Ferocem.

Cum ab eo qui fundum alii obligatum habebat quidam sic emptum rogasset, ut esset is sibi emptus, si eum liberasset, dummodo ante kalendas Iulias liberaret, quaesitum est, an utiliter agere possit ex empto in hoc, ut uenditor eum liberaret. responsit: uideamus, quid inter ementem et uendentem actum sit. nam si id actum est, ut omni modo intra kalendas Iulias uenditor fundum liberaret, ex empto erit actio, ut liberet, nec sub condicione emptio facta intellegetur, ueluti si hoc modo emptor

---

1. 13, 10); as to the meaning of *manu sata*, see L. 80 pr. *infra*.

For *actum*.* Mommsen conjectures *satum*.

§ 4. *Arundo* was used for vine poles. Cujas is probably right in joining *siluam caeduam*; strictly it means copse or underwood, which, by proper management, can be cut down yearly so as to grow again (D. 50. 16. 30 pr.). It might be cut by a usufructuary for stakes and posts (D. 7. 1. 9, 7; ib. 10). Cp. Stair, ii. 3. 74, on liferenter's right to wood cut in haggs.

L. 41 pr.—The decision is that a clause in a contract of sale as to purging the encumbrances on lands by a certain date may, according to the intention of the parties, amount to an *engagement* (*dictum promissumve*), the non-fulfilment of which will

and some corn having sprouted from the ears left on the land, the question was asked, Did it fall under the reservation? The answer was that it turned very much on the intention of the parties; but, to judge by the expressions used, the growth that sprang up from the ears was not within the view of the parties, any more than grains let fall from the corn sack, or the growth from seeds dropped by birds in their flight.

4. The seller of a farm reserved for himself all the produce; an opinion was given that reeds and coppice-wood were included under produce.

5. Where it had been announced that the vats which were on the proprietor's lands would pass as pertinents, an opinion was given that those which the slave who cultivated the lands had bought out of his *peculium* would also pass to the purchaser.

6. The wheel which serves to raise the water is a pertinent of a house no less than the bucket.

41. JULIAN.

A person negotiated with the proprietor of an encumbered estate for a purchase, on the terms that he should be held to have bought if the owner cleared off the encumbrances, provided that were done before the 1st of July; the query was put whether he can by bringing the action on purchase in an adapted form compel the seller to discharge the burden? The answer was: the real intention of the parties must be ascertained. If the bargain was that the seller was to disburden the lands in any event by the 1st of July, an action on purchase will lie to have him ordained to do it, and the sale will not be regarded as subject to a condition, if *e.g.* the buyer has ground a modified action on the contract for performance or damages, or may have the effect of a *condition* merely, in which case the owner has a free hand. Whether a guarantee or a condition was meant is a question of intention: it cannot be settled by simply looking to the form of the clause, *e.g.* there are many ways of expressing a condition besides the common hypothetical form.

interrogauerit: 'erit mihi fundus emptus ita ut eum intra kalendas Iulias liberes,' uel 'ita ut eum intra kalendas a Titio redimas.' si uero sub condicione facta emptio est, non poterit agi ut condicio impleatur.

1. Mensam argento coopertam mihi ignoranti pro solida uendidisti imprudens: nulla est emptio pecuniaque eo nomine data condicetur.

42. MARCIANUS libro I institutionum.

Domini neque per se neque per procuratores suos possunt saltem criminosos seruos uendere, ut cum bestiis pugnarent. et ita diui fratres rescripserunt.

43. FLORENTINUS libro VIII institutionum.

Ea quae commendandi causa in uenditionibus dicuntur, si palam appareant, uenditorem non obligant, ueluti si dicat seruum speciosum, domum bene aedificatam: at si dixerit hominem litteratum uel artificem, praestare debet: nam hoc ipso pluris uendit.

---

§ 1. See L. 14 *supra*, and notes on pp. 30, 36. Here the buyer is misled by the seller innocently, as to the kind of merchandise he is buying. The table was sold expressly as solid silver; it is really only coated over (*cooperta*) with silver. The error voids the contract, and the buyer can recover the price.

It has been proposed to take *inauratum* (L. 14) as meaning 'inlaid with gold' as opposed to solid gold: in which case a *vas inauratum* might quite well pass as '*aureum*,' because it consists in part of gold, very much as we speak of a 'gold' watch, a 'silver' knife.

L. 43 pr., § 1.—*Apparent* is the reading of P⁴., 'if the quality is patent' or 'obvious on inspection.' Obvious faults were also excepted in the edict of the curule aediles, *ad eos enim morbos uitiaque pertinere edictum aedilium probandum est, quae quis ignorauit uel ignorare potuit*, such as blindness or an ulcer on the head (D. 21. 1. 14, 10; ib. 1, 6). That title contains several illustrations of the difference between a mere affirmation

stipulated as follows: 'the purchase shall take effect on the understanding that you free the lands by the 1st of July,' or 'that you redeem the lands from Titius by the 1st.' But if the purchase was made subject to a condition, no action is competent to compel performance of the condition.

1. You have unwittingly sold me a table overlaid with silver for one of solid silver without my knowing it to be so: the sale is void and a *condictio* will lie to recover the money paid for it.

42. MARCIAN.

Masters cannot either personally or by their agents sell their slaves, even if guilty of crime, to fight with wild beasts. There is a rescript by the brothers of blessed memory to that effect.

43. FLORENTINE.

Statements made at the time of sale in praise of the goods, if they refer to patent qualities, *e.g.* that a slave is finely made or that a house is well built, do not bind the seller: but if he represents a slave as well educated or a skilled workman, he is responsible for that, because it directly enhances the price.

made at the time of the sale to recommend the wares and a proper *dictum promissumve*, 'warranty': *Sciendum tamen est, quaedam etsi dixerit, praestare cum non debere, scilicet ea quae ad nudam laudem serui pertinent, ueluti si dixerit frugi probum dicto audientem: ut enim Pedius scribit, multum interest commendandi serui causa quid dixerit, an uero praestaturum se promiserit quod dixit. Plane si dixerit aleatorem non esse, furem non esse, ad statuam nunquam confugisse, oportet cum id praestare* (L. 19. pr., § 1). The law as to mere puffery is clearly stated in D. 4. 3. 37: *Quod uenditor ut commendet dicit sic habendum quasi neque dictum neque promissum est: si uero decipiendi emptoris causa dictum est, aeque sic habendum est, ut non nascatur aduersus dictum promissumue actio, sed de dolo actio.* The law as to special assurances is that the vendor who gives them undertakes thereby a guarantee for the condition and qualities of the article, provided the buyer might reasonably take them as such, but not if they are mere vaunts which none but a credulous person would take

1. Quaedam etiam pollicitationes uenditorem non obligant, si ita in promptu res sit, ut eam emptor non ignorauerit, ueluti si quis hominem luminibus effossis emat et de sanitate stipuletur: nam de cetera parte corporis potius stipulatus uidetur, quam de eo in quo se ipse decipiebat.

2. Dolum malum a se abesse praestare uenditor debet, qui non tantum in eo est qui fallendi causa obscure loquitur, sed etiam qui insidiose obscure dissimulat.

44. MARCIANUS libro III regularum.

Si duos quis seruos emerit pariter uno pretio, quorum alter ante uenditionem mortuus est, neque in uiuo constat emptio.

---

seriously: *ea autem sola dicta siue promissa admittenda sunt, quae sic dicuntur ut praestentur, non ut jactentur* (D. 21. 1. 19, 3). When binding as guarantees, they were to be construed favourably ('*cum quodam temperamento*'); thus if the seller engages that a slave knows a trade, the buyer is not to expect a first-rate workman,—he must be content if the slave will pass muster as a tradesman according to ordinary parlance (*loc. cit.* § 4); if the seller says a slave is steady or laborious, you must not look for the gravity of a philosopher or for one who will work night and day; but if he promises a first-rate cook, he is responsible if the slave is only of average skill (ib. L. 18). For the general rules about warranty, see Windscheid, § 395.

§ 2. *Dolum malum abesse* is a warranty implied in the nature of a *bonae fidei* contract, and no contracting party can stipulate for exemption from it: *non ualere si conuenerit ne dolus praestetur* (D. 50. 17. 23; cp. *infra* L. 68; Pothier, § 233 sq.). See further, D. 19. 1. 1, 1; ib. 6, 8.

Many editors remove the second '*obscure*,' and thus get a sharp contrast between ambiguous language and crafty concealment. On the other hand, the MS. reading is confirmed by the *Basilika*, and it must be kept in view that silence as well as speech is often a means of equivocation.

For the treatment of warranty in English law, see S. G. B., §§ 12–16; Scots law was, to a large extent, assimilated to the English by the Mercantile Law Amendment Act (1856) § 5. Warranty is defined as 'an agreement with reference to goods

1. In some cases even warranties do not bind the seller, if the thing is so obvious that the purchaser could not help knowing it, as for example when a man buys a slave who has lost his eyes and takes a warranty of soundness: for he is held to have stipulated for soundness of body in other respects and not in that particular on which he was self-deceived.

2. The seller must always warrant his innocence of fraud—a term which includes not only ambiguous statements intended to mislead, but also studied and equivocal concealment.

44. MARCIAN.

A man bought two slaves together for a slump sum, and one dies before the sale is carried through; the purchase does not hold for the survivor either.

which are the subject of a contract of sale, but collateral to the main purpose of such contract, the breach of which gives rise to a claim of damages, but not to a right to treat the contract as repudiated' (S. G. B. § 62; cp. § 54). The following rules, which hold both in England and Scotland, will serve to illustrate the present lex. Any affirmation made at the time of sale may amount to a warranty, provided it is intended as such—that is, if it enters into the bargain as part of it (Benj. p. 609 sq; Bell, *Com.* i. 466, note): the criterion still is whether it was intended and understood that the buyer might rely on the representations of the seller. Again, 'the eulogies which dealers are accustomed to make of their goods are not to be received as warranties; they are understood in the ordinary intercourse of trade as boastful recommendations, which the buyer is to take or reject according to his prudence' (Bell, *Prin.* § 111); so *simplex commendatio non obligat* (*Power* v. *Barham* (1836) 4 A. & E. 473; Pothier, § 263). Lastly, the buyer's eye is his merchant where the defect is obvious; a general warranty is not binding unless the vice was *latent* at the time of the sale. Pothier, *Vente*, § 207; cases in Benj. p. 613 sq.

L. 44.—Where the several *corpora* embraced in a single contract are related to each other in such a way that the buyer must have meant the contract to be executed as an entire contract or not at all, the contract is wholly void as soon as the prestation

54. MARCIANUS libro IV regularum.

Labeo libro posteriorum scribit, si uestimenta interpola quis pro nouis emerit, Trebatio placere ita emptori praestandum quod interest, si ignorans interpola emerit. quam sententiam et Pomponius probat, in qua et Iulianus est, qui ait, si quidem ignorabat uenditor, ipsius rei nomine teneri, si sciebat, etiam damni quod ex eo contingit: quemadmodum si uas aurichalcum pro auro uendidisset ignorans, tenetur ut aurum quod uendidit praestet.

---

of any one *corpus* becomes impossible. Cp. D. 45. 1. 29 : *sed et familiae et omnium seruorum stipulatio una est : itemque quadrigae aut lecticariorum stipulatio una est.* So when a troupe of comic actors or a team of horses is bought, the death of one of them, before the sale is complete, cancels the bargain as regards the rest (D. 21. 1. 34-38).

L. 45.—It is difficult to reconcile this text with the principles laid down in LL. 9-11 (p. 30 *supra*) regarding the effect of the so-called *error in substantia, i.e.* mistake as to the qualities of the *res uendita*. According to the most probable view of these passages, the test of the materiality of such error is whether the difference between the real and the supposed qualities is so great as to put the commodity in a different class of merchandise and give it a different denomination ; if it is, the error is essential and the contract is a nullity. But here *uestimenta interpola (i.e.* cast-off clothes done up to look like new, cp. Plautus, *Most.* 272) are bought *pro nouis*, which is clearly a case of non-essential error, and yet the buyer gets relief from the vendor, who must make good the difference in value if he innocently sold them as new, and the full *interesse* if he did so fraudulently. The obligation in the latter case is quite clear ; but it is difficult to account for the liability of the *bona fide* seller except by assuming that he warranted the clothes as new, either expressly, or impliedly as by supplying them to a purchaser who asked for new clothes. In any case there is a great array of authorities cited for this decision : Marcian quotes most of the lex from Labeo, who adopts part of the decision from Trebatius, and the complement of it from Pomponius and Julian. The words '*quam sententiam. . . . ex eo contingit*' seem to be a parenthesis inserted

45. MARCIAN.

Labeo says in his *Posteriora* that, if one buys second-hand clothes furbished up, thinking they are new, Trebatius held that the vendee has a claim for damages, provided he did not know the clothes were second-hand. That opinion is approved of by Pomponius, and also by Julian, who remarks that—if the vendor did not know, he owes an indemnity only for the goods; but if he did know, he is liable for all loss resulting therefrom. For example, if he sells a vessel of brass for a gold one, believing it to be so, he is bound to indemnify the vendee for not supplying a gold vessel as promised.

---

by Marcian, as is indicated both by the change of construction, and by the fact that Julian would not have concurred in the opinion stated in the last clause about the *vas aurichalcum* (cp. L. 41, 1); the last clause is thus the conclusion of the quotation from Labeo. The example there given is the sale of a brazen vessel for a gold one, and the opinion meant to be conveyed is obviously the same as in the former case, that the contract is valid and a claim for compensation will lie. But according to the previous texts on this subject the error in question would certainly be essential, and the contract would be void. Savigny explains the contradiction on historical grounds. The nullity of a contract, as the result of error about a material quality of the object, was not always recognised; Marcellus combated this doctrine (L. 9, 2), Julian maintained it (L. 41, 1), Paul and Ulpian established it (LL. 9, 11, 14), and it was adopted in the *Pandects*. But the compilers failed to observe that in this lex they admitted a testimony by Labeo in favour of the older view which they had discarded everywhere else. *Syst.* iii. 285.

Aurichalcum is said by Pliny to be a mixture of copper and tin: Festus says, '*quidam putant ex aere et auro.*' If it could be taken as an alloy of gold with some base metal, the decision here given would harmonise exactly with L. 10 *supra*.

The expressions used in the first example to indicate the measure of damages are noticeable. Trebatius holds that the innocent seller is liable to indemnify the buyer for all loss attributable to his failure to supply new clothes as he undertook to do (*quod interest*, which is not used of a mere reduction of the

46. Marcianus *libro singulari de delatoribus.*

Non licet ex officio, quod administrat quis, emere quid, uel per se uel per aliam personam: alioquin non tantum rem amittit, sed et in quadruplum conuenitur secundum constitutionem Seueri et Antonini: et hoc ad procuratorem quoque Caesaris pertinet. sed hoc ita se habet, nisi specialiter quibusdam hoc concessum est.

47. Ulpianus *libro* xxix *ad Sabinum.*

Si aquae ductus debeatur praedio, et ius aquae transit ad emptorem, etiamsi nihil dictum sit, sicut et ipsae fistulae per quas aqua ducitur,

48. Paulus *libro* v *ad Sabinum.*

licet extra aedes sint:

49. Ulpianus *libro* xxix *ad Sabinum.*

et quamquam ius aquae non sequatur, quod amissum est, attamen fistulae et canales dum sibi sequuntur, quasi pars aedium ad emptorem perueniunt. et ita Pomponius libro decimo putat.

50. Ulpianus *libro* xi *ad edictum.*

Labeo scribit, si mihi bibliothecam ita uendideris, si decuriones

---

price). Marcian seems to modify this in the parenthesis which follows; he would exact the full *interesse* only where the seller was *in dolo*, and would limit the claim against a *bonâ fide* seller to the difference in value between old and new clothes (*ipsius rei nomine tenetur*). Mom. *Beit.* i. p. 204.

The closing words *ut aurum*, etc., admit of the meaning that the vendor must actually furnish a gold vessel, but the real sense must be (as Cujas pointed out) that the seller owes an indemnity because he promised a golden article at the time of sale. It seems plain in this instance that a promise or warranty was given, and it may therefore be assumed the more easily in the parallel case of the clothes.

L. 46.—See L. 34, 7 *supra;* Pothier, *Vente*, § 13. The sale

46. MARCIAN.

It is illegal for any one, either directly or through another person, to purchase any property of which he has the administration: the penalty for contravention is fixed by a constitution of Severus and Antonine at four times the price in addition to forfeiture of the property: this applies even to an agent for the emperor. Special exemption may, however, be granted to particular persons.

47. ULPIAN.

If a house enjoys a servitude right of bringing in water, the right passes to a purchaser without express mention of it, and so do the pipes conveying the water,

48. PAUL.

though they are outside the house:

49. ULPIAN.

and even if the right to the water should not pass because it has been lost, still the pipes and conduits, as each attaches to the next, become the property of the purchaser as a part of the house. Pomponius expresses the same opinion.

50. ULPIAN.

Labeo lays it down that, if you have sold me a library on con-

---

was not void, but voidable. When there was no risk of fraud, a tutor might buy his ward's property (D. 26. 8. 5; ib. 6).

LL. 47-49.—For the rule that *'fistulae'* pass by accession, see L. 78 pr. *infra*; D. 19. 1. 38, 2; ib. 15; for the law about laying them down, etc., see D. 8. 2. 18 and 19. If *dum sibi sequuntur* is right, the meaning seems to be that each part cedes to the next, and so the continuous whole forms a pertinent: Mommsen proposes to read *dum ibi relinquuntur*.

L. 50.—*Decuriones* were the members of the municipal senate, which was often called *curia* in later times. This body was a close corporation entrusted with the local government of the municipalities throughout the empire.

Campani locum mihi uendidissent, in quo eam ponerem, et per me stet quo minus id a Campanis impetrem, non esse dubitandum, quin praescriptis uerbis agi possit. ego etiam ex uendito agi posse puto quasi impleta condicione, cum per emptorem stet quo minus impleatur.

51. Paulus libro XXI ad edictum.

Litora quae fundo uendito coniuncta sunt in modum non computantur quia nullius sunt sed iure gentium omnibus uacant: nec uiae publicae aut loca religiosa uel sacra. itaque ut proficiant uenditori caueri solet, ut uiae, item litora et loca publica in modum cedant.

52. Paulus libro LIV ad edictum.

Senatus censuit, ne quis domum uillamue dirueret quo plus

Though the condition attached to a contract was not fulfilled, still if that were due to the fault of either party the contractual tie produced certain effects. Cp. L. 8 pr. *supra*. For the rule that the condition is held to be fulfilled when the debtor prevents its fulfilment, see D. 50. 17. 161: *In iure ciuili receptum est, quotiens per eum, cuius interest condicionem non impleri, fiat quominus impleatur, perinde haberi ac si impleta condicio fuisset*; ib. 174: *Qui potest facere ut possit condicioni parere iam posse uidetur*; D. 45. 1. 85, 7: *Quicumque sub condicione obligatus curauerit ne condicio existeret, nihilo minus obligatur*; D. 35. 1. 81, 1: *Tunc demum pro impleta habetur condicio, cum per eum stat, qui si impleta esset, debiturus erat.* In such a case Ulpian was satisfied of the competency of an action on the contract; Labeo thought it necessary to bring an *actio praescriptis verbis*, which was the ordinary remedy for enforcing an innominate contract, and was so called because a clause setting forth the special facts on which the pursuer relied was inserted at the head of the formula. Probably the purchaser in the case put in the text failed to apply for a site.

This doctrine has been generally adopted. See Pothier, *Obl.* §§ 212–214; Bell, *Prin.* § 50. In *Pirie* v. *Pirie* (1873) 11 Macp. 941, where the above texts were commented on, a condition attached to a bequest in favour of a third party was held fulfilled when the third party had voluntarily rendered its fulfil-

dition that the council of Campania sell me a site for a building to contain it, and if it is my fault that I do not get one from them, there is no doubt that you can maintain an action on the circumstances against me. In my opinion an action on the contract is equally competent, the condition being held as fulfilled when the buyer renders its fulfilment impossible.

51. PAUL.

Shores or river banks within the bounds of an estate that is sold are not reckoned in the measurement, because they belong to no one, but are by the law of nations free and open to all; the same is true of public roads, and religious and sacred places. Hence it is customary, if they are to count in favour of the seller, to make it a condition that roads, shores, and public places shall be included in the measurement.

52. PAUL.

The Senate passed a decree forbidding anyone to pull down a

---

ment impossible. In that case the general principle was thus expressed: 'if the accomplishment of a condition is prevented by that one of the contracting parties who has an interest that it should not arrive, whether it depend on his own act or not, the condition so far as he is concerned shall be held as accomplished.' In *Mackay* v. *Dick* (1881) 6 App. Ca. 251, the House of Lords held that, where the fulfilment of a condition by one party is prevented by the other, the condition is waived.

L. 51.—Cp. D. 18. 6. 7, 1: *Quod uenditur, in modum agri cedere debet, nisi si id actum est, ne cederet: at quod non uenit, in modum cedendum, si id ipsum actum est ut cederet, ucluti uiae publicae, limites, luci qui fundum tangunt: cum uero neutrum dictum est, cedere non debet, et ideo nominatim caueri solet, ut luci uiae publicae quae in fundo sint totae in modum cedant.* See also L. 73, 1 *infra;* D. 11. 7. 10 and 11. Pothier, *Vente*, § 251 sq.

L. 52.—The reference is to the *SC. Volusianum* of the year 56 A.D., in the reign of Nero (Orelli, *Insc.* 3115). It had been preceded by *SC. Hosidianum* (A.D. 47), referred to in the same

sibi adquireretur, neue quis negotiandi causa eorum quid emeret uenderetue: poena in eum qui aduersus senatus consultum fecisset constituta est, ut duplum eius quanti emisset in aerarium inferre cogeretur, in eum uero qui uendidisset, ut irrita fieret uenditio. plane si mihi pretium solueris, cum tu duplum aerario debeas, repetes a me: quod a mea parte irrita facta est uenditio. nec solum huic senatus consulto locus erit si quis suam uillam uel domum, sed et si alienam uendiderit.

53. GAIUS libro XXVIII ad edictum prouinciale.

Ut res emptoris fiat, nihil interest, utrum solutum sit pretium an eo nomine fideiussor datus sit. quod autem de fideiussore diximus, plenius acceptum est, qualibet ratione si uenditori de pretio satisfactum est, ueluti expromissore aut pignore data, proinde fit ac si pretium solutum esset.

54. PAULUS libro I ad edictum aedilium curulium.

Res bona fide uendita propter minimam causam inempta fieri non debet.

55. PAULUS libro II ad edictum aedilium curulium.

Nuda et imaginaria uenditio pro non facta est et ideo nec alienatio eius rei intellegitur.

---

inscription, which seems to have enacted severe penalties against any person pulling down a house in order to sell the site for more than he gave for it. Probably the Volusian SC. added a prohibition against trafficking in the materials and fixtures incorporated in a building in order to make money (*negotiandi causa*), the only check upon speculation we find in the *Digest*. Cp. D. 39. 2. 48 : *Si quis ad demoliendum negotiandi causa uendidisse domum partemue domus fuerit conuictus: ut emptor et uenditor singuli pretium, quo domus distracta est, praestent, constitutum est: ad opus autem publicum si transferat marmora uel columnas, licito iure facit*: probably in that case the thing was not delivered, which would account for the difference in the penalty. In the present case the sale is annulled, the effect of which is to make the seller lose the property which he has delivered, and also his action for the price; the property may very likely have been

town or country house in order to make a profit, or to traffic in the sale or purchase of the materials, and fixing as the penalty for a contravention, in the case of the buyer, the forfeiture to the Treasury of double the amount of the purchase-price, and in the case of the seller the cancelling of the sale. Clearly if you have paid me the price, as you have to pay the double of it to the Treasury, you can bring an action for repayment, because on my side also the sale is avoided. The decree applies to the sale of a town or country house belonging to another as well as to the sale of one's own.

53. GAIUS.

As regards passing the property in a thing to the buyer, it is all one whether the price has been paid, or security given for it. The expression 'security,' however, is to be interpreted liberally; any method by which the price is secured to the seller—for example, by a surety or by pledge—is equivalent to payment.

54. PAUL.

A sale carried through in good faith ought not to be set aside for a trifling cause.

55. PAUL.

A merely colourable sale is an absolute nullity, and so the object is not held to have been alienated at all.

---

confiscated. The same desire to secure the permanence of buildings, and protect the amenity of the city, may be traced in a SC. of the time of Trajan, *ea quae aedibus iuncta sunt legari non possunt* (D. 30. 1. 41, 1; Pothier, § 12).

L. 53.—See L. 19 *supra*, p. 41 sq. *Expromissor* was a cautioner or surety who intervened in the room of the debtor as principal in a distinct and separate obligation; the *adpromissor* or *fideiussor* on the other hand, simply became joint-debtor under an accessory obligation. The first is a form of privative intercession; the other two are forms of cumulative intercession. See *Inst.* iii. tit. 20.

L. 55.—See D. 45. 7. 54: *contractus imaginarii etiam in*

56. Paulus libro L ad edictum.

Si quis sub hoc pacto uendiderit ancillam, ne prostituatur et, si contra factum esset, uti liceret ei abducere, etsi per plures emptores mancipium cucurrerit, ei qui primo uendidit abducendi potestas fit.

57. Paulus libro V ad Plautium.

Domum emi, cum eam et ego et uenditor combustam ignoraremus. Nerua Sabinus Cassius nihil uenisse, quamuis area maneat, pecuniamque solutam condici posse aiunt. sed si pars domus maneret, Neratius ait hac quaestione multum interesse, quanta pars domus incendio consumpta [sit, quanta] permaneat, ut, si quidem amplior domus pars exusta est, non compellatur emptor perficere emptionem, sed etiam quod forte solutum ab eo est repetet: sin uero uel dimidia pars uel minor quam dimidia exusta fuerit, tunc coartandus est emptor uenditionem adimplere aestimatione uiri boni arbitratu habita, ut, quod ex pretio propter incendium decrescere fuerit inuentum, ab huius praestatione liberetur.

---

emptionibus iuris uinculum non obtinent, cum fides facti simulatur, non intercedente ueritate. Cp. D. 50. 17. 16 : *Imaginaria uenditio non est pretio accedente.* A sale may be merely a cover for donation (L. 36, p. 80), in which case it breaks down for want of a price seriously meant; and if the price is elusory, it is still only a fictitious sale (*uenditio uno nummo*).

L. 56.—Where a clause such as '*ut manumittatur*' or '*ne prostituatur*' was introduced in the sale of a slave, it was often accompanied by a pact that in case of default the seller was to be entitled to recover the property in the slave, *manum inicere et mancipium sibi adducere*. The law jealously enforced the clause *ne prostituatur* in favour of the slave: if the seller consented to a breach of it he lost the right of *manus iniectio*, and the slave became free. The condition attached to the slave, though she were bought and sold over and over again without any mention of it. Unless the seller stipulated expressly for the right to recover her, she became *ipso facto* free if the condition was violated, and the contravener lost the rights of patron (C. iv. 56. 1; D. 18. 7. 6).

56. PAUL.

If a female slave is sold under an agreement that she is not to be made a public prostitute, and that the seller in case of a breach of this covenant shall be entitled to reclaim her, the original seller is at liberty to remove her though she has passed through the hands of several purchasers.

57. PAUL.

I bought a house, neither the seller nor myself being aware that it had been burnt down. Nerva Sabinus and Cassius hold that although the site is left there has been no sale of anything, and that the purchase-price is recoverable by personal action. But if a part of the house remains standing, Neratius says this question turns very largely on how much of the house is burnt down and how much is left standing; thus if the larger part of the house is destroyed, the buyer cannot be compelled to go through with the contract, indeed he may demand back any money he may have paid; but if the half or less than the half is burnt down, then the purchaser has no alternative but to implement the contract at a valuation made in accordance with the opinion of a reasonable man for the purpose of ascertaining the depreciation in value due to the fire and deducting it from the price.

L. 57.—A series of somewhat arbitrary rules is stated in this lex and the following one regarding the legal effects of accidental damage happening to the subject-matter of a contract of sale prior to the completion of the contract. They form a supplement to L. 15 pr. (p. 36 *supra*), discussing the consequences of partial extinction of the *res vendita* from the same point of view as was there taken in considering the result of total destruction. The latter was held to make the inchoate contract a nullity by rendering performance quite impossible, and here similarly partial destruction excludes anything more than partial performance. The other possible category to which cases of this kind are often referred is error. But the attempt here seems to be to lay down rules as to the validity and the effects of the contract, conform-

1. Sin autem uenditor quidem sciebat domum esse exustam, emptor autem ignorabat, nullam uenditionem stare, si tota domus ante uenditionem exusta sit: si uero quantacumque pars aedificii remaneat, et stare uenditionem et uenditorem emptori quod interest restituere.

2. Simili quoque modo ex diuerso tractari oportet, ubi emptor quidem sciebat, uenditor autem ignorabat: et hic enim oportet et uenditionem stare et omne pretium ab emptore uenditori, si non depensum est, solui uel si solutum sit, non repeti.

3. Quod si uterque sciebat et emptor et uenditor domum esse exustam totam uel ex parte, nihil actum fuisse, dolo inter utramque partem compensando, et iudicio * quod ex bona fide descendit, dolo ex utraque parte ueniente, stare non concedente.

---

able at once to equity and to the probable intention of the innocent party or parties as to entering into the contract, supposing them to have known how much of the *res uendita* was prestable and how much was not. The example given is the sale of a house, where it is to be assumed that the building is the primary object, and the site a secondary consideration with the purchaser; for although the site is prestable after the house is burnt to the ground, it is treated as a negligeable quantity (*nihil uenisse quamuis area maneat*), so that practically this is a case of total extinction of the object sold.

The various possible cases are taken up in the four sections of this lex *seriatim*, according to the state of the parties' information and the extent of the damage.

I. Neither of the parties knew of the fire (pr.). In case of total loss, the sale is null on the principle of L. 15 pr., and the price, if paid, can be recovered. In case of partial loss, a further distinction is drawn according to the proportion which the part left standing bears to the whole. If it is less than a half, it appears to be left to the vendee's option to hold to the contract (paying, of course, a reduced price), or to reject it and have back his money (*non compellatur emptor perficere emptionem*). If, on the other hand, half or more than half of the building is saved, the contract is valid; the vendee cannot throw it up, but he has only to pay what may in view of all the circumstances be held to be a fair price. The reading in the pr. is doubtful in two

1. But if the seller knew of the fire and the buyer did not, the sale is set aside entirely if the whole house was burnt to the ground before the sale; but if any part whatever of the building remains, the sale stands and the seller must reimburse the purchaser for his loss.

2. The same principles must be applied in the converse case of the buyer knowing and the seller not knowing: here too the sale should be sustained, and the buyer should pay the seller the full price if he has not done so, and, if he has, he should have no claim for repayment.

3. But if both parties knew that the house was wholly or partly consumed, the bargain has no result, because the fraud on the one side is set off against the fraud on the other, and an action which has its source in good faith will not allow a transaction tainted with mutual fraud to be upheld.

---

places; the Florentine MS. gives '*hane quaestionem*' and '*consumpta*.' The former should probably be *hac quaestione*; and the latter should be altered to *consumptae*, or if retained, some words must be inserted, as *sit, quanta* (Mommsen). Some civilians consider a great part of this lex to be a fabrication by Tribonian, partly because the diction is unlike Paul's, and partly because some of the rules are unsatisfactory: why, for instance, should the *bonâ fide* buyer be bound to take a half-burnt house, which may be of no use to him? And how is the exact fraction to be ascertained?

II. The vendor alone knew of the fire (§ 1). If the house is wholly destroyed, the sale is void as before; but we should expect besides that the vendor would be liable for any prejudice the vendee suffered through his deceit. If any portion at all is saved from the flames, the sale stands; the buyer gets what is left, and can sue for the full *interesse*, in effect a penalty is thus imposed on the fraudulent vendor.

III. The vendee alone knew of the fire (§ 2). Total loss is not expressly mentioned, and it seems as if the words were closely linked to the second half of § 1, so that the hypothesis here is that some part of the building remains standing: if so, the point decided is that the *malâ fide* vendee is bound by the

58. Papinianus libro x quaestionum.

Arboribus quoque uento deiectis uel absumptis igne dictum est emptionem fundi non uideri esse contractam, si contemplatione illarum arborum, ueluti oliueti, fundus comparabatur, siue sciente siue ignorante uenditore: siue autem emptor sciebat uel ignorabat uel uterque eorum, haec optinent quae in superioribus casibus pro aedibus dicta sunt.

---

contract, and must pay the full price for what is left of the house; and, if he has paid the price, he cannot recover it by a *condictio indebiti*. It is, however, a very general opinion that this section applies to total as well as partial destruction, so that the contract is good though nothing escapes the fire; the purchaser must pay the price, according to Voet, as a punishment for his fraud, or, as others hold, because he must have intended to give that sum for the site, or else to make a donation of it. But how can there be a good sale *sine re?* To regard the *area* as the ' res ' in this case is to contradict the plain words of the pr. (*nihil uenisse*).

IV. Both knew of the fire (§ 3). In that case, whether the whole or only part has perished, the contract is void. Each side being chargeable with fraud, *dolus dolo compensatur* (D. 2. 10. 3, 3); neither can sue the other for implement (D. 4. 3. 36), and if the contract has been implemented, neither can bring an action for damages on the ground of fraud (D. 44. 4. 4, 13; D. 50. 17. 154).

Iudicio * is the reading of F; other MSS. have *iudicium*. The above decisions should be compared with those given in corresponding circumstances regarding stolen property. L. 34, 3, p. 62 *supra*.

L. 58.—The end of this lex beginning with the words *siue autem*, etc. is probably a Tribonianism, the reference being to the preceding lex which is an excerpt from Paul. It is just possible that Papinian may have written it, referring back to similar *dicta* of his own about destruction by fire. It is plain in any case that the compilers of the *Digest* considered the rules of L. 57 to be generally applicable where accident makes the performance of an obligation impossible to a greater or less extent. They are,

58. PAPINIAN.

It has been laid down that a contract for the purchase of land is held to be abandoned when the trees on it have been uprooted by the wind or destroyed by fire, if the trees, olives for example, were the motive for buying the land, no matter whether the seller knew the fact or not: the principles stated above for the several cases regarding a house apply here also, according as the buyer or both parties knew or did not know the state of things.

---

indeed, more reasonable in the example here put,—the sale of an olive-garden, where the trees are, in the contemplation of the parties, the main object of the contract. If half the trees are blown down, that will scarcely affect the value of the rest; and it is always possible to supply the blanks by transplanting or otherwise. But the ruins of a half-burnt house are usually worth little or nothing, and restoration is out of the question if the building had any features or ornaments peculiar to it. Pothier felt that these rules must often do violence to the intention of the buyer, and consequently he proposed to allow him to sue for a dissolution of the contract; but he is wrong in citing this lex as an authority for an equitable remedy of that kind (*Vente*, § 4). The French Civil Code, adopting Pothier's view, provides by art. 1601 that, in case of partial loss, the buyer may either abandon the sale or claim what is left of the thing at a reduced price fixed by valuation. No such rule exists in English law; see *Burr* v. *Gibson* (1838) 3 M. & W. 390, and note on p. 37 *supra*. To the cases of total destruction there given, add *Taylor* v. *Caldwell* (1863) 3 B. & S. 826, where, in an action for breach of a promise to give a music-hall for certain days, it was held a sufficient answer that the hall had been destroyed by accidental fire; and the rule was laid down that ' in contracts in which the performance depends on the continued existence of a given person or thing, a condition is implied that the impossibility arising from the perishing of the person or thing shall excuse the performance.' The civil law, which implies such an exception in all cases of obligation *de certo corpore* (*e.g.* D. 46, 3. 107), was relied upon in the judgments in that case.

59. CELSUS libro VIII digestorum.

Cum uenderes fundum, non dixisti 'ita ut optimus maximusque:' uerum est, quod Quinto Mucio placebat, non liberum, sed qualis esset, fundum praestari oportere. idem et in urbanis praediis dicendum est.

60. MARCELLUS libro VI digestorum.

Comprehensum erat lege uenditionis dolia sexaginta emptori accessura: cum essent centum, in uenditoris fore potestate responsum est quae uellet dare.

61. MARCELLUS libro XX digestorum.

Existimo posse me id quod meum est sub condicione emere, quia forte speratur meum esse desinere.

62. MODESTINUS libro V regularum.

Qui officii causa in prouincia agit uel militat, praedia comparare in eadem prouincia non potest, praeterquam si paterna eius a fisco distrahantur.

L. 59.—To sell an estate '*uti optimus maximusque*' was to give an express warranty of its freedom from all burdens of the nature of praedial servitudes: *qui 'uti optimae maximaeque sunt' aedes tradit, non hoc dicit seruitutem illis deberi; sed illud solum, ipsas aedes liberas esse, hoc est, nulli seruire* (D. 50. 16. 90; ib. 126; 41. 1. 20). The circumstances here contemplated are, that the seller of the lands gives no such undertaking and that there is no question of fraud (*e.g.* non-disclosure of burdens known to exist, D. 19. 1. 1, 1); and Mucius holds that the buyer in that case must submit to the exercise of any servitudes that may prove to exist, and cannot claim relief from his author. The passage cannot be taken, as the gloss takes it, of the case where the seller has expressly refused to be responsible for servitudes; and no sufficient authority can be adduced for the view of some writers that, if servitudes affecting the lands emerge after the sale, the purchaser is entitled, independent of express warranty by the seller, to sue for a reduction of the price by the *actio quanti minoris*, on the ground that such burdens amount to a secret fault

59. CELSUS.

If in selling a piece of land you did not promise it 'free of incumbrances of every kind,' Quintus Mucius rightly held that the land does not require to be handed over free of burdens, but simply in such condition as it was. The same remark applies to urban tenements.

60. MARCELLUS.

The conditions of sale contained a statement that sixty vats would pass as an accessory to the purchaser; it turned out there were one hundred of them; an opinion was given that the seller would be free to select those he should hand over.

61. MARCELLUS.

In my opinion a man may buy conditionally what belongs to him, if he thinks his ownership is defeasible.

62. MODESTINE.

No public official or soldier can acquire land in the province where he is serving, except it be his family estate which the fisc is selling.

---

in the thing sold. See D. 21. 2. 75, where it is again laid down that, when no mention was made at the time of sale of servitudes over the property, but they are subsequently exercised by the parties in right of them, the purchaser cannot claim indemnity as for eviction; if he wishes to be protected against such risks, he must bargain expressly for a *fundus optimus maximusque*,—there is no *implied* warrandice against incumbrances of this kind.

L. 60.—Compare D. 19. 1. 54, 1.

L. 61.—See note on p. 39 *supra;* and D. 45. 1. 31: *si rem meam sub condicione stipuler, utilis est stipulatio, si condicionis existentis tempore mea non sit.*

L. 62 pr.—The object of this prohibition was '*ne* [*milites*] *studio culturae militia sua auocentur*'; consequently a soldier was at liberty to buy a house. Officials might, of course, acquire lands in another province. The penalty for a breach of the

110 XVIII. 1. *DE CONTRAHENDA EMPTIONE.* [L. 63.

1. Qui nesciens loca sacra uel religiosa uel publica pro priuatis comparauit, licet emptio non teneat, ex empto tamen aduersus uenditorem experietur, ut consequatur quod interfuit eius, ne deciperetur.

2. Res in auersione empta, si non dolo uenditoris factum sit, ad periculum emptoris pertinebit, etiamsi res adsignata non sit.

63. IAUOLENUS libro VII ex Cassio.

Cum seruo dominus rem uendere certae personae iusserit, si alii uendidisset quam cui iussus erat, uenditio non ualet: idem iuris in libera persona est: cum perfici uenditio non potuit in eius persona, cui dominus uenire eam noluit.

1. Demonstratione fundi facta fines nominari superuacuum est: si nominentur, etiam ipsum uenditorem nominare oportet, si forte alium agrum confinem possidet.

---

regulation was confiscation of the property to the fisc, provided an information was laid during the period of service. Cp. D. 49. 16. 9; ib. 13.

§ 1. It seems clear that Modestine agrees with Ulpian (LL. 22–24 *supra*) that the sale of a *res extra commercium* is a nullity notwithstanding the *bona fides* of the purchaser, and he adds that it grounds a claim for damages against the seller.

Unfortunately, some of his expressions are ambiguous. Thus '*licet emptio non teneat*' should mean according to usage, 'although the sale is invalid'; but some writers, who deny the absolute nullity of such dispositions, would translate thus, 'although the sale does not bind' *sc.* the buyer to pay (or, *sc.* the seller to deliver the *res extra commercium*, that being impossible). Again, the word '*decipi*' sometimes implies that a person is the victim of the fraud or deceit of another, sometimes only that he is mistaken or misled without suggesting any intention on the part of another to take advantage of him; so that we cannot infer from the use of the word here that *dolus* or *culpa lata* on the part of the seller was necessary to ground the action for indemnity. The true inference from the texts seems to be, that when a seller makes a contract which is invalid on general grounds of law, or owing to facts personal to himself (as by selling a thing exempt from commerce or a non-existent inherit-

1. When a man purchases holy, or religious, or public ground in the honest belief that it is private property, although the sale is not binding, yet he can bring the action on purchase to recover from the vendor what he has lost by being misled.

2. Except there be fraud on the part of the vendor, a thing sold *en bloc* is at the risk of the vendee, although it has not been delivered to him.

63. JAVOLEN.

If a slave, when ordered by his owner to sell a thing to a person named, sells it to a different person, the sale is void,—and the result is the same where a free man is the agent,—for a sale cannot be concluded in favour of a person to whom the owner did not consent to sell.

1. If the lands have been sufficiently set forth, it is superfluous to name the boundaries; when these are specified, it is the seller's duty to do so in the case where he possesses other conterminous lands.

---

ance, D. 18. 4. 8, 9; D. 11. 7. 8, 1; *Inst.* iii. 23. 5), he is liable in damages to the other party even for *culpa levis*, *e.g.* for not knowing better; in other words, the Roman law held the seller answerable for *diligentia* in entering into a contract, and allowed action against him for any *culpa in contrahendo* (Ihering).

Lastly, the measure of the damages is left in doubt by the use of a phrase *quod interfuit eius ne deciperetur*, which sometimes denotes the full interest which the creditor has in the fulfilment of an obligation (*quanti interest rem emptam habere*, D. 19. 1. 13, §§ 1, 2), sometimes only the expense and loss caused by entering into a contract. Here it seems to follow from the nullity of the contract that the *actio ex empto* would lie merely for compensation in the latter sense ('the negative *interesse*' of German writers); if the buyer could have sued for all he would have gained had the contract been executed ('*erfüllungs-interesse*'), that would imply that the transaction was valid.

§ 2. See p. 76 *supra*.

L. 63, § 1.—If the lands sold have been pointed out, or are sufficiently ascertained in some other way, it is unnecessary to

64. Iauolenus libro ii epistularum.

Fundus ille est mihi et Titio emptus : quaero, utrum in partem an in totum uenditio consistat an nihil actum sit. respondi personam Titii superuacuo accipiendam puto ideoque totus fundi emptionem ad me pertinere.

65. Iauolenus libro xi epistularum.

Conuenit mihi tecum, ut certum numerum tegularum mihi dares certo pretio : quod ut faceres, utrum emptio sit an locatio ? respondit, si ex meo fundo tegulas tibi factas ut darem conuenit, emptionem puto esse, non conductionem : totiens enim conductio alicuius rei est, quotiens materia, in qua aliquid praestatur, in eodem statu ciusdem manet : quotiens uero et immutatur et alienatur, emptio magis quam locatio intellegi debet.

---

give the name of the boundaries ; but if the seller retains lands marching with those sold, he is bound to specify the marches, for, as appears from D. 19. 1. 48, it was the seller's duty to clear up any doubtful question as to boundaries.

L. 64.—There seems to be no other text dealing with the effect of a purchase *sibi et alii.* Javolen decides in the same sense that if in selling land I reserve a servitude over it *ut mihi et uicino seruiat*, the mention of my neighbour is surplusage, and the servitude belongs wholly to me (D. 8. 4. 5); the principle apparently is that what is void accresces to what is valid. This was in accordance with the Sabinian view. The Proculians held the opinion that a stipulation by A for payment of a sum to A and B entitled A as promisee to payment of half the sum, and was void for the remainder, and Justinian gave legislative sanction to this opinion in the case of unilateral obligations (*Inst.* iii. 19. 4 ; cp. Gaius, iii. 103). Both schools agreed that B acquired no right. The principle of the Roman law was that an agreement between A and B whereby A undertakes that C shall do something for B or receive something from him, so as to be immediate debtor or creditor of B, is in general invalid ; C is not bound by it and takes nothing under it, even if A is his mandatory, and it is inoperative also between A and B. See D.

64. JAVOLEN.

The query was put whether, suppose I have bought a piece of land for Titius and myself, the sale is valid for the whole of the land or for the half only, or is entirely void. My answer was, 'the mention of Titius is, in my opinion, to be construed as a superfluity, and therefore I am the purchaser of the whole of the land.'

65. JAVOLEN.

I have made an agreement with you to supply me with a certain number of tiles for a fixed price: does the transaction fall under sale or hiring? The answer was: 'an agreement by me to furnish to you tiles made with the clay on my land is, in my opinion, not hiring, but sale. For there is hiring of something whenever the material on which labour is spent remains with its owner in its former state; but when it is transformed and the property passes, we must understand sale rather than hiring.'

44. 7. 11, and, for the exceptions from this rule, Vangerow, § 608. If, as here, the bargain is that B shall sell something *to A and C*, it was still held that C was invested with no right, and the controversy between the schools was about the disposal of the share intended for him.

L. 65.—The criterion here set up for distinguishing sale from location has been referred to already on p. 65. Some inferior MSS. give *quas tu* for *quod ut*, a reading supported by the clear version in *Basil.* xix. 1. 63: *Conuenit mihi tecum ut certum numerum tegularum pro certo pretio faceres. Si quidem materia tua est, ex qua fiunt, uenditio est; si uero ego eam dedi, conductio est; nam in uenditione dominium materiae mutatur; in conductione uero eiusdem manet.* The form of hiring suggested by the circumstances would be *locatio conductio operis.*

The decision covers all products of the soil which the owner spends labour in preparing or working, and then disposes of for a fixed sum, as stones, coals, etc. If the person who wanted the bricks had arranged to work the clay on the other's land and make the bricks for himself, that would be a case of letting to hire.

66. Pomponius libro XXXI ad Quintum Mucium.

In uendendo fundo quaedam etiam si non dicantur, praestanda sunt, ueluti ne fundus euincatur aut usus fructus eius, quaedam ita demum, si dicta sint, ueluti uiam iter actum aquae ductum praestatu iri: idem et in seruitutibus urbanorum praediorum.

1. Si cum seruitus uenditis praediis deberetur nec commemorauerit uenditor, sed sciens esse reticuerit et ob id per ignorantiam rei emptor non utendo per statutum tempus eam seruitutem amiserit, quidam recte putant uenditorem teneri ex empto ob dolum.

2. Quintus Mucius scribit, qui scribsit 'ruta caesa quaeque aedium fundiue non sunt,' bis idem scriptum: nam ruta caesa ea sunt quae neque aedium neque fundi sunt.

67. Pomponius libro XXXIX ad Quintum Mucium.

Alienatio cum fit, cum sua causa dominium ad alium transferimus, quae esset futura si apud nos ea res mansisset, idque

---

L. 66 pr.—If the buyer has the usufruct of the property carried off from him, that is partial eviction, and the seller must indemnify him for losing the beneficial use and enjoyment (D. 21. 2. 15, 1; ib. 39, 5; ib. 49).

Quaedam ita demum, etc. This clause is often taken to mean that the lands sold enjoyed servitude rights over the adjacent lands, which rights the seller had conveyed, and was bound to make effectual. But, looking to the context, it is better to understand the words of servitudes affecting the lands sold for which the seller has engaged to indemnify the purchaser. Pomponius wishes to contrast the implied warrandice against the existence of personal servitudes (*e.g.* usufruct) over the lands with the express warrandice necessary to protect the purchaser against the burden of any praedial servitudes that may emerge (*e.g. iter*, etc.). Cp. L. 59.

§ 1. Cp. D. 19. 1. 1, 1; ib. 21, 1.

§ 2. For a definition of *ruta caesa* see D. 50. 16. 241: *In rutis caesis ea sunt, quae terra non tenentur, quaeque opere structili tectorioue non continentur.* It was an old expression embracing all plenishing and stores that did not pass to the buyer as accessories,—everything falling into the category of *instrumentum* (D. 33, tit. 7) or *suppellex* (D. 33, tit. 10); it was opposed to *iuncta*

66. Pomponius.

In a sale of lands the seller is subject to certain obligations without express mention, *e.g.* to warrant against eviction from the lands or the usufruct: to certain others he is subject only by express undertaking, *e.g.* to indemnify for a right of way, of passage, of driving, or of conducting water over the lands: and the same holds of servitudes over urban estates.

1. If the estate sold had a servitude right attached to it, and the seller has not informed the buyer but has knowingly concealed it, in consequence of which the purchaser has lost the servitude by non-user for the prescriptive period, it is rightly held by some that the seller is amenable to the action on purchase on account of his bad faith.

2. Quintus Mucius remarks that it is tautology to employ this style, 'what is dug up and cut down, and all that does not pertain to the house or lands,' for it is just what can be dug up or cut that does not belong to the house or lands.

67. Pomponius.

When we alienate anything, we transfer the ownership to another with all the accessories that would have attached to it if it had remained in our hands: this holds good in the whole

(*seu uineta*) *fixaque* as 'moveables' are to 'fixtures' with us. The above definition is not quite correct, at least for the classical law, *e.g.* dung and straw went to the purchaser with the lands (D. 19. 1. 17, § 2); see ib. § 6, where Ulpian gives examples of *ruta caesa*.

Though a clause of reservation was not necessary, it was very often employed: Cic. *Topic.* c. 26: *fecique quod saepe liberales uenditores facere solent, ut quum aedes fundumue uendiderint rutis caesis receptis, concedant tamen aliquod emptori quod ornandi causa apte et loco positum uideatur.*

Mommsen would insert *si* before *qui scribsit*, and *habere* after *scriptum*.

L. 67.—*Alienatio* is here equal to transfer of property (see p. 9). Cp. D. 41. 1. 20, 1: *Quotiens autem dominium transfertur, ad eum qui accipit tale transfertur, quale fuit apud eum qui tradit.*

toto iure ciuili ita se habet, praeterquam si aliquid nominatim sit constitutum.

68. PROCULUS libro VI epistularum.

Si, cum fundum uenderes, in lege dixisses, quod mercedis nomine a conductore exegisses, id emptori accessurum esse, existimo te in exigendo non solum bonam fidem, sed etiam diligentiam praestare debere, id est non solum ut a te dolus malus absit, sed etiam ut culpa.

1. Fere aliqui[1] solent haec uerba adicere: 'dolus malus a uenditore aberit,' qui etiam si adiectum non est, abesse debet.

Cum sua causa contains a reference to burdens as well as advantages (C. iv. 49. 13). It includes all accessions that have not been reserved. Pothier, § 47.

L. 68 pr.—See D. 19. 1. 13, 16; ib. 53 pr.

§ 1. *Dolus* has somewhat different meanings in different departments of law. The most general notion is that of deliberate intention, an evil *animus* directed to an infraction of the law or an offence against good conscience. In the sphere of contract the Romans made *bonâ fides* so prominent an idea that there is always an implied warranty against *dolus*, which is really the antithesis of it, and covers any trickery or treachery inconsistent with the confidence necessary to social life. This may take the form of false or misleading representations, or of dishonest concealment (see pp. 92, 115). It may be deception intended to influence the other party's motives, to capture his consent by surprise, or it may be actual circumvention employed to overreach another. Labeo gave a definition which Ulpian accepts as correct: *Dolum malum esse omnem calliditatem fallaciam machinationem ad circumueniendum fallendum decipiendum alterum adhibitam* (D. 4. 3. 2). It is in general best rendered by 'dole' or 'fraud,' though sometimes the idea is more exactly given by 'bad faith' as opposed to good faith, by 'cheating' as opposed to honesty, or by 'intentionally' as opposed to mistakenly.

If the fraud consists in inducing another to believe in the existence of some essential of the contract which does not really exist, as in the fraudulent sale of a *res extra commercium*, the contract is a nullity because an element essential to its validity

---

[1] nequiquam? (*Mom.*)

range of the common law in the absence of any special arrangement.

68. Proculus.

If you state in the conditions of sale of a farm that all the rent you may collect from the lessee shall belong to the purchaser, you are bound, in my opinion, to be diligent as well as honest in collecting it—that is to say, you are answerable for fault as well as bad faith.

1. It is the practice of some to stipulate expressly that 'there shall be no bad faith on the part of the vendor,' but he is responsible for bad faith independently of such a clause.

---

is wanting, and the fraud serves only to let in a claim for damages. But if a contract be *primâ facie* unobjectionable, is proof of fraud sufficient to invalidate it? In this connection the older civilians used to distinguish between *dolus causam dans* (fraud which gave rise to the contract, without which it would not have been made) and *dolus incidens* (fraud which was not the inductive cause, but an accompaniment of the contract); the former was held to avoid the contract absolutely, the latter merely to ground a claim for damages. The distinction is not formulated in the texts, but was thought to be implied in such passages as D. 19. 1. 11, 5 and D. 4. 3. 7, contrasted with D. 19. 1. 13, 4. Pothier, *Obl.* § 31. But the modern civilians have in general abandoned this position. They lay it down that fraud does not *ipso iure* annul a *bonae fidei* contract at all, there being an actual assent of the will, though induced by fraudulent means; but it entitles the party defrauded to bring an action on the contract for indemnification, a remedy the effects of which will vary with the circumstances of the case. If, for instance, the fraud attaches merely to a modality of the contract (as in D. 19. 1. 13, 4), an award of damages will be given; but if the contract would never have been entered into at all but for the fraud, it will be rescinded in the interest of the sufferer by the fraud (D. d. t. 11, 5). Instances of a contract-suit for damages for fraud occur in D. 4. 3. 9; D. 19. 1. 4 pr.; ib. 6, 9; ib. 30, 1: in the following places it is brought to set aside the transaction, C. iv. 44. 5, 8 and 10; C. viii. 28. 10; D. 19. 2. 23. On the old doctrine the anomalous result would be reached that action is

2. Nec uidetur abesse, si per eum factum est aut fiet, quo minus fundum emptor possideat. erit ergo ex empto actio, non ut uenditor uacuam possessionem tradat, cum multis modis accidere poterit, ne tradere possit, sed ut, si quid dolo malo fecit aut facit, dolus malus eius aestimaretur.

69. PROCULUS libro XI epistularum.

Rutilia Polla emit lacum Sabatenem Angularium et circa eum

---

maintainable on a contract which is *ab initio* a nullity. See, for a full argument, Vangerow, § 605, where the circumstances under which redress was obtainable by (1) a suit on the contract, or (2) *exceptio doli*, or (3) *actio doli*, are also explained. The special title *De dolo* is D. iv. tit. 3.

As to the idea of fraud in connection with contract in English law, see *dicta* cited on p. 54 *supra*. The distinction above mentioned has no place, except in the sense that it is only *material* fraud (*dolus dans causam*) that founds any claim for relief. The purchaser, if he has been induced to enter into the contract by the fraudulent misrepresentations or concealment of the vendor, may at his option rescind the contract within a reasonable time, provided that it is still possible to restore the parties to their original position, and that no third parties have in good faith and for value acquired rights under the contract; or, instead of rescinding, or where the right to rescind is lost in one of the above ways, he may stand to the contract and claim damages in an action of deceit. See Benj. p. 432 sq.

Some of the older Scotch authorities certainly do recognise the distinction between *dolus causam dans* as grounding an action for reducing the contract and *dolus incidens* as giving relief by damages only; but, though the expressions are still in use as synonyms for material and non-material fraud, the rule of law must now be held to be that fraud of the latter kind has no legal effect. Bell, *Com.* i. 262; *Prin*, §§ 13, 14, with the editors' notes. There must be material fraud, *i.e.* fraud inducing the contract, in order to entitle to relief even by damages. When there is such fraud, the party defrauded has a choice of remedies so long as matters are entire: the contract is not void, but voidable at his option, on condition that *restitutio in integrum* is still possible, and that the rights onerously acquired by third

2. The vendor is guilty of fraud if it has been or is due to him that the purchaser has not obtained possession of the land. An action on purchase will therefore lie, not to compel the vendor to hand over the exclusive possession, for there are many causes which may render that impossible, but for the purpose of fixing the damages for any breach of good faith, past or present.

69. Proculus.

Rutilia Polla bought the lake Sabatenes Angularius and ten

---

parties in good faith would not be defeated by its rescission; if reduction is barred, or in any case if he prefers the alternative remedy, he has his action to recover the damage he has sustained by reason of the fraud. There is thus substantial agreement between Scots and English law as to the effect of fraudulent representations giving rise to a contract for the sale of goods, as was assumed in *Houldsworth* v. *Glasgow Bank* (1880) 5 App. Ca. at p. 323. Hence, though the *actio quanti minoris* is rejected by the law of Scotland generally both in the case of heritage and of moveables, there seems to be an exception where fraud is proved; that is to say, the buyer may retain the goods and claim an abatement of the price in respect of the fraudulent representations of the vendor (*Amaan* v. *Handyside* (1865) 3 Macp. 526; *Dobbie* v. *Duncanson* (1872) 10 Macp. 810). This is contrary to the general rule, which is that, where goods are delivered disconform to contract, the buyer must return them without delay, or at least reject them by some distinct act, otherwise he is held to be satisfied and must pay the full price. Bell, *Prin.* § 99. In England the *actio quanti minoris* is allowed generally, so that the buyer, though he has accepted the goods and though no fraud is alleged, may set up against the seller a breach of warranty in diminution or extinction of the price. See S. G. B. § 54.

§ 2. Proculus seems to rest the seller's obligation to deliver (*tradere*) on the basis of the implied warranty against fraud. But he must not be taken to mean that the seller satisfied his obligation by showing that, through no default of his, it had become impossible for him to give full legal possession; that would be contrary to what is stated in D. 19. 1. 2 and 3. Cp. L. 25 *supra*.

L. 69.—Various guesses have been made at the meaning of *Angularius*, as 'angular in shape' 'lying in a bend,' etc.

lacum pedes decem: quaero, numquid et[1] decem pedes, qui tunc accesserunt, sub aqua sint, quai lacus creuit, an proximi pedes decem ab aqua Rutiliae Pollae iuris sint. Proculus respondit: ego existimo eatenus lacum, quem emit Rutilia Polla, uenisse, quatenus tunc fuit, et circa cum decem pedes qui tunc fuerunt, nec ob eam rem, quod lacus postea creuit, latius eum possidere debet quam emit.

70. LICINNIUS RUFINUS libro VIII regularum.

Liberi hominis emptionem contrahi posse plerique existimauerunt, si modo inter ignorantes id fiat. quod idem placet etiam, si uenditor sciat, emptor autem ignoret. quod si emptor sciens liberum esse emerit, nulla emptio contrahitur.

71. PAPIRIUS IUSTUS libro I constitutionum.

Imperatores Antoninus et Uerus Augusti Sextio Uero in haec uerba rescripserunt: 'quibus mensuris aut pretiis negotiatores uina compararent, in contrahentium potestate esse: neque enim quisquam cogitur uendere, si aut pretium aut mensura displiceat, praesertim si nihil contra consuetudinem regionis fiat.'

72. PAPINIANUS libro X quaestionum.

Pacta conuenta, quae postea facta detrahunt aliquid emptioni,

L. 70.—The sale was valid to the effect of grounding an *actio empti*. See note on p. 15 *supra*. The words *plerique existimauerunt* imply that this conclusion was not reached without some hesitation; the younger Celsus was the first to put forward the view, so far as we know (L. 6 pr.). Cp. D. 40. 13. 4.

L. 71.—It appears from D. 4. 3. 18, 3 that if the bargain bore expressly that the goods were to be weighed by a particular set of weights, there was nothing illegal in that, though the weights were light or heavy. The last clause of the above rescript implies that there was a presumption that the parties intended to employ the scales in use in the *locus contractus*.

L. 72 pr.—In the *bonae fidei* contracts the parties were, to a large extent, free to settle the terms of their bargain for themselves, and the special agreements by which they did so were

[1] num quia ü? (*Mom.*)

feet of land round it: I ask whether, supposing the ten feet which then bordered the lake are submerged owing to an increase in its size, the ten feet now nearest the water are the property of Rutilia Polla. Proculus answered: 'I am of opinion that Rutilia Polla bought the lake just as it was at the time of sale and the ten feet of land which then surrounded it, and that she cannot claim any greater extent than she bought on the ground of the subsequent increase of the lake.'

70. Licinnius Rufinus.

It has been the opinion of most jurists that the sale of a free man is valid provided the parties do not know his condition. The same view is accepted where the seller knows but the buyer is ignorant. But if the buyer knew he was buying a free man the purchase is void.

71. Papirius Justus.

The Emperors Antoninus and Verus issued a rescript to Sextius Verus in the following terms: 'in the wine trade the contracting parties are allowed to use any scale of measures or prices they like (for nobody is forced to sell if he is not pleased with the price or the measure employed), particularly if these are in accordance with the custom of the district.'

72. Papinian.

Special agreements made subsequent to a sale count as part of called *pacta conventa* or *adiecta*. They might be made at the time of the contract as accessory to it (*ex* or *in continenti*), or separately after an interval (*ex intervallo*). In the first case the pact formed part of the contract, and could be sued on under the classical law by the action on the contract, *ea pacta insunt quae legem contractui dant, id est quae in ingressu contractus facta sunt* (D. 2. 14. 7, § 5). They are sometimes called *pacta vestita* as opposed to *pacta nuda*. In the second case the pact, being made subsequently (*postea facta*), did not form part of the contract, and being without a '*causa*' did not give rise to an action, but only to a plea in defence, according to the rule *nuda pactio obligationem non parit sed parit exceptionem* (§ 5 cit.; C. ii. 3. 13).

As regards pacts of the latter kind, the general rules laid

contineri contractui uidentur: quae uero adiciunt, credimus non inesse. quod locum habet in his quae adminicula sunt emptionis, ueluti ne cautio duplae praestetur aut ut cum fideiussore cautio duplae praestetur. sed quo casu agente emptore non ualet pactum, idem uires habebit iure exceptionis agente uenditore. an idem dici possit aucto postea uel deminuto pretio, non immerito quaesitum est, quoniam emptionis substantia constitit ex pretio. PAULUS notat: si omnibus integris manentibus de augendo uel deminuendo pretio rursum conuenit, recessum a priore contractu et noua emptio intercessisse uidetur.

1. PAPINIANUS: Lege uenditionis illa facta 'si quid sacri aut religiosi aut publici est, eius 'nihil uenit,' si res non in usu publico, sed in patrimonio fisci erit, uenditio eius ualebit, nec uenditori proderit exceptio, quae non habuit locum.

down here and in D. 2. 14. 7, 6 and 27, 2 are as follows:—A distinction was made according as they affected the essence (*substantia*) or only some modality (*adminiculum*) of the contract. If a pact touched an essential of the contract, if for instance it raised or lowered the price, it was held, provided matters were entire, that the original contract had been abandoned and a new one entered into embodying the modification (§ 6 *cit.*; D. 18. 5. 2). By this piece of legal analysis the *nuda pactio*, which could only serve as a plea in defence, was transformed into a ground of action. The postulate of a new contract was necessary to a Roman jurist, because he held that the price must be definite from the first; in modern practice we should conceive the matter simply as a modification of an existing obligation. If, on the other hand, a pact touched a mere subsidiary part of the contract, leaving its essence intact, it could not give rise to an action, but could be pleaded as an equitable exception. Pothier, *Vente*, § 327 sq.

Papinian gives two examples of special agreements of this kind, touching only the collateral rights and duties of the parties (*adminicula*). The first '*ne cautio duplae praestetur*' operates as a release to the seller from an obligation that naturally belonged to the contract, viz. to answer for eviction; the buyer was entitled to demand a penal stipulation from the seller binding him to pay double the amount of the price in that event, but by the above clause he waives his right in favour of the seller—hence the ex-

the contract if they abate some of its terms, but not if they add a new term. This applies to all provisions subsidiary to the contract; for example, a covenant dispensing with the penalty of the double for eviction, or one requiring it and a surety as well. If the pact does not form a good ground of action at the instance of the vendee, it will receive effect as an equitable defence in favour of the vendor. It has with good reason been questioned whether this holds good when the price is subsequently increased or diminished, because the price goes to the essence of the contract. PAUL remarks: 'if while matters are entire a new agreement is made to raise or lower the price, I consider the parties have abandoned the first contract, and that a fresh sale has taken place.'

1. Where the conditions of sale contained this clause, 'if any part of the land is sacred, or religious, or public, it is excepted from the sale,' a parcel of land which is the property of the State but not dedicated to the use of the public will be validly sold, and the vendor will take no benefit from the reservation, which does not apply here.

---

pressions *detrahere emptioni* here and *imminuere contractum* in L. 27, § 2 *cit*. In the other example, '*ut cum fideiussore cautio duplae praestetur*,' not only is the stipulation claimed by the buyer, but caution for it as well, which he was not entitled to apart from this clause (D. 21. 2. 4 pr.)—hence it is said *adicere emptioni*, to increase the original obligation. The result was, that if the seller refused to give the stipulated surety, the buyer could not demand it by an action on the pact, but he could plead the pact by way of exception when the seller sued him for the price. It may be inferred from L. 7, § 6 *cit*. that Ulpian went further and held that in this case also the old contract was revoked and a new one concluded, so that the buyer would have a title to sue the seller for implement of his promise.

The rest of the passage deals with a pact altering the price, as an example of a covenant going to the essence of the original contract and setting up a new one in its stead. Probably the compilers of the Digest inserted Paul's observation because Papinian appeared to leave the question of the discharge of the original contract open.

§ 1. See note on p. 16 *supra*.

73. PAPINIANUS libro III responsorum.

Aede sacra terrae motu diruta locus aedificii non est profanus et ideo uenire non potest.

1. Intra maceriam sepulchrorum hortis uel ceteris culturis loca pura seruata, si nihil uenditor nominatim excepit, ad emptorem pertinent.

74. PAPINIANUS libro I definitionum.

Clauibus traditis ita mercium in horreis conditarum possessio tradita uidetur, si claues apud horrea traditae sint: quo facto confestim emptor dominium et possessionem adipiscitur, etsi non aperuerit horrea: quod si uenditoris merces non fuerunt, usucapio confestim inchoabitur.

L. 73, § 1.—Rich people usually had a burying-place (*sepulcrum*) on their lands, enclosed by a wall; but only the ground where interments had actually been made was '*religiosus*,' all the rest within the wall being '*purus*,' i.e. *profanus*. A special clause of reservation was necessary in order to prevent this profane ground from passing to the purchaser; the general clause *si quid sacri*, etc., was only sufficient to reserve the actual graves. If there was no reservation at all, the whole passed as an accessory of the lands. See LL. 22–24 *supra*, p. 49; and D. 19. 1. 53, 1.

L. 74.—The civilians (as Pothier, *Vente*, §§ 313, 314) speak of delivery as being either real or feigned (*ficta*), and under the latter head they include 'symbolical' delivery, that is, the giving of something as a symbol of the thing delivered; *e.g.* the keys of the building where goods are stored, cp. D. 41. 1. 9, 6, *item si quis merces in horreo repositas uendiderit, simulatque claues horrei tradiderit emptori, transfert proprietatem mercium ad emptorem* (a text which occurs also in *Inst.* ii. 1. 45), or the title-deeds of slaves (C. viii. 53. 1), *emptionum mancipiorum instrumentis donatis et traditis et ipsorum mancipiorum donationem et traditionem factam intellegis*. But the Roman texts do not give an allegorical meaning to the keys or the title-deeds, and they never speak of *ficta traditio*; Paul says in D. 41. 2. 1, 21: *si iusserim uenditorem procuratori rem tradere, cum ea in praesentia sit, uideri*

73. Papinian.

If a sacred building be destroyed by an earthquake, the site remains consecrated and therefore cannot be sold.

1. The unconsecrated space within the walls of a burying-ground, kept as a garden or shrubbery, belongs to the purchaser, unless expressly reserved by the seller.

74. Papinian.

The delivery of the keys of a warehouse is considered equivalent to delivery of the possession of the goods stored there, provided it is done at the warehouse: when that has taken place, the purchaser instantly acquires the property and the possession, even without opening the warehouse: while if the goods therein were not the property of the seller, usucapion at once begins to run.

mihi traditam Priscus ait . . . non est enim corpore et actu necesse adprehendere possessionem, sed etiam oculis et affectu argumento esse eas res, quae propter magnitudinem ponderis moueri non possunt, ut columnas, nam pro traditis eas haberi, si in re praesenti consenserint; et uina tradita uideri, cum claues cellae uinariae emptori traditae fuerint. Accordingly, Savigny, in his treatise on Possession, and the modern school generally, reject the distinction between real and fictitious delivery as foreign to the civil law. They hold that in the delivery by transfer of title-deeds (*Code, loc. cit.*) it must be understood that the slaves were present when the gift was made, so that it was really a case of *traditio longa manu*, just as a sum of money was held to be delivered when the debtor placed it by the creditor's orders in a place where the latter could see it (D. 46. 3. 79)—a passage which may explain why it is here said that the key must be given *at the warehouse*. So where delivery is given by handing over the keys, the point is not that the keys represent the goods in any sense, but they are necessary to give the buyer control over the goods; consequently he who has the keys comes to be recognised as in possession of the contents of the building.

In modern law it is not necessary that the key be handed over at the warehouse. See French Code, art. 1606; S. G. B. § 31, 3. In Scotland the giving of the key has always been held an act of

75. HERMOGENIANUS libro II iuris epitomarum.

Qui fundum uendidit, ut cum certa mercede conductum ipse habeat uel, si uendat, non alii sed sibi distrahat, uel simile aliquid paciscatur: ad complendum id quod pepigerunt ex uendito agere poterit.

76. PAULUS libro VI responsorum.

Dolia in horreis defossa, si non sint nominatim in uenditione excepta, horreorum uenditioni cessisse uideri.

1. Eum qui in locum emptoris successit isdem defensionibus uti posse quibus uenditor eius uti potuisset, sed et longae possessionis praescriptione, si utriusque possessio impleat tempora constitutionibus statuta.

77. IAUOLENUS libro IV ex posterioribus LABEONIS.

In lege fundi uendundi lapidicinae in eo fundo ubique essent exceptae erant, et post multum temporis in eo fundo repertae

real or actual delivery, and not symbolical (Bell, *Com.* i. 186; *Maxwell* v. *Stevenson* (1831) 5 W. & S. 269); and the circumstance that the seller has means of access by a master key, or retains control of an outer gate, will not affect the reality of the buyer's possession.

L. 75.—See Paul to the same effect in D. 19. 1. 21, §§ 4–5. Conditions forbidding or restricting alienation, such as the *pactum de retrouendendo* binding the buyer to sell the thing back to the vendor if he demanded it, and the *pactum*, προτιμήσεως, giving the seller the right of pre-emption if the buyer wished to sell, had purely obligatory, not real effects. The validity of pacts between buyer and seller in restraint of the natural rights of property (*e.g.* restraining the purchaser from selling the land without his author's consent, or from making it sacred or religious) was denied in the classical law, because of the want of interest in the seller (D. 2. 14. 61). But Justinian, holding the interest of good neighbourhood to be sufficient, decreed that an obligation undertaken in a sale or other contract not to build a tomb or otherwise put the land *extra commercium* was to be upheld (C. iv. 54. 9).

75. Hermogenian.

If the seller of a piece of land stipulates with the buyer for a lease of it at a certain rent, or for a re-sale to himself alone if the buyer wishes to sell, or for any such condition, he can bring the action on sale to enforce execution of the bargain.

76. Paul.

Vats sunk in the ground in a wine-store count as accessories when the store is sold, unless they are expressly reserved.

1. A person who succeeds to the rights of the buyer can employ the same defences as his author could, and also the plea of the long prescription if the possession of both taken together completes the period required by the constitutions.

77. Javolen.

In the contract for the sale of an estate there was a reservation of all quarries wherever situate; and long afterwards quarries

L. 76 pr.—*Dolium* ($\pi i\theta os$) was the largest vessel in use for storing wine, oil, corn, etc., having a capacity of 100 gallons and over. It was of globular shape, with a wide mouth, and was made of earthenware. *Dolia* were often sunk deep in sand or earth in the cellar or store. Owing to their size they were usually sold along with the house or lands. Vat, tun, or pipe conveys the idea better than cask or barrel. Cp. D. 19. 1. 17 pr.; ib. 54, 1.

§ 1. *Accessio temporis seu possessionis* was allowed first to universal successors and later to singular successors on the principle *Qui in ius dominiumue alterius succedit, iure eius uti debet* (D. 50. 17. 177 pr.; cp. ib. 156, § 2). See *Inst.* ii. 6, §§ 12, 13. Paul alludes here to a constitution of Severus and Caracalla which granted to vendees the right to join their possession to that of their authors', in order to make a title by completing the long possession; cp. D. 41. 4. 2, 20: *emptori tempus uenditoris ad usucapionem procedit.*

L. 77.—In D. 50. 17. 34 Ulpian enunciates the rule for the construction of contracts: *id sequimur quod actum est, aut, si non pareat quid actum est, erit consequens ut id sequamur, quod in*

erant lapidicinae. eas quoque uenditoris esse Tubero respondit: Labeo referre quid actum sit: si non appareat, non uideri eas lapidicinas esse exceptas: neminem enim nec uendere nec excipere quod non sit, et lapidicinas nullas esse, nisi quae apparent et caedantur: aliter interpretantibus totum fundum lapidicinarum fore, si forte toto eo sub terra esset lapis. hoc probo.

78. Labeo libro IV posteriorum a Iauoleno epitomatorum.

Fistulas emptori accessuras in lege dictum erat: quaerebatur, an castellum, ex quo fistulis aqua duceretur, accederet. respondi apparere id actum esse, ut id quoque accederet, licet scriptura non continetur.

1. Fundum ab eo emisti cuius filii postea tutelam administras, nec uacuam* accepisti possessionem. dixi tradere te tibi possessionem hoc modo posse, ut pupillus et familia eius decedat de fundo, tunc demum tu ingrediaris possessionem.

2. Qui fundum ea lege emerat, ut soluta pecunia traderetur ei possessio, duobus heredibus relictis decessit. si unus omnem pecuniam soluerit, partem familiae herciscundae iudicio seruabit; nec, si partem soluat, ex empto cum uenditore aget, quoniam ita contractum aes alienum diuidi non potuit.

---

regione in qua actum est frequentatur. quid ergo, si neque regionis mos appareat, quia uarius fuit? ad id, quod minimum est, redigenda summa est. Accordingly, a clause reserving the right to work quarries or the like is, in the absence of any clear evidence of the intention of the parties, held to apply only to things known to exist at the time of the contract; the parties are not taken to have had in view things absolutely unknown when they fixed the price; *paria sunt, non esse et non apparere*, as it has been tersely put. But the bequest of a usufruct of lands (somewhat like an 'estate for life' or 'liferent') carried the right to open new mines and quarries, as well as to work the stone and minerals known to exist at the date of the bequest (D. 7. 1. 9, 3; ib. 13, 5).

L. 78 pr.—All works for drawing, pumping, or bringing in water, including an artificial reservoir outside a house (*castellum*),

were opened upon the lands. Tubero gave it as his opinion that they also belonged to the seller: but Labeo held that it depended upon the intention of the parties; if that was not clear, he thought those quarries had not been reserved, for no one sells or reserves what is non-existent, as quarries are until they are opened up and worked: on any other construction, the whole estate would fall under the clause of reservation, if it turned out that there was a bed of stone underlying the whole of it. This latter opinion I adopt.

78. LABEO.

In the conditions of sale it was provided that the water-pipes should pass to the purchaser as an accessory; the question arose whether the reservoir from which the water was conveyed by these pipes was also an accessory. I replied that the intention plainly was to treat it as an accessory, although the clause did not expressly mention it.

1. You bought an estate from a man, and (on his death) you became tutor to his son, without ever having been put in possession. I gave an opinion that you can deliver possession to yourself in this way—by the pupil and his slaves removing from the estate before you enter into possession.

2. A man who had bought an estate on the terms that the price must be paid before possession was given, died leaving two heirs. If one of them pays the whole price, he will retain the half in the action for division of the inheritance; but if he pays only his share, he cannot bring the action on purchase against the seller, because a debt contracted in this way is not severable.

---

were held to be parts and pertinents. L. 40, 6 *supra*; D. 19. 1. 15; ib. 17, 7; ib. 38, 2.

§ 1. *Nec uacuam* is an emendation proposed for *nequaquam* (Flor.).

§ 2. A purchaser had to tender the price in full as a condition of getting judgment against the vendor in an action on the contract (D. 19. 1. 13, 8; cp. D. 18. 4. 22); similarly, if an owner

3. Frumenta quae in herbis erant cum uendidisses dixisti te, si quid ui aut tempestate factum esset, praestaturum : ea frumenta niues corruperunt : si immoderatae fuerunt et contra consuetudinem tempestatis, agi tecum ex empto poterit.

---

wished to recover on a sale made to his slave, it was not enough for him to tender the price up to the amount of the slave's *peculium* merely (D. 21. 1. 57 pr.). On the same principle it is here decided that one of several heirs of the purchaser cannot by the *actio ex empto* compel delivery of his share of the *res vendita* without tendering the full price,—the prestation is indivisible, unless the seller chooses to sever it. Pothier, §§ 63, 64.

In the case here figured it was a special term (*lex*) in the contract that payment of the price should be held a condition precedent to delivery of the possession. We may conclude that, apart from such special agreement, the vendor and the vendee were bound to make or be ready and willing to make their prestations simultaneously. It appears from Gaius, iv. § 126, that if the vendor brought an action for the price before he had given delivery, the vendee could plead what is called in C. viii. 45. 5 the *exceptio doli*, in D. 44. 4. 5, 4 the *exceptio mercis non traditae*, and by modern civilians the *exceptio non adimpleti contractus*, viz. '*ut ita demum ei emptor damnetur, si ei res quam emerit tradita sit*,' that is to say, he could plead non-implement by the seller, not as a bar to the action, but as a bar to judgment; the plea could be met in the ordinary case by the pursuer offering delivery in the course of the process, or it could be elided *replicando* by averring a special agreement respecting the sequence of the prestations (*si praedictum est ne aliter emptori res traderetur quam si pretium soluerit*). The plea would thus lead to concurrent performance of the obligations under the contract, unless there was a special condition to the contrary. So far as the texts show, there was no difference between the position of the buyer and the seller—either could competently plead the *exceptio* when sued by the other.

The view here stated seems to be the correct one. It should be added, however, that some writers hold that the pursuer was bound, as a condition of raising an action on the contract, to

3. In selling a crop of corn in the blade, you undertook to be responsible for damage done by stormy weather: the corn was completely spoiled by a fall of snow; if it was exceptional and unusually severe, an action on purchase will lie against you.

---

prove that he had fulfilled the obligation incumbent on him, or was willing to do so. But as a concluded contract of sale produced mutual obligations which, unless otherwise agreed, were immediately prestable, there was a sufficient ground of action independent of actual or preferred performance (D. 19. 4. 1, §§ 1, 2); and the equity of the case was sufficiently met by allowing the defender, when convened, the *exceptio doli*, that is, he could plead that he should not be ordained to perform while his counter-claim arising out of the same agreement remained unsatisfied.

In English and Scots law the rule is that 'unless otherwise agreed, delivery of the goods and payment of the price are concurrent conditions' (S. G. B. § 30). 'Where the bargain is simple and without special stipulation, the buyer's obligation is to pay immediately; and the seller is entitled to demand and have action for payment, on offering delivery of the thing, or proving the delivery made, or on showing that the thing has perished by accident' (Bell *on Sale*, p. 103). See the cases in Benj. p. 582 sq., and Bell, *Prin.* § 100.

§ 3. Possibly *ui* has here the same force as *uis maior* 'unavoidable calamity,' 'act of God.' For *tempestatis* Salmasius conjectured *tempestates*, which is ingenious but not necessary.

The decision is that the undertaking in question does not cover ordinary losses, such as might occur in any average year, but only damage due to some extraordinary catastrophe, which goes to show that, if one undertook to answer for *casus*, he was in general responsible whether the damage was preventible by human care and foresight or not, and even for *casus insolitissimi* (Mommsen). It is to be inferred from this passage that, where there is no stipulation throwing the risk on the seller, a *standing* crop is at the risk of the buyer from the moment the sale is completed; the sale is not conditional like that of a *future* crop (L. 8 pr. p. 24 *supra*).

79. Iauolenus libro V ex posterioribus Labeonis.

Fundi partem dimidiam ea lege uendidisti, ut emptor alteram partem, quam retinebas, annis decem certa pecunia in annos singulos conductam habeat. Labeo et Trebatius negant posse ex uendito agi ut id quod conuenerit fiat. ego contra puto, si modo ideo uilius fundum uendidisti ut haec tibi conductio praestaretur: nam hoc ipsum pretium fundi uideretur, quod eo pacto uenditus fuerat: eoque iure utimur.

80. Labeo libro V posteriorum a Iauoleno epitomatorum.

Cum manu sata in uenditione fundi excipiuntur, non quae in perpetuo sata sunt excipi uiderentur, sed quae singulis annis seri solent, ita ut fructus eorum tollatur: nam aliter interpretantibus uites et arbores omnes exceptae uidebuntur.

1. Huius rei emptionem posse fieri dixi: 'quae ex meis aedibus in tuas aedes proiecta sunt, ut ea mihi ita habere liceat,' deque ea re ex empto agi.

2. Silua caedua in quinquennium uenierat: quaerebatur, cum glans decidisset, utrius esset. scio Seruium respondisse, primum

---

L. 79.—Here, as in L. 75 *supra* and D. 19. 1. 21, 4, the contract of sale contains within itself a completed contract of location in favour of the vendor, and in two of these texts it is expressly said that the subsidiary contract formed part of the consideration for the sale. Consequently, the later jurists were of opinion that the ordinary action on the contract was competent to enforce the promise to give or take the lease; the earlier jurists held the contrary view, probably on the ground that the lease was itself an actionable contract. In the example here given the arrangement is in favour of the seller; but it would in some cases be for the buyer's interest to get a lease of the lands retained by the seller, and he might pay a higher price in view of that (Bechmann).

Uidetur has been proposed for *uideretur* here, and *uidentur* for *uiderentur* in L. 80 pr.

L. 80 pr.—Compare L. 40, 3, p. 88 *supra*.

79. Javolen.

You have sold one half of an estate on condition that the purchaser shall take a ten years' lease of the other half which you retained at a fixed yearly rent. According to Labeo and Trebatius you cannot bring an action on sale to enforce the execution of this bargain. I hold the contrary opinion, provided that you took a lower price for the land in consideration of the lease being effected, for the fact that the sale was concluded subject to this agreement may be regarded as a consideration for the lands: this is now settled law.

80. Labeo.

When a contract for the sale of land contains a clause reserving 'all that is sown,' the reservation is not held to cover things laid down once for all, but only what is sown and cropped every year; for if the other construction were adopted, vines and trees of all kinds would fall within the clause.

1. In my opinion the right to continue to rest the beams of my house on your wall can be a valid subject of purchase, and an action on purchase will lie to enforce the right.

2. The cuttings of a coppice for five years were sold, and the question arose to which of the parties did the acorns which fell off belong. I know that Servius' opinion was that we must be

---

§ 1. The owner of property could create both praedial and personal servitudes by sale; see for examples, D. 8. 1. 20 (*uia aut aliquod ius fundi*); D. 18. 6. 8, 2 (*ususfructus*); D. 19. 1. 3, 2; ib. 6, 5. In the present case the purchase legalises the encroachment already made on the neighbouring property. *Proiecta sunt* refers to resting a beam on a neighbour's wall, which is usually called *ius tigni immittendi*; sometimes *proiectum* means a balcony (*macnianum*) projecting over another's land, but not supported by it (D. 43. 17. 3, 5).

§ 2. On *silua caedua* see L. 40, 4, p. 88 *supra*. *Glans* (acorn) was used in a general sense of all fruits growing on trees or plants (D. 50. 16. 236, 1).

Hae is probably the right reading in place of *haec.**

sequendum esse quod appareret actum esse: quod si in obscuro esset, quaecumque glans ex his arboribus quae caesae non essent cecidisset uenditoris esse, eam autem quae in arboribus fuisset eo tempore cum haec* caederentur emptoris.

3. Nemo potest uideri eam rem uendidisse, de cuius dominio id agitur, ne ad emptorem transeat, sed hoc aut locatio est aut aliud genus contractus.

81. SCAEUOLA libro VII digestorum.

Titius cum mutuos acciperet tot aureos sub usuris, dedit pignori siue hypothecae praedia, et fideiussorem Lucium, cui promisit intra triennium proximum se eum liberaturum: quod si id non fecerit die supra scripta et soluerit debitum fideiussor creditori, iussit praedia empta esse, quae creditoribus obligauerat. quaero, cum non sit liberatus Lucius fideiussor a Titio, an, si soluerit creditori, empta haberet supra scripta praedia. respondit, si non ut in causam obligationis, sed ut empta habeat, sub condicione emptio facta est et contractam esse obligationem.

1. Lucius Titius promisit de fundo suo centum milia modiorum frumenti annua praestare praediis Gaii Seii: postea Lucius Titius uendidit fundum additis uerbis his: 'quo iure quaque condicione ea praedia Lucii Titii hodie sunt, ita ueneunt itaque habebuntur:'

---

§ 3. If the intention is to reserve the property in the thing, the transaction is either letting to hire, or else an innominate contract, if the counter-prestation be something other than money; in any case it is not sale. This does not mean that the obligation in sale is always to give a good title, but only that the seller must do so if he can, that is, if he is owner. The purpose of the buyer is to acquire such right and title as the seller actually has, and the seller's intention must not be at variance with that purpose. See L. 25, 1, p. 50 *supra*, and D. 19. 1. 11, 2. On the other hand, a special covenant obliging the seller to pass the property was, according to Celsus, equally inconsistent with the idea of sale (D. 12. 4. 16).

L. 81 pr.—Compare the circumstances in D. 13. 7. 34. A

§ 1.]   XVIII. 1. *DE CONTRAHENDA EMPTIONE.*   135

guided in the first place by the actual meaning of the parties if that could be ascertained; but if it was matter of doubt, then all acorns that had fallen off the trees not yet lopped belonged to the vendor, but those which remained on the trees at the time of lopping belonged to the vendee.

3. A thing cannot be considered as sold, if the intention is that the property in it shall not pass to the vendee: such a transaction is either hiring or some other kind of contract.

81.   SCAEVOLA.

Titius borrowed a sum of money at interest, and pledged or hypothecated certain lands and gave Lucius as his surety, promising to release him within the next three years: in the event of his failing to do so within the period mentioned, and the surety paying up the debt to the creditor, he declared the lands pledged to the creditors to be his by purchase. Titius having failed to release Lucius his surety, the question was put whether the latter, provided he satisfied the creditor's claim, acquired by purchase the lands foresaid. The opinion was to the effect that, if there was a conditional sale of the lands, not by way of security but as a purchase outright, that constituted a binding obligation.

1. Lucius Titius promised to supply from his land 100,000 bushels of corn a year to the lands of Gaius Seius; thereafter Lucius Titius sold his land, with an express clause that ' the lands are sold and shall be held subject to the same rights and burdens under which they are now held by Lucius Titius ': Query, is the

---

creditor who holds a pledge in security of a debt past due, and is about to exercise his power of sale (*distractio* used, as often, of *forced* sale) is begged by his debtor to become the purchaser himself at a certain price. He agrees, and the debtor writes a letter bearing that he has sold to him. *Held*, that the debtor cannot revoke the sale by offering to pay up the debt with interest.

§ 1. The ground of the opinion is that the prestation of the corn is a personal obligation, and therefore does not run with the

quaero, an emptor Gaio Seio ad praestationem frumenti sit obnoxius. respondit emptorem Gaio Seio secundum ea quae proponerentur obligatum non esse.

---

lands. The proprietor could bind himself, but the law did not admit the possibility of charging the property with an obligation transmissible to his successors. No doubt the owner could

purchaser bound to deliver the corn to Gaius Seius? The answer was that, in the circumstances stated, the purchaser was not liable to Gaius Seius.

---

burden the lands with servitudes, but the rule was *servitus in faciendo consistere nequit,* 'the servitude could not degenerate into an obligation' (Ihering).

BOOK XIX.

TITLE I.

DE ACTIONIBUS EMPTI UENDITI.

LIBER DECIMUS NONUS.

TIT. I.

DE ACTIONIBUS EMPTI UENDITI.[1]

1. ULPIANUS libro XXVIII ad Sabinum.

Si res uendita non tradatur, in id quod interest agitur, hoc est quod rem habere interest emptoris: hoc autem interdum pretium egreditur, si pluris interest quam res ualet uel empta est.

L. 1 pr.—On the measure of damages for delay in delivery and for non-delivery, see this title LL. 3, §§ 3, 4; 11, §§ 9–14; 13, 9; 21, §§ 2, 3; 22; 23; 25; 32; 43; *Code* iv. 49. 12; Pothier, *Vente*, §§ 69–80.

The English common law rule is that the party sustaining loss by breach of contract is, so far as money can do it, to be placed in the same position as if the contract had been performed. This is limited by the rule in *Hadley* v. *Baxendale* (1854) 9 Ex. 341, which, putting out of view what the parties may be supposed to have had in contemplation, sets up as an objective standard of damages what a reasonable man, with the same information as the parties had, would have contemplated as the probable result of the breach, if he had directed his mind to the question. The measure of general or ordinary damages (*i.e.* in a contract where there are no special circumstances) is the estimated loss arising directly and naturally from the breach itself. If the contract was made under special circumstances known to both parties, which, in the ordinary course of events, would occasion a special loss if the contract were broken, there is an implied liability to pay special damages for the special loss. See S. G. B. § 55, and *Hammond & Co.* v. *Bussey* (1887) 20 Q. B. Div. 86, where, the seller having failed to supply coals answering the description 'steam coal,' and the buyer having resold with a similar warranty, the buyer received from the seller the costs of defending an action by the sub-purchaser for breach. The general rule in *Hadley* v.

---

[1] Cp. *Code* iv. 49.

BOOK XIX.

TITLE I.

OF THE ACTIONS ON PURCHASE AND ON SALE.

1. ULPIAN.

If the thing sold is not delivered, the buyer may maintain an action for damages, that is to say, for all the interest he can show in having the thing: of which the price is not always the measure—he may have an interest exceeding the value of the thing or the price put on it.

Baxendale is stated in S. G. B. § 52, 2; it resolves in many cases into the convenient rule in sub-section 3—that, where there is an available market for the goods in question, the proper measure of damages is the difference between the contract price and the market price at the date of the breach.

The principles applied in Scotland are stated in Bell, *Com.* i. p. 478 sq.; *Prin.* §§ 31, 33, 115. They are substantially similar to the above-mentioned rules, with the exception that there is no absolute rule as to market price (*Dunlop* v. *Higgins* (1848) 1 H. L. Ca. at p. 403); there are cases in which the highest price after the day of sale, or the average price between the stipulated day of delivery and the date of the action, has been taken as the criterion of damages; but the only rule is that the whole circumstances of the case must be taken into account in assessing the amount. See, as to delay in delivery, *Webster* v. *Cramond Iron Co.* (1875) 2 R. 752; and English cases in Chalmers, *Sale*, p. 80.

This topic may be completed by a short reference to the question, Is the vendor held entitled to satisfy his obligation by paying damages, or can the vendee compel him to give delivery where that has not become impossible *interitu rei* or otherwise? This has been considered a doubtful point in the civil law; Pothier quotes the authorities, particularly Paul, *Sent.* i. 13. 4, *si id quod emptum est neque tradatur neque mancipetur, uenditor cogi potest ut tradat aut mancipet,* and decides that the buyer

1. Uenditor si, cum sciret deberi, seruitutem celauit, non euadet ex empto actionem, si modo eam rem emptor ignorauit: omnia enim quae contra bonam fidem fiunt ueniunt in empti actionem. sed scire uenditorem et celare sic accipimus, non solum si non admonuit, sed et si negauit seruitutem istam deberi, cum esset ab eo quaesitum. sed et si proponas eum ita dixisse: 'nulla quidem seruitus debetur, uerum ne emergat inopinata seruitus, non teneor,' puto eum ex empto teneri, quia[1] seruitus debebatur et scisset. sed [et] si id egit, ne cognosceret emptor aliquam seruitutem deberi, opinor eum ex empto teneri. et generaliter dixerim, si improbato more uersatus sit in celanda seruitute, debere eum teneri, non si securitati suae prospectum noluit. haec ita uera sunt, si emptor ignorauit seruitutes, quia non uidetur esse celatus qui scit, neque certiorari debuit qui non ignorauit.

2. PAULUS libro V ad Sabinum.

Si in emptione modus dictus est et non praestatur, ex empto est actio.

1. Uacua possessio emptori tradita non intellegitur, si alius in ea legatorum fideiue commissorum seruandorum causa in

---

could sue by the *actio empti* for specific performance, which the magistrate would enforce by execution *militari manu*, if necessary (*Vente*, § 68). In England the remedy of specific performance was for long a privilege occasionally granted in the Equity Courts, and, though now somewhat extended, the right to it is still dependent upon the discretion of the judge: see S. G. B. §˙53, reproducing § 2 of the Merc. Law Amendment Act, 1856 (which was intended to assimilate English to Scots law in this respect, but did not go nearly the whole way). In Scotland, on the contrary, there is an absolute right to insist for implement of the contract by delivery of the goods, unless delivery is shown to be impossible. Bell, *Com.* i. p. 477; cp. *Stewart* v. *Kennedy* (1890) 15 App. Ca. at pp. 95, 102, 105.

§ 1. For *dolus* in connection with servitudes, see L. 39 *infra*; D. 21. 2. 69, 5; and note on p. 108. This section aims at showing that fraud always grounds a claim against the seller, whether

[1] si qua? (*Mom.*)

1. If the seller knew of the existence of a servitude, and has concealed it, he cannot escape the action on purchase, provided the buyer did not know, for all dishonest dealing comes within the compass of that action. When I speak of the seller knowingly concealing a servitude, I refer not only to the case of his failing to give notice of it, but also of his denying its existence when the question is put to him. Even take it that he has said expressly 'No servitude actually exists, but I give no warranty against such unexpectedly coming to light,' he is in my opinion liable in an action on purchase if a servitude existed and he knew of it. If, again, he has schemed to keep the buyer in ignorance of a servitude burden, he is in my opinion liable under the same action. In short, the rule is that he is responsible for any misconduct in concealing a servitude, but not for seeking simply to protect himself against liability. These rules apply only where the buyer is ignorant of the existence of any such burden; for there can be no concealment from one who knows, and no duty of disclosure to one already informed.

2. Paul.

The action on purchase lies where the quantity delivered is less than was promised at the time of the sale.

1. The purchaser is not considered as having full possession delivered to him, so long as another is in possession for the pur-

---

it takes the shape of *suppressio ueri* or *suggestio falsi*, and whatever legal devices may be employed to avert its consequences. If *quia* is the right reading, it must mean 'in so far as' (*quatenus*).

L. 2 pr.—The following passages deal with declarations by the seller as to the size of a piece of ground :—h. t. LL. 4, 1; 6 pr.; 13, 14; 22; 42; D. 21. 2. 69, 6; ib. 45; C. viii. 45. 10. Cp. note, p. 86 *supra*.

§ 1. In the case supposed the heir has sold, but he cannot put the buyer in possession, because a legatee or some one on his behalf is already in possession *custodiae causa* (D. 36. 3. 1, 2), or the estate is bankrupt and in the hands of creditors, or the *venter* is in possession (see *Digest*, 37, tit. 9).

possessione est, aut creditores bona possideant. idem dicendum est, si uenter in possessione sit: nam et ad hoc pertinet uacui appellatio.

3. Pomponius libro IX ad Sabinum.

Ratio [1] possessionis, quae a uenditore fieri debeat, talis est, ut, si quis eam possessionem iure auocauerit, tradita possessio non intellegatur.

1. Si emptor uacuam possessionem tradi stipulatus sit et ex stipulatu agat, fructus non uenient in eam actionem, quia et qui fundum dari stipularetur, uacuam quoque possessionem tradi oportere [2] stipulari intellegitur nec tamen fructuum praestatio ea stipulatione continetur, neque rursus plus debet esse in stipulatione. sed ex empto superesse ad fructuum praestationem.

2. Si iter actum uiam aquae ductum per tuum fundum emero, uacuae possessionis traditio nulla est: itaque cauere debes per te non fieri quo minus utar.

3. Si per uenditorem uini mora fuerit, quo minus traderet, condemnari eum oportet, utro tempore pluris uinum fuit, uel quo

---

For the obligation to give exclusive possession, see note on p. 50. The seller's primary obligation to deliver implies a duty to free the *res uendita* of all burdens and charges in order to hand over the full legal possession (L. 52 *infra*). *Ex his praediis quae mercata es, si aliqua a uenditore obligata et necdum tibi tradita sunt, ex empto actione consequeris ut ea a creditore liberentur* (C. viii. 45. 5; Cp. Pothier, §§ 42-46). This applies generally to all burdens not disclosed or known to the vendee, except praedial servitudes (p. 108 *ante*).

It does not seem clear whether there is an implied warranty of freedom from charges by English law (Benj. p. 705); but it is an important doctrine of Scots law that the seller is bound to discharge all incumbrances in the case of heritage, and all duties, warehouse rents, and other charges in the case of goods.

L. 3 pr.—*Non uidetur possessionem adeptus is, qui ita nactus est ut eam retinere non possit* (D. 41. 1. 22). The seller must give jural possession, *possessio ad interdicta*. Cp. L. 11, § 13.

[1] traditio? (*Cuj.*)   [2] oportere *del.*

pose of securing legacies or trusts, or if creditors have entered upon the estate; and the same is true where the mother possesses for behoof of her unborn child, for that is also inconsistent with 'full' possession.

3. POMPONIUS.

The possession which the seller is bound to give is of such a nature that, if it be set aside by legal process, it is held that delivery has never been given.

1. If a purchaser has stipulated for full possession and brings an action on the stipulation, he cannot sue for the fruits of the thing in that action; for even a stipulation that a piece of land shall be given [in property] to a person, although it is held to imply a stipulation that full possession shall also be given, does not include the prestation of the fruits, and on the other hand nothing can be imported into the stipulation: but the action on purchase is still available for enforcing the claim to the fruits.

2. If I buy the right to a footpath, or to a drove-road, or to a carriage-road, or to an aqueduct over your lands, there is no possible mode of delivering full possession; you must therefore give security that you will do nothing to impede me in the exercise of the right.

3. In a sale of wine, if there has been delay on the part of the seller in giving delivery, regard must be had, in assessing the damages, to the time when the highest price ruled, whether it be the date of the sale or of final judgment in the process, and to

---

§ 1. It appears from D. 45. 1. 52, 1, *siquis uacuam possessionem tradi promiserit, non nudum factum hace stipulatio continebit, sed causam bonorum* (cp. D. 22. 1. 4), that Ulpian and Papinian held that a stipulation '*possessionem tradi*' carried the right to the fruits from the time it was made.

§§ 3, 4. On damages for delay, see note to L. 1 *supra*, and Pothier, §§ 58, 74 sq.

If no place of delivery is stipulated, the vendor's duty is to deliver at the place where the goods are at the time of the contract, and nowhere else, and the vendee must send for them. Pothier, § 52.

uenit uel quo lis in condemnationem deducitur, item quo loco pluris fuit, uel quo uenit uel ubi agatur.

4. Quod si per emptorem mora fuisset, aestimari oportet pretium quod sit cum agatur, et quo loco minoris sit. mora autem uidetur esse, si nulla difficultas uenditorem impediat, quo minus traderet, praesertim si omni tempore paratus fuit tradere. item non oportet eius loci pretia spectari in quo agatur, sed eius ubi uina tradi oportet: nam quod a Brundisio uinum uenit, etsi uenditio alibi facta sit, Brundisi tradi oportet.

     4. PAULUS libro V ad Sabinum.

Si seruum mihi ignoranti, sciens furem uel noxium esse, uendideris, quamuis duplam promiseris, teneris mihi ex empto, quanti mea intererit scisse, quia ex stipulatu eo nomine agere tecum non possum antequam mihi quid abesset.

1. Si modus agri minor inueniatur, pro numero iugerum auctor obligatus est, quia, ubi modus minor inuenitur, non potest aestimari bonitas loci qui non exstat. sed non solum si modus agri totius minor est, agi cum uenditore potest, sed etiam de partibus eius, ut puta si dictum est uineae iugera tot esse uel oliueti et minus inueniatur: ideoque his casibus pro bonitate loci fiet aestimatio.

     5. PAULUS libro III ad Sabinum.

Si heres testamento quid uendere damnatus sit et uendiderit,

L. 4 pr.—*Noxius* 'not free from *noxa* (guilt),' *i.e.* guilty of some delict for which the owner has not made amends, and for which the purchaser might therefore be called on to make amends or else surrender the slave. The rule was *noxalis actio caput sequitur. Inst.* iv. 8. 5.

§ 1. Pothier, § 258.

L. 5 pr.—The heir was sometimes charged to sell to a legatee, sale being made the vehicle for bestowing the legacy, generally in the form *per damnationem*. Gaius, ii. § 201 sq. The legatee had an action on the will to compel the heir to conclude a contract of sale with him, and the same action lay to enforce

the place where the price was highest, whether it be the place where the contract was made or where action is brought upon it.

4. But if the delay has been on the side of the buyer, the damages should be assessed with reference to the price current at the time when the action is brought and at the place where it is lowest. Now the buyer is considered to be in delay, if there has been no impediment to hinder the seller from delivering, and especially if he has all the time been ready to deliver. Further, the prices current at the stipulated place of delivery will supersede the prices of the place where the action is brought; for if wine 'in Brundisium' be sold, delivery must be given at Brundisium, although the contract was made elsewhere.

4. Paul.

If you sell me a slave whom you know and I do not know to be a thief or liable to a noxal action, notwithstanding that you have engaged to pay the double, I can maintain the action on purchase against you for all the interest I had in being informed, because I cannot sue you under the stipulation in that behalf until I have actually sustained some loss.

1. If a piece of ground is found to measure less than was stated, the seller's warranty renders him liable in proportion to the acreage wanting, because where the quantity falls short it is impossible to estimate the quality of the deficiency. But action lies against the seller not only in respect of deficiency in the lands as a whole, but also when the separate portions are deficient,— as where it is found that there is less than the stated number of acres under vines or olives: and in such cases the valuation will be made with reference to the quality of the ground.

5. Paul.

An heir, who is bound by the will to sell something and has

---

performance of the contract as an alternative to the *actio ex empto*. The obligations on the heir were exactly the same as in any other sale.

de reliquis, quae per consequentias emptionis propria sunt, uel ex empto uel ex testamento agi cum eo poterit.

1. Sed si falso existimans se damnatum uendere uendiderit, dicendum est agi cum eo ex empto non posse, quoniam doli mali exceptione actor summoueri potest, quemadmodum, si falso existimans se damnatum dare promisisset, agentem doli mali exceptione summoueret. Pomponius etiam incerti condicere eum posse ait, ut liberetur.

6. Pomponius libro IX ad Sabinum.

Tenetur ex empto uenditor, etiamsi ignorauerit[1] minorem fundi modum esse.

1. Si uendidi tibi insulam certa pecunia et ut aliam insulam meam reficeres, agam ex uendito, ut reficias : si autem hoc solum, ut reficeres eam, conuenisset, non intellegitur emptio et uenditio facta, ut et Neratius scripsit.

2. Sed si aream tibi uendidi certo pretio et tradidi, ita ut insula aedificata partem dimidiam mihi retradas, uerum est et ut aedifices agere me posse ex uendito et ut aedificatam mihi

---

§ 1. If the whole essentials of an agreement are correctly understood, an error in the motives or interest operating on the will as an inducement to agree has in general no effect. Assent may be given owing to an unfounded expectation of some advantage, and the other contractor may be aware of the mistake; still this is irrelevant in law, provided the latter did not induce the false hope. *Id quoque quod ob causam datur, puta quod negotia mea ab eo adiuta putaui, licet non sit factum, quia donari uolui, quamuis falso mihi persuaserim, repeti non posse* (D. 12, 6. 65, 2, cp. ib. 52, 2 ; D. 12. 4. 3, 7 ; D. 18. 1. 34 pr., p. 60 *supra*). But if a person is, as here, induced to give a promise by the mistaken idea that he is under a legal obligation to do so, such a case forms an exception. The error here vitiates the consent; it grounds a *condictio indebiti* for release from the promise, and serves also as an equitable defence to an action by the promisee. This is sometimes called *falsa causa* ('*fausse cause*,' French Civil Code, art. 1131).

[1] agnoverit F.

done so, can be sued by an action either on the contract or on the will for all claims necessarily arising out of the contract of sale.

1. But if he has sold under a mistaken idea that the will ordained him to sell, it must be observed that the action on the contract is incompetent against him, for he can elide the claim by the plea of fraud, just as that defence would defeat an action upon a stipulation to give something where the promiser had been under the mistaken belief that he was legally bound to give it. Pomponius remarks that he can also bring a *condictio incerti* to obtain his release.

6. POMPONIUS.

The seller is subject to the action on purchase, although he was unaware that the lands contained less than he stated.

1. If I have sold you a tenement for a fixed sum and an undertaking that you will repair another tenement of mine, I can bring an action on sale against you to have the repairs done: but if the only consideration agreed on was that you should repair the house, that is not regarded as a contract of sale, as Neratius also remarks.

2. But if I have sold you a vacant plot for a fixed price, and have delivered it on condition that, after building a block of houses on it, you shall re-convey one half of it to me, I can bring an action against you both to compel you to build and to

---

L. 6 pr.—*Ignoraverit* is a necessary emendation. Cp. L. 11, § 7.

§ 1. There must be a price in numbered moneys, but the whole consideration need not be in money. The buyer may, as the complement of the price, bind himself *ad factum praestandum*. Cp. L. 28 *post*. He might also supplement the fixed price by undertaking to share with the seller the profit made on a re-sale, or to give him the whole profit (L. 13, § 24 *post*; D. 18. 1. 7, § 2, p. 22 *ante*).

§ 2. This is a somewhat complicated sale; the buyer of the site is taken bound to build and then to give back half the block. The ordinary course was for the owner of the ground to give out

retradas: quamdiu enim aliquid ex re uendita apud te superesset, ex uendito me habere actionem constat.

3. Si locum sepulchri emeris et propius cum locum, antequam mortuus ibi inferatur, aedificatum a uenditore fuerit, poteris ad eum reuerti.

4. Si uas aliquod mihi uendideris et dixeris certam mensuram capere uel certum pondus habere, ex empto tecum agam, si minus praestes. sed si uas mihi uendideris ita, ut adfirmares integrum, si id integrum non sit, etiam id quod eo nomine perdiderim praestabis mihi: si uero non id actum sit, ut integrum praestes, dolum malum dumtaxat praestare te debere. Labeo contra putat et illud solum obseruandum, ut, nisi in contrarium id[1] actum sit, omnimodo integrum praestari debeat: et est uerum. quod et in locatis doliis praestandum Sabinum respondisse Minicius refert.

5. Si tibi iter uendidero, ita demum auctorem me laudare poteris, si tuus fuerit fundus cui adquirere seruitutem uolueris: iniquum est enim me teneri, si propter hoc adquirere seruitutem non potueris, quia dominus uicini fundi non fueris.

6. Sed si fundum tibi uendidero et ei fundo iter accessurum dixero, omnimodo tenebor itineris nomine, quia utriusque rei quasi unus uenditor obligatus sum.

7. Si filius familias rem uendiderit mihi et tradiderit, sic ut pater familias tenebitur.

---

a contract for putting up the buildings (*locatio conductio operis*). See p. 46 *ante*. A similar transaction to the present is discussed in D. 19. 5. 13, 1, with this difference, that no price is to be paid for the site; consequently, it is not sale, but an innominate real contract with the usual remedy of *actio praescriptis verbis*.

§ 3. The law prescribed a certain free space to be left round burial-grounds. From L. 13 of the title *Finium regundorum* (*Digest*, 10, tit. 1), we learn there was a law at Rome, on the model of Solon's, that if a man dug a grave on his land near his neighbour's march he must leave a margin as wide as the grave was deep.

§ 4. For express warranty, compare L. 13, § 3 *post*. The opinion of Sabinus that there is no implied warranty of soundness in the sale of a *ras* is set aside by Labeo and Pomponius, who

[1] ut id, nisi in contrarium? (*Mom.*)

re-convey the building; for it is settled that so long as any part of the subject sold remains in your hands I can bring an action on sale against you.

3. If you buy a place for a burying-ground, and the seller, before any interment takes place, erects a building [on his own ground] without observing the prescribed distance, you will have legal recourse against him.

4. If you sell me a vessel declaring it to be of a certain capacity or a certain weight, an action on purchase will lie if you supply a smaller one. But if you sell me a vessel with an assurance that it is sound, and it proves not to be sound, you will also have to compensate me for any loss thereby incurred: but if it was not agreed that you should supply a sound one, you will only be responsible for fraud. Labeo, on the contrary, is of opinion that the rule is simply that soundness is always implied, unless there is an arrangement to the contrary; and this is the correct view. According to an opinion of Sabinus, reported by Minicius, the same rule applies to vats let to hire.

5. If I have sold you a right to a footpath, you cannot cite me as your author unless the land for which you desired to acquire the servitude belongs to you; for it is not fair that I should be responsible if you were precluded from acquiring the servitude by the fact that you were not proprietor of the lands adjoining.

6. But if I have sold you a piece of ground and promised a path to it as an accessory, I shall certainly be held liable in respect of the access, having come under the same obligation as if I had sold the two things together.

7. If a *filius familias* has sold and delivered a thing to me, he is responsible just like a *pater familias*.

---

extended to this case the principle of the edict that the seller is liable even for secret faults if they are so serious as to prevent the purchaser having the use of the thing. For the same rule where vats are hired, see D. 19. 2. 19, 1.

§ 5. The rule was *nemo potest seruitutem adquirere uel urbani uel rustici praedii, nisi qui habet praedium* (D. 8. 4. 1, 1).

§ 7. Speaking generally, a *filius familias* could be debtor but

8. Si dolo malo aliquid fecit uenditor in re uendita, ex empto eo nomine actio emptori competit: nam et dolum malum eo iudicio aestimari oportet, ut id, quod praestaturum se esse pollicitus sit uenditor emptori, praestari oporteat.

9. Si uenditor sciens obligatum aut alienum uendidisset et adiectum sit ' neue eo nomine quid praestaret,' aestimari oportet dolum malum eius, quem semper abesse oportet in iudicio empti, quod bonae fidei sit.

7. Pomponius libro X ad Sabinum.

Fundum mihi cum uenderes deducto usu fructu, dixisti eum usum fructum Titii esse, cum is apud te remansurus esset. si coeperis eum usum fructum uindicare, reuerti aduersus te non potero, donec Titius uiuat nec in ea causa esse coeperit, ut, etiamsi eius usus fructus esset, amissurus eum fuerit: nam tunc, id est si capite deminutus uel mortuus fuerit Titius, reuerti potero ad te uenditorem. idemque iuris est, si dicas eum usum fructum Titii esse, cum sit Sei.

8. Paulus libro V ad Sabinum.

Si tibi liberum praedium tradidero, cum seruiens tradere debe-

---

not creditor in a contract; *filius familias ex omnibus causis tanquam pater familias obligatur* (D. 44. 7. 39; cp. *Inst.* iii. 19. 6). But he was capable of contract to the fullest extent in respect of his *peculium castrense* (see p. 10 *ante*).

§ 8. See p. 92 *ante*.

§ 9. If the seller's conduct is fraudulent, *e.g.* if he knowingly sells a *res aliena* without informing the vendee, a proviso that he is not to answer for eviction (*pactum de non praestanda euictione*) will not shield him from liability for any damage sustained. The buyer's remedy is the *actio empti*, which, as an equitable (*bonae fidei*) action, covers all claims on account of fault or fraud.

L. 7.—Mancipation and *in iure cessio* were both competent modes of creating a usufruct in the way here contemplated, *i.e.* where the owner transfers the bare ownership and reserves the usufruct (*deducto usufructu*); it could not be done by delivery

8. If the vendor has done some intentional harm to the subject sold, the vendee can obtain redress by the action on purchase; for fraudulent intent should be taken into account in that action, in order that all engagements by the vendor to the vendee may be made good.

9. If a man has sold what he knows to be pledged or to belong to another, and has stipulated 'that he shall not be responsible on such grounds,' damages should be given for the fraud; for fraud should never show itself in the action on sale where regard is had to equity.

7. POMPONIUS.

In selling me a piece of ground with a reservation of the usufruct, you stated that it belonged to Titius, whereas it was really reserved for yourself. If you bring an action claiming the usufruct as yours, I shall have no recourse against you during Titius' lifetime unless his position undergoes such a change that he would forfeit the usufruct supposing it belonged to him; in which case, that is to say, if Titius die or lose his status, I shall have recourse against you as the seller. The law is the same, if you represent Titius as owner of the usufruct, when it really belongs to Seius.

8. PAUL.

If I deliver to you an estate free from servitude, when I

(Vat. Frag. 47). Here the seller falsely represents that Titius is fructuary, but that causes no damage; the only effect is that he is held to his statement, so that the usufruct is at an end on the death or *capitis diminutio* of Titius. In the classical law the right of usufruct lapsed on the slightest change of *status* (as by adoption or adrogation); Justinian settled that only *maxima* or *media capitis diminutio* should extinguish the right. *Inst.* ii. 4. 3.

L. 8 pr.—Marcian says that the *actio ex uendito* or the *incerti condictio* would be available to have the servitude imposed which had been omitted at delivery (D. 8. 2. 35). Cp. D. 12. 6. 22, 1.

rem, etiam condictio incerti competit mihi, ut patiaris eam seruitutem, quam debuit,¹ imponi.

1. Quod si seruum praedium in traditione fecero, quod liberum tibi tradere debui, tu ex empto habebis actionem remittendae eius seruitutis gratia, quam pati non debeas.

9. Pomponius libro xx ad Sabinum.

Si is qui lapides ex fundo emerit tollere eos nolit, ex uendito agi cum eo potest, ut eos tollat.

10. Ulpianus libro xlvi ad Sabinum.

Non est nouum, ut duae obligationes in eiusdem persona de eadem re concurrant: cum enim is qui uenditorem obligatum habebat ei qui eundem uenditorem obligatum habebat heres exstiterit, constat duas esse actiones in eiusdem persona concurrentes, propriam et hereditariam, et debere heredem institutum, si uelit separatim duarum actionum commodo uti, ante aditam hereditatem proprium uenditorem conuenire, deinde adita hereditate hereditarium: quod si prius adierit hereditatem, unam quidem actionem mouere potest, sed ita, ut per eam utriusque contractus sentiat commodum. ex contrario quoque si uenditor uenditori heres exstiterit, palam est duas euictiones cum praestare debere.

L. 9.—It is the duty of the vendee to carry away the thing sold, and he may be called on to do so immediately if there is no agreement or custom to the contrary. Cp. D. 18. 6. 1, 3 (sale of wine); Pothier, *Vente*, § 290 sq.

The leading case in English Law is *Greaves* v. *Ashlin* (1813) 3 Camp. 425. In that case the seller, after some delay, gave the buyer notice that if the goods were not carried away immediately he should re-sell them, and he did so. The buyer sued him for non-delivery. It was laid down on the one hand that the buyer's neglect did not entitle the seller to put an end to the contract, and sell the goods to another; and on the other hand that 'if the buyer does not carry away the goods bought, within a reasonable time, the seller may charge him warehouse room, or he may bring an action for not removing them, should he be prejudiced by the delay.' See S. G. B. § 39; Benj. p. 708.

¹ debui. Pᵇ.

ought to have delivered it burdened with a servitude, I can bring a *condictio incerti* to compel you to submit to the servitude which is due being set up.

1. But if in giving delivery I have burdened an estate with a servitude, when I was bound to deliver it unencumbered, you can bring an action on purchase to obtain release from a servitude you ought not to be subject to.

9. POMPONIUS.

If a man buys the stones off a piece of ground and refuses to take them away, an action on sale may be brought to enforce their removal.

10. ULPIAN.

It is not unusual for two obligations to concur in the same person in respect of the same thing: thus when one has incurred the obligations of a seller first to one person and then to another, and one of these succeeds the other as heir, it is quite settled that two rights of action meet in him, his own and that which he acquires as heir; and if the institute desires to avail himself of the two actions separately, he must before entering on the inheritance sue on the sale to himself, and then after entry on the sale to the deceased: but if he enters first, he can bring only one action, which, however, will secure him the benefit of both contracts. And, conversely, if one has sold a thing and then succeeds to another person, who has also sold it, it is clear he must answer for eviction under both sales.

L. 10.—The hypothesis is that A sells the same thing first to B and then to C, and incurs the penalty for eviction to each of them; B dies and C becomes his heir. Two actions, his own and B's, now concur in C, but there is no merging (*confusio*), because they arise from different *causae;* the object of each is to recover from A the penalty for eviction under a separate contract. *Non est nouum ut fideiussor duabus obligationibus eiusdem pecuniae nomine teneatur: nam si in diem acceptus mox pure accipiatur, ex utraque obligatur, et si fideiussor confideiussori heres exstiterit, idem erit* (D. 46. 1. 21, 1; cp. ib. 5). When he has entered, he must

11. ULPIANUS libro XXXII ad edictum.

Ex empto actione is qui emit utitur.

1. Et in primis sciendum est in hoc iudicio id demum deduci, quod praestari conuenit: cum enim sit bonae fidei iudicium, nihil magis bonae fidei congruit quam id praestari quod inter contrahentes actum est. quod si nihil conuenit, tunc ea praestabuntur quae naturaliter insunt huius iudicii potestate.

2. Et in primis ipsam rem praestare uenditorem oportet, id est tradere: quae res, si quidem dominus fuit uenditor, facit et emptorem dominum, si non fuit, tantum euictionis nomine uenditorem obligat, si modo pretium est numeratum aut eo nomine satisfactum. emptor autem nummos uenditoris facere cogitur.

3. Redhibitionem quoque contineri empti iudicio et Labeo et Sabinus putant et nos probamus.

4. Animalium quoque uenditor cauere debet ea sana praestari, et qui iumenta uendidit solet ita promittere 'esse, bibere, ut oportet.'

---

combine the separate penalties due under the two obligations in one *petitio*; if he did not, probably the seller could plead as an equitable defence that the actions should be conjoined. *Si plures sint inter eosdem societates coitae, ad omnes societates sufficere hoc unum iudicium constat* (D. 17. 2. 52, 14).

L. 11, § 1.—When the parties do not express their intentions, it is presumed they mean to abide by the *naturalia* of the contract, as established by custom and usage: *ea enim quae sunt moris et consuetudinis in bonae fidei iudiciis debent uenire* (D. 21. 1. 31, 20).

§ 2. See note, pp. 50, 51 *ante*. The seller can perform his part of the contract if he has *possessio*. He *may* have the ownership also, and, if so, it passes on delivery to the buyer; but that is a mere accident, not an essential. For the obligation on the buyer to make the seller owner of the price, see D. 19. 4. 1 pr. *Emptor nisi nummos accipientis fecerit, tenetur ex uendito*. If slaves were sold and the buyer paid the price out of their *peculia* (which belonged to the seller, p. 57), he could still be sued for the price, *cum proprii uenditoris nummi soluti non praestant emptori liberationem* (C. iv. 49. 7).

11. ULPIAN.

The buyer's remedy is the action on purchase.

1. It is important to note that this action extends to everything for which the parties have agreed to be responsible; for it is an equitable action, and what can be more agreeable to equity than to give effect to the intentions of the contracting parties? In the absence of any agreement, the measure of their responsibility will be the obligations that naturally fall within the scope of this action.

2. The primary obligation on the seller is to make good, that is, to deliver the actual thing; the result of which is to make the purchaser owner if the seller was owner, and if he was not, to make the seller responsible for eviction, provided always the price has been paid or security given for it. The purchaser, on the contrary, is obliged to make the seller owner of the price.

3. I concur in the opinion of Labeo and Sabinus, that the action on purchase may have for its object the rescission of the contract.

4. One who sells live animals should give security that they are sound when delivered, and the seller of beasts of burden usually gives a guarantee that 'they feed and drink properly.'

§ 3. *Redhibitio* was the right based on the edict of the curule aediles to have the thing sold taken back, and the price restored on the ground of deficient quality; *redhibere est facere ut rursus habeat uenditor quod habuerit: et, quia reddendo id fiebat, idcirco redhibitio est appellata, quasi redditio* (D. 21. 1. 21 pr.) It could be enforced by the *actio redhibitoria*, or *actio quanti minoris*, but the existence of special remedies did not make the action on the contract incompetent. The *actio empti* could be brought whenever there was a claim of indemnity for damage actually sustained.

§ 4. Warranties as to the condition of slaves and animals were also based upon the edict of the aediles, who had the supervision of the markets. The edict made the seller responsible for all defects or vices of any consequence, unless he had expressly pointed them out to the buyer. Ignorance of the existence of the faults, though excusable, did not relieve him. It appears

5. Si quis uirginem se emere putasset, cum mulier uenisset, et sciens errare eum uenditor passus sit, rehibitionem quidem ex hac causa non esse, uerum tamen ex empto competere actionem ad resoluendam emptionem, et[1] pretio restituto mulier reddatur.

6. Is qui uina emit arrae nomine certam summam dedit: postea conuenerat, ut emptio irrita fieret. Iulianus ex empto agi posse ait, ut arra restituatur, utilemque esse actionem ex empto etiam ad distrahendam, inquit, emptionem. ego illud quaero: si anulus datus sit arrae nomine et secuta emptione pretioque numerato et tradita re anulus non reddatur, qua actione agendum est, utrum condicatur, quasi ob causam datus sit et causa finita sit, an uero ex empto agendum sit. et Iulianus diceret ex empto agi posse: certe etiam condici poterit, quia iam sine causa apud uenditorem est anulus.

7. Uenditorem, etiamsi ignorans uendiderit, fugitiuum non esse praestare emptori oportere Neratius ait.

8. Idem Neratius, etiamsi alienum seruum uendideris, furtis noxisque solutum praestare te debere ab omnibus receptum ait et ex empto actionem esse, ut habere licere emptori caueatur, sed et ut tradatur ei possessio.

9. Idem ait non tradentem quanti intersit condemnari:

---

from the following sections and C. iv. 49, 14, that the buyer of a slave was entitled to demand caution from the seller for the absence of such defects (*stipulatio duplae*): *emptor seruorum . . . de eorum fuga, itemque sanitate, erronesque non esse, aut noxa solutos, repromitti sibi recte postulat.*

§ 5. Cp. D. 18. 1. 11, 1, where it was simply a case of error; here it is a case of fraud, the seller taking advantage of the buyer's ignorance by concealing a fact which he knew would have kept him from buying. Although the edict did not require a warranty in this case, and the slave could not be returned on that ground, yet the seller's fraud let in an action on the contract with the effects stated in the text. The passage is not to be read in the sense that the buyer could sue directly for rescission on this ground by the *actio empti*. That action would lie only for damages, but it might result in the cancelling of the contract,

[1] ut (*dett.*).

5. If one believed he was buying a virgin, whereas the woman on sale was a mother, and the seller knowing his mistake lets him carry out the transaction, though it does not ground the action for return, yet an action on purchase is competent to have the sale cancelled, the woman taken back, and the price restored.

6. A person buying wine paid so much by way of earnest; it was afterwards agreed to depart from the sale. Julian holds that the action on purchase is competent to get back the earnest, and that in a modified form it is available also for rescinding the sale. I put this query: if a ring be given as earnest, and a sale has followed and the price has been paid and the article has been delivered, but the ring is not restored, what action should be brought—a condiction on the ground that it was given for a consideration which is at an end, or an action on the contract? According to Julian it would be the action on purchase; undoubtedly a condiction is also competent to recover the ring, because it is now in the hands of the seller without consideration given for it.

7. Neratius remarks that the seller of a slave, though ignorant of his character at the time of the sale, is bound to warrant him not to be a runaway.

8. Neratius also says that, though the slave you sell belongs to another, it is universally admitted that you are bound to warrant him free from liability for theft or delict, and that the buyer can bring the action on purchase to require you both to give security for undisturbed possession and also to deliver the possession to him.

9. He says that, for failure to deliver, the seller should be

---

where the defect rendered the thing totally useless, and rescission was therefore the only mode of compensating the buyer.

§ 6. See pp. 68, 69 *ante*.

§ 7. *Fugitiuus* and *erro* are used of slaves whose disposition it is to run away or play truant when they have the chance, even if they have never done so (D. 50. 16. 225).

§ 9. *Quanti plurimum auctorem periclitari oportet* means the highest sum the seller could be called upon to pay in case of

satis autem non dantem, quanti plurimum auctorem periclitari oportet.

10. Idem Neratius ait propter omnia haec satis esse quod plurimum est praestari, id est ut sequentibus actionibus deducto eo quod praestitum est lis aestimetur.

11. Idem recte ait, si quid horum non praestetur, cum cetera facta sint, nullo deducto condemnationem faciendam.

12. Idem libro secundo responsorum ait emptorem noxali iudicio condemnatum ex empto actione id tantum consequi, quanti minimo defungi potuit: idemque putat et si ex stipulatu aget: et siue defendat noxali iudicio, siue non, quia manifestum fuit noxium seruum fuisse, nihilo minus uel ex stipulatu uel ex empto agere posse.

13. Idem Neratius ait uenditorem in re tradenda debere praestare emptori, ut in lite de possessione potior sit: sed Iulianus libro quinto decimo digestorum probat nec uidere traditum, si superior in possessione emptor futurus non sit: erit igitur ex empto actio, nisi hoc praestetur.

14. Cassius ait eum qui ex duplae stipulatione litis aestimationem consecutus est, aliarum rerum nomine, de quibus in uenditionibus caueri solet, nihil consequi posse. Iulianus deficiente dupla ex empto agendum putauit.

---

eviction, *i.e.* double the price: *si dupla non promitteretur, et eo nomine agetur, dupli condemnandus est reus* (D. 21. 2. 2; cp. L. 44 *post*).

§§ 10, 11. These sections come to this, that the buyer can recover the *duplum* for a single breach of the seller's duties, and no more than the *duplum* for two or more distinct breaches.

§ 12. It would thus appear that the buyer may, if a third party produces irrefragable evidence of his right to the *res vendita*, at once hand it over, without notice to his author, and does not thereby lose his recourse against him. *Defungi* means 'to get clear of,' 'to be quit of' the action on certain terms.

§ 13. This section defines precisely the extent of the seller's obligation to deliver: he must convey such a title of possession as will secure to the buyer the protection of the interdicts, and

found liable in damages; and for refusal to give security, in the highest sum for which a seller can be held responsible.

10. He adds that all the buyer's claims are fully satisfied by payment of such highest sum; that is to say, the amount already paid must be deducted in assessing the damages in any subsequent actions.

11. He also says, quite rightly, that if the seller has failed in any one of his obligations, though he has fulfilled the rest, judgment will be given for the full sum without deduction.

12. He observes, in the second book of his *Responsa*, that the buyer of a slave, if condemned in a noxal action, can recover by the action on purchase no more than the lowest sum that would have discharged the claim, and he holds it is the same if the action be laid on the stipulation; and the buyer can sue on the stipulation or on the contract at his option, no matter whether he defends the noxal action or lets judgment go by default, the liability to make amends being indisputable.

13. Neratius says further, that the seller when giving delivery must guarantee that the buyer shall prevail in any possessory suit; while Julian, in the fifteenth book of his *Digesta*, holds there is no delivery at all unless the buyer is enabled to maintain his possession; an action on purchase will therefore lie, unless he is put in a position to do so.

14. According to Cassius, when the buyer has once been awarded damages in an action on the stipulation for the double, he can recover nothing more under any of the other heads in respect of which it is usual for the seller to give security. But where the stipulation for the double has not been made, Julian thought that the action on purchase must be employed.

---

give him the better claim in any question that may be raised about the possession. See notes on pp. 50, 65 *ante*.

The adversative conjunction (*sed Iulianus*) is used because Julian was of the opposite school from Neratius (Pothier).

§ 14. With *deficiente dupla* compare *Sed et si stipulatio nulla fuisset interposita, de ex empto actione idem dicemus* (D. 21. 2. 19 pr.).

15. Denique libro decimo apud Minicium ait, si quis seruum ea condicione uendiderit, ut intra triginta dies duplam promitteret, postea ne quid praestaretur, et emptor hoc fieri intra diem non desiderauerit, ita demum non teneri uenditorem, si ignorans alienum uendidit: tunc enim in hoc fieri,[1] ut per ipsum et per heredem eius emptorem habere liceret : qui autem alienum sciens uendidit, dolo, inquit, non caret et ideo empti iudicio tenebitur.

16. Sententiam Iuliani uerissimam esse arbitror in pignoribus quoque : nam si iure creditoris uendiderit, deinde haec fuerint euicta, non tenetur nec ad pretium restituendum ex empto actione creditor : hoc enim multis constitutionibus effectum est. dolum plane uenditor praestabit, denique etiam repromittit de dolo : sed et si non repromiserit, sciens tamen sibi non obligatam[2] uel non esse eius qui sibi obligauit uendiderit, tenebitur ex empto, quia dolum eum praestare debere ostendimus.

17. Si quis rem uendiderit et ei accessurum quid dixerit, omnia quidem quae diximus in re distracta in hoc quoque sequenda sint,[3] ut tamen euictionis nomine non in duplum teneatur, sed in hoc tantum obligetur, ut emptori habere liceat, et non solum per se, sed per omnes.

18. Qui autem habere licere uendidit, uideamus quid debeat

---

§§ **15, 16.** A special agreement *de non praestanda euictione* does not avail the fraudulent seller; he can be sued by the *actio empti* for the full *interesse*. Cp. LL. 1, 1 ; 6, 9 *supra*. § 18 discusses the effect of such a pact where the seller has acted in good faith.

For the rule that the creditor selling a pledge did not warrant against eviction, but was liable for fraud, *e.g.* selling when he knew that he had no right of sale, or that his debtor was not owner of the pledge, see D. 21. 2. 50 : *Si pignora ueneant per apparitores praetoris . . . nemo unquam dixit dandam in eos esse actionem re euicta ; sed si dolo rem uiliori pretio proiecerunt, tunc de dolo actio datur aduersus eos domino rei.* Cp. D. 20. 5. 10 ; C. viii. 45. 1 and 2.

§ **17.** An express stipulation for the double in case of eviction does not apply to the accessories or produce; it is construed strictly.

[1] teneri ? (*Cuj.*)   obligata ? (*Mom.*)   [3] sunt ?

15. He is quoted by Minicius as saying, in his tenth book, that where a man has sold a slave on the condition that he will give security for double the price within a month, and thereafter be free of responsibility, and the purchaser has let the time expire without requiring security, the seller will not escape liability for selling another man's slave, unless he did it in ignorance; in which case he and his heirs are bound merely to do nothing to disturb the buyer's possession: but if he knowingly sells a slave belonging to another, that is fraud, and it will expose him to the action on purchase.

16. I think the opinion given by Julian is equally true of things pledged: for if a creditor in the exercise of his rights has sold a pledge, he cannot be compelled even to restore the price if the buyer is subsequently evicted and brings the action on purchase: that has been enacted by several constitutions. Of course the seller will be responsible for fraud; in fact he undertakes to answer for fraud: but even though he has given no undertaking, if he sells a thing knowing it is not pledged to him, or that the man who pledged it was not the owner, he can be sued by the action on purchase, because, as we have shown above, he is responsible for fraud.

17. If a man, when selling a thing, declares that some other thing will go with it as an accessory, the same principles apply to the accessory as have been laid down for sale in general, with this exception, that the seller is not liable to the penalty of the double in the event of eviction; he is only bound to secure the purchaser in undisturbed possession both as regards himself and all others.

18. We have to consider next what liability is incurred by

§ **18.** The connection of ideas in this section requires some attention. In the first part down to *non tenebitur*, Ulpian distinguishes between what in Scotland is called 'absolute warrandice' and 'warrandice from fact and deed'; under the former the seller is liable *contra omnes mortales* for every defect in the right which he has granted; under the latter he and his heirs are bound to do nothing inconsistent with the grant, but he is

praestare. et multum interesse arbitror, utrum hoc polliceatur per se uenientesque a se personas non fieri, quo minus habere liceat, an uero per omnes. nam si per se, non uidetur id praestare, ne alius euincat : proinde si euicta res erit, siue stipulatio interposita est, ex stipulatu non tenebitur, siue non est interposita, ex empto non tenebitur. sed Iulianus libro quinto decimo digestorum scribit, etiamsi aperte uenditor pronuntiet per se heredemque suum non fieri, quo minus habere liceat, posse defendi ex empto eum in hoc quidem non teneri, quod emptoris interest, uerum tamen ut pretium reddat teneri. ibidem ait idem esse dicendum et si aperte in uenditione comprehendatur nihil euictionis nomine praestatum iri : pretium quidem deberi re euicta, utilitatem non deberi : neque enim bonae fidei contractus hac patitur[1] conuentione, ut emptor rem amitteret et pretium uenditor retineret. nisi forte, inquit, sic quis omnes istas supra scriptas conuentiones recipiet, quemadmodum recipitur, ut uenditor nummos accipiat, quamuis merx ad emptorem non pertineat, ueluti cum futurum iactum retis a piscatore eminus aut indaginem plagis positis a uenatore uel pantheram[2] ab aucupe : nam etiamsi nihil capit, nihilo minus emptor pretium praestare necesse habebit. sed in supra scriptis conuentionibus contra erit dicendum : nisi forte sciens alienum uendit : tunc enim secundum supra a nobis relatam Iuliani sententiam dicendum est ex empto eum teneri, quia dolo facit.

---

absolutely protected from action at the instance of the buyer on account of eviction at the hands of any other person,—there is implied, in fact, a tacit *pactum de non praestanda euictione*, which shuts out any possible demand for return of the price in such a contingency. In the succeeding passage (*sed Iulianus . . . praestare necesse habebit*) Ulpian quotes a rather hesitating opinion of Julian to the effect that such a pact, whether express or implied, releases the seller merely from the obligation to make good the *interesse*, but not from an obligation to return the price, for he considers it to be inequitable that the buyer should lose both the property and the price, unless indeed a sale with such

[1] utitur ? (*Mom.*)   [2] pantheran ?

the seller under the warranty of full possession and enjoyment. Now in my opinion it makes a great difference whether the undertaking is that the seller and his successors in title will not disturb the buyer, or that no person whatever shall do so. In the former case he cannot be held answerable for eviction at the hands of a third party: accordingly, if the property be carried off, he is not liable therefor either under the stipulation if he has entered into one, or under the contract if he has not. Julian, however, says, in the fifteenth book of his *Digesta*, that even where the seller has declared explicitly that he and his successors will not disturb the buyer's possession, it may be argued that he is liable under the contract, not certainly in full damages to the buyer, but for repayment of the price merely. He goes on to say that the same rule applies even when it is an express term of the contract that the seller is not to be responsible for eviction: if eviction follows, he is bound to restore the price, but not to pay an indemnity: for an agreement that the purchaser is to lose the property while the seller keeps the price is inconsistent with a contract based on equity. But perhaps, he adds, all such covenants are to be brought under the legal principle which sanctions a bargain that the seller shall get the price though the thing sold should never reach the buyer, as for instance when we buy all the fish that may be caught in a haul of the net, or all the game a hunter may take in the toils, or all the birds a fowler may enclose: though nothing be caught, the purchaser is bound to pay the price. But the contrary is true of the covenants above mentioned, except where one knowingly sells what belongs to another; in that case it is true, in accordance with the opinion of Julian referred to above, that the seller is liable under the contract, on the ground that he has acted fraudulently.

an adjected pact is to be justified by the analogy of the *emptio spei* (p. 25 *ante*), in which the seller gets the price though the buyer should get nothing. In the concluding words (*sed in supra scriptis . . . dolo facit*) Ulpian reasserts the principle he stated at the outset, adding the qualification that, if the seller is in bad

12. CELSUS libro XXVII digestorum.

Si iactum retis emero et iactare retem piscator noluit, incertum eius rei aestimandum est: si quod extraxit piscium reddere mihi noluit, id aestimari debet quod extraxit.

13. ULPIANUS libro XXXII ad edictum.

Iulianus libro quinto decimo inter eum qui sciens quid aut ignorans uendidit differentiam facit in condemnatione ex empto: ait enim, qui pecus morbosum aut tignum uitiosum uendidit, si quidem ignorans fecit, id tantum ex empto actione praestaturum quanto minoris essem empturus, si id ita esse scissem: si uero sciens reticuit et emptorem decepit, omnia detrimenta, quae ex ea emptione emptor traxerit, praestaturum ei: siue igitur aedes uitio tigni corruerunt, aedium aestimationem, siue pecora contagione morbosi pecoris perierunt, quod interfuit idonea uenisse erit praestandum.

1. Item qui furem uendidit aut fugitiuum, si quidem sciens,

---

faith, the *actio empti* will lie, notwithstanding such a *pactum de non praestanda euictione*.

Some writers, however, maintain that Ulpian does not mean in the closing words to express his dissent from Julian, but only to remove the doubt suggested by the reference to *emptio spei* (Puchta). The result of the passage would then be that the pact in question relieves the seller of the expenses, etc., incident to eviction, but not of the obligation to restore the price to the buyer, and that it has no effect whatever if the seller is in bad faith. Pothier so understands it (*Vente*, § 185 sq.). Cp. French Civil Code, art. 1629.

But it may be inferred from the final words that as the *actio empti* is competent only where there is fraud, it is not allowed where the seller makes the covenant honestly to secure himself against possible risks; consequently, though the title should prove to be bad, he will be entitled to keep the price. This result is more consistent with the decisions elsewhere, as D. 21. 2. 68 pr.: *Cum ea condicione pignus distrahitur, ne quid euictione secuta creditor praestet; quamuis pretium emptor non soluerit, sed uenditori cauerit, euictione secuta nullam emptor exceptionem habebit, quo minus pretium soluat.* Cp. D. 18. 4. 10 and 11.

12. CELSUS.

If I buy the draught of a net and the fisherman refuses to cast his net, the uncertain value of the catch must be taken into account; if he casts the net but refuses to hand over the fish, the value of the haul will be the measure of the damages.

13. ULPIAN.

Julian in his fifteenth book draws a distinction, as regards the damages to be awarded in the action on purchase, between selling a thing with and without knowledge of its defects: for he says, if a man sells me diseased cattle or rotten beams without knowing it, all he has to make good in the action on purchase is the difference between the price I gave and what I would have given had I known their condition; but if he knows it and says nothing, and so deceives the buyer, he is responsible to him for all loss resulting from the purchase: for example, if a house collapses because of the rottenness of the beams he must pay its value, and if other stock dies through contact with the tainted herd he must reimburse the buyer for all it has cost him that he did not get sound cattle.

1. Similarly, if a man sells a slave whom he knows to be a

Compare generally for the effect of a stipulation '*habere licere*' D. 45. 1. 38.

L. 12.—In the ordinary examples of *emptio spei* given in the texts, the chance or expectation can only be realised by some act on the part of the seller. If the act is done, it is immaterial whether it has any result or not. By selling a haul of his net, a fisherman binds himself to cast his net,—the hiring of a service is involved; see note on p. 25. For *incertum* compare D. 18. 4. 11, *nam hoc modo admittitur esse uenditionem, 'si qua sit hereditas, est tibi empta' et quasi spes hereditatis: ipsum enim incertum rei ueneat, ut in retibus.*

L. 13 pr.—§ 2.—The liability of the seller for defects in the *res uendita* rested partly on the principles of the common law

praestare debebit, quanti emptoris interfuit non decipi : si uero ignorans uendiderit, circa fugitiuum quidem tenetur, quanti minoris empturus esset, si eum esse fugitiuum scisset, circa furem non tenetur : differentiae ratio est, quod fugitiuum quidem habere non licet et quasi euictionis nomine tenetur uenditor, furem autem habere possumus.

2. Quod autem diximus 'quanti emptoris interfuit non decipi,' multa continet, et[1] si alios secum sollicitauit ut fugerent, uel res quasdam abstulit.

3. Quid tamen si ignorauit quidem furem esse, adseuerauit autem bonae frugi et fidum et caro uendidit ? uideamus, an ex empto teneatur, et putem teneri. atqui ignorauit : sed non debuit facile quae ignorabat adseuerare. inter hunc igitur et

---

(*ius civile*), partly on the edict of the curule aediles ; in the first case it was enforced by the action on the contract, in the second by the actions introduced by the edict. The action on the contract was limited to cases of fraud (cp. L. 4. pr.) and breach of express warranty ; the actions under the edict applied in all sales of a certain class, wherever there were defects which had not been pointed out, irrespective of the seller's knowledge or ignorance of their existence. Cicero states expressly that the *actio empti* was limited in the above manner (*de Off.* iii. 16, 17); yet we are told here that it could be brought against a seller who knew nothing of the defects. It must, therefore, have undergone some modification. The most probable explanation is that the jurists, after the principles of the edict had become settled, imported them into the common law *actio empti*. It would be easy to remodel a *bonae fidei* action in the manner suggested, because the recognised custom was regularly adopted into actions of that kind (D. 21. 1. 31, 20). The *actio empti* as thus extended to cover the case of an innocent seller followed very closely the lines of the *actio quanti minoris* introduced by the edict; for example, it applied, as the edict did, only to *uitia corporis*, not to *uitia animi*, and it concluded not for full damages but for reduction of the price by striking off the excess over the worth of the thing with its defects (*vera rei aestimatio*); it is only where the seller acts fraudulently that he is liable under the *actio empti* for other

[1] ut?

thief or a runaway, he will have to make good what the buyer loses by being deceived; but if he does not know, he is liable, in the case of the runaway slave, for the surplus over the price the purchaser would have paid had he known he was a runaway : but he is not liable in the case of the thief: the reason for the distinction being, that possession of a runaway slave is impossible, and the seller is liable just as for eviction, whereas possession of the thief is possible.

2. The expression used above, 'what the buyer loses by being deceived,' embraces many elements of damage; *e.g.* the slave may have incited others to run away with him, or have stolen some property of the buyer's.

3. But what if the seller, without knowing that the slave was a thief, certifies him as well behaved and honest, and sells him dear ? Can he be reached by the action on purchase ? I am inclined to think he can. But it may be urged, he did not know; the answer is, he should not lightly have asserted what he did not know. There is therefore not much difference between

---

defects and for indirect damages. Cp. note to D. 18. 1. 45; D. 21. 1. 1, §§ 9, 10; ib. 4 pr., § 4. Vangerow, § 609. Pothier, *Obl.* § 162 sq.

The expression '*quanti emptoris interfuit non decipi*' is in itself ambiguous (see note p. 111 *ante*); but the context makes it clear that the measure of damages against a fraudulent seller was the interest the buyer had in getting a sound article (*quod interfuit idonea venisse*), whereas the damages against a *bona fide* seller resolved into a reduction of the price.

For the rules as to fugitive slaves, see D. 21. 1. 17; C. iv. 58. 1; Paul, *Sent.* ii. 17. 11.

The edict did not lay upon the seller the duty of pointing out that a slave is given to stealing (*furem esse*), because that is not inconsistent with peaceable possession as the vice of running away is. But he is liable for fraud if he knows him to be a thief and conceals the fact (L. 4 pr. *supra*, D. 21. 1. 14, 9).

§ 3. This passage and texts such as L. 6, § 4 *supra* and D. 18. 6. 15, *Si uina . . . antequam ab emptore tollerentur sua natura corrupta fuerint, si quidem de bonitate eorum adfirmauit uenditor,*

qui scit [et tacuit non multum interest: nam qui scit[1]] praemonere debuit furem esse, hic non debuit facilis esse ad temerariam indicationem.

4. Si uenditor dolo fecerit, ut rem pluris uenderet, puta de artificio mentitus est aut de peculio, empti eum iudicio teneri, ut praestaret emptori quanto pluris seruum emisset,[2] si ita peculiatus esset uel eo artificio instructus.

5. Per contrarium quoque idem Iulianus scribit, cum Terentius Uictor decessisset relicto herede fratre suo, et res quasdam ex hereditate et instrumenta et mancipia Bellicus quidam subtraxisset, quibus subtractis facile, quasi minimo ualeret hereditas, ut sibi ea uenderetur persuasit: an uenditi iudicio teneri possit? et ait Iulianus competere actionem ex uendito in tantum quanto pluris hereditas ualeret, si hae res subtractae non fuissent.

6. Idem Iulianus dolum solere a uenditore praestari etiam in huiusmodi specie ostendit: si, cum uenditor sciret fundum pluribus municipiis legata[3] debere, in tabula quidem conscripserit uni municipio deberi, uerum postea legem consignauerit, si qua tributorum aut uectigalis indictionisue quid[4] nomine aut ad uiae collationem praestare oportet, id emptorem dare facere praestareque oportere, ex empto eum teneri, quasi decepisset emptorem: quae sententia uera est.

---

tenebitur emptori ; quodsi nihil adfirmauit, emptoris erit periculum, are authority for the general rule that goods had to be delivered in such condition as to conform to the seller's assurances whether in stipulatory form or not (*dicta et promissa*). There was no difference, as in English law, between representation and warranty. See p. 90 sq. *ante*.

We are not expressly told here what the *actio ex empto* embraced —whether it lay for damages for non-performance or only for reduction of the price. The lacuna in the text has been filled up as Mommsen suggests.

§ 4. According to Paul (*Sent.* ii. 17. 6), the seller who made a false representation of this kind was bound either to make good the difference in value or to submit to a rescission of the sale

---

[1] *Mom. suppl. secundum Basil.*
[2] seruus esset? (*Krueg.*)
[3] tributa?
[4] cuius? (*Mom.*)

him and one who conceals what he knows: for the latter, knowing the slave was a thief, ought to have disclosed the fact, and the former should not have been so ready to make rash assertions.

4. If a thing fetches a higher price owing to some dishonesty on the seller's part, such as telling a falsehood about the technical skill or the *peculium* of a slave, he is liable under the action on purchase to make up to the buyer the difference in value as compared with a slave really possessing the *peculium* or training he represented.

5. Julian deals also with the converse case: Terentius Victor dies leaving a brother as heir, and one Bellicus secretly removes various articles, title deeds, and slaves belonging to the estate, thereby making it appear of very small value, and inducing a sale of it to himself cheap; can he be reached by the action on sale? Julian says the action is competent to recover the surplus which the estate would have been worth if the foresaid items had not been purloined.

6. Julian also points out that the seller is regularly held answerable for fraud in circumstances like the following: suppose the seller, knowing that a landed estate is burdened with legacies in favour of several city corporations, states in the announcement of the sale that it is liable only to one corporation, but subsequently makes it a condition of the contract that, if any taxes, dues, impost or road-rate should prove to be exigible, the purchaser shall be bound to pay, perform, or satisfy the same, the seller is nevertheless liable under the action on purchase for having imposed upon the buyer,—a sound opinion in my judgment.

(cp. C. iv. 49. 9). Reduction of the price and not the full *interesse* is said to be the object of the *actio empti* in this case, which seems to conflict with the preceding sections; but the explanation may be that in certain cases, in particular where there is an available market, the two standards of damages are practically coincident. In the example here put, the buyer might have no interest in getting the trained slave other than the difference in value; if he recovers that he can go into the market and buy.

7. Sed cum in facto proponeretur tutores hoc idem fecisse, qui rem pupillarem uendebant, quaestionis esse ait, an tutorum dolum pupillus praestare debeat. et si quidem ipsi tutores uendiderunt, ex empto eos teneri nequaquam dubium est: sed si pupillus auctoribus eis uendidit, in tantum tenetur, in quantum locupletior ex eo factus est, tutoribus in residuum perpetuo condemnandis, quia nec transfertur in pupillum post pubertatem hoc quod dolo tutorum factum est.

8. Offerri pretium ab emptore debet, cum ex empto agitur, et ideo etsi pretii partem offerat, nondum est ex empto actio: uenditor enim quasi pignus retinere potest eam rem quam uendidit.

9. Unde quaeritur, si pars sit pretii soluta et res tradita postea euicta sit, utrum eius rei consequetur pretium integrum ex empto agens an uero quod numerauit? et puto magis id quod numerauit propter doli exceptionem.

10. Si fructibus iam maturis ager distractus sit, etiam fructus emptori cedere, nisi aliud conuenit, exploratum est.

---

§ 7. Compare D. 4. 3. 15 pr.: *Sed et ex dolo tutoris, si factus est locupletior, puto in eum dandam actionem, sicut exceptio datur.* See also D. 26, tit. 9, 3.

§ 8. It has been a good deal discussed whether the party suing on the contract of sale was bound, as a condition of raising his action, to show that he had fulfilled his part (see note to D. 18. 1. 78, § 2 *supra*, and L. 25 *infra*). If the buyer's duty is to pay the price as a counterpart to receipt of the goods, the proper inference would seem to be not that he must prepay the price in order to have a title to sue, but that he cannot ask judgment except on condition of payment. This is quite consistent with the seller's right of retention. Cp. D. 21. 1. 57 pr.: *nam et si ex empto dominus agat, nisi pretium totum soluerit, nihil consequitur.*

The *res uendita nondum tradita* is not strictly speaking a pledge, because the seller is undivested owner, and no one can have a right of pledge over his own property; but it may be described as *quasi pignus*, for the seller has a right of retention till he is paid the full price, just as a pignorate creditor has a

7. But when a case was submitted where the tutors had acted in this way in selling the pupil's property, he said the question was whether the pupil was bound to answer for the fraud of his tutors. If the tutors sold at their own hand, there is no doubt whatever that they are liable in an action on purchase; but if they only authorised a sale by the pupil, he is responsible so far as he has been enriched thereby, but his tutors are liable in damages for the balance without relief, because the liability for their dishonest dealing is not shifted to the pupil when he attains puberty.

8. When the buyer brings the action on purchase, he should tender payment of the price; consequently, if only a part be tendered, the action is ineffectual: for the seller is entitled to retain the subject sold as a sort of pledge.

9. Hence the question arises whether, if part of the price be paid and delivery given, and the buyer be then evicted, he can recover in the action on purchase the full price, or only the part he paid? In my opinion he will be prevented by the plea of fraud from getting more than he actually paid.

10. If land be sold when its produce is ripe, it is settled that the crop passes to the purchaser in the absence of any agreement to the contrary.

---

right to retain the pledge till the debt is extinguished. See D. 18. 4. 22: *Hereditatis venditae pretium pro parte accepit: reliquum emptore non solvente, quaesitum est an corpora hereditaria pignoris nomine teneantur. respondi, nihil proponi cur non teneantur.* Cp. D. 21. 2. 31, 8: *nam venditor pignoris loco quod vendidit retinet quoad emptor satisfaciat.* Pothier, § 63 sq.

In England the plaintiff in an action for non-delivery need not prove he was ready and willing to pay till the seller shows he was ready to give delivery, payment and delivery being concurrent conditions. *Wilks v. Atkinson* (1815) 1 Marshall, 412; S. G. B. § 30. For the right of lien in England and of retention in Scotland, see note on p. 21 *ante.*

§ 10. See C. iv. 49. 13, and for a special agreement to the contrary D. 18. 1. 40, §§ 3, 4. Pothier, § 47.

11. Si in locatis ager fuit, pensiones utique ei cedent qui locauerat: idem et in praediis urbanis, nisi si quid nominatim conuenisse proponatur.

12. Sed et si quid praeterea[1] rei uenditae nocitum est, actio emptori praestanda est, damni forte infecti uel aquae pluuiae arcendae uel Aquiliae uel interdicti quod ui aut clam.

13. Item si quid ex operis seruorum uel uecturis iumentorum uel nauium quaesitum est, emptori praestabitur, et si quid peculio eorum accessit, non tamen si quid ex re uenditoris.

14. Si Titius fundum, in quo nonaginta iugera erant, uendiderit et in lege emptionis dictum est in fundo centum esse iugera et antequam modus manifestetur, decem iugera alluuione adcreuerint, placet mihi Neratii sententia existimantis, ut, si quidem sciens uendidit, ex empto actio competat aduersus eum, quamuis decem iugera adcreuerint, quia dolo fecit nec dolus purgatur: si uero ignorans uendidit, ex empto actionem non competere.

---

§ 11. See examples of special agreement that the rents shall go to the buyer in D. 18. 1. 68 pr; § 16 *infra*; L. 53 pr. *infra*; D. 19. 2. 58 pr; Pothier, *Louage*, § 288. It must be remembered that by the Roman law the tenant farmer (*colonus*) had no real right over the lands, only a *jus ad rem*; and so, when the owner sold the lands, the purchaser was not bound to respect the lease, but might turn out the tenant, whose only remedy was by suing his landlord for damages: *emptorem quidem fundi ncccsse non est stare* [sinere] *colonum, cui prior dominus locauit, nisi ea lege emit* (C. iv. 65. 9). It is surprising that rents were not regarded as representing the natural fruits of the subject sold, and therefore as passing to the purchaser from the date of the contract, especially when we are told (§ 13) that the hire paid for a vessel or a draught animal was treated as *in fructu*. This difficulty has led Voet and others to hold that the rents were apportioned,—a view which necessitates a rather forced interpretation of this section, viz. that as the seller alone has privity of contract with the tenant, he must exact the rent, but is bound to account to the purchaser for the proportion effeiring to the period after the sale, or else he must assign his right of action.

[1] postea? (*Husch.*, cp. *Basil.*)

11. If the land be let, the rents will naturally go to the lessor; and the same applies to urban tenements, unless an express agreement was come to on the subject.

12. Further, if any damage is done to the subject sold, the right of action must be ceded to the purchaser—to avert threatened damage, or to have rain-water kept off, or under the Aquilian law, or for interdict against forcible or stealthy dispossession, as the case may be.

13. Moreover, any profits made from the services of slaves, or by letting to hire beasts of burden or ships, and also any additions to the *peculium* of slaves except such as are derived from the seller's estate, must be accounted for to the purchaser.

14. If Titius sells a piece of land which extends to 90 acres, but was stated in the contract of sale to contain 100, and if before the measurement is verified 10 acres have been added by alluvion, I concur in the opinion of Neratius that, if the seller knew the extent of the land, an action on purchase will lie against him, notwithstanding the accrual of 10 acres, because his conduct was fraudulent and the fraud is not purged; but if he did not know, the action on purchase is incompetent.

§ 12. An example of the *actio damni infecti*, to compel the adjoining proprietor to give security for damage threatened by the dangerous state of his property, will be found in L 36 *infra*. Every owner had a right to be protected against the danger of flooding by rain-water owing to any alterations on his neighbour's land (*aquae pluuiae arcendae*, D. 39, tit. 3); the action was *in personam*, against the owner who had made the structural change. The Aquilian law introduced the *actio damni iniuriae* to give compensation for wrongful damage to property (D. 9, tit. 2). The interdict *quod vi aut clam* provided the owner with a remedy against wrongful acts done secretly or forcibly (*i.e.* without his consent or against his will) which interfered with the use of the land or other immoveable (D. 43, tit. 24).

§ 14. *Antequam modus manifestetur.* Cp. D. 18. 1. 40 pr.

In strict law the *actio empti* for a reduction of the price should be allowed even against the *bonâ fide* seller, where the lands sold do not come up to the measurement announced; and the opinion of

15. Si fundum mihi alienum uendideris et hic ex causa lucratiua meus factus sit, nihilo minus ex empto mihi aduersus te actio competit.

16. In his autem quae cum re empta praestari solent, non solum dolum, sed et culpam praestandam arbitror : nam et Celsus libro octauo digestorum scripsit, cum conuenit, ut uenditor praeteritam mercedem exigat et emptori praestet, non solum dolum, sed et culpam eum praestare debere.

17. Idem Celsus libro eodem scribit : fundi, quem cum Titio communem habebas, partem tuam uendidisti et antequam traderes, coactus es communi diuidundo iudicium accipere. si socio fundus sit adiudicatus, quantum ob eam rem a Titio consecutus es, id tantum emptori praestabis. quod si tibi fundus totus adiudicatus est, totum, inquit, cum emptori trades, sed ita, ut ille soluat quod ob eam rem Titio condemnatus es. sed ob eam quidem partem, quam uendidisti, pro euictione cauere debes, ob alteram autem tantum de dolo malo repromittere : aequum est enim eandem esse condicionem emptoris quae futura esset si cum ipso actum esset communi diuidundo. sed si certis regionibus fundum inter te et Titium iudex diuisit, sine dubio partem, quae adiudicata est, emptori tradere debes.

18. Si quid seruo distracto uenditor donauit ante traditionem, hoc quoque restitui debet : hereditates quoque per seruum ad-

---

Neratius can only be justified on special considerations of equity. The seller is seeking to avoid a penalty, whereas the buyer stands to win 10 acres more than he bargained for, if the strict rule were applied ; in these circumstances equity comes to the aid of the seller, whose overstatement was made in good faith, by establishing a kind of compensation between the deficiency and the gain by alluvion. Compare the decision in L. 42 *infra*, and Pothier, *Vente*, § 256.

§ 15. See L. 29 *infra*; Pothier, *Vente*, § 96. To take *ex causa lucratiua* is to take a gratuitous right, without a valuable consideration, as opposed to acquiring for an onerous cause.

§ 16. Compare D. 18. 1. 68, and § 11 *supra*.

§ 17. If a co-owner sells his share in common property and

15. If you have sold me land not belonging to you, although I subsequently become owner of it on a gratuitous title, an action on purchase against you is competent to me notwithstanding.

16. As regards ordinary accessories of the thing sold, the seller is in my opinion answerable for negligence as well as for fraud: thus, as Celsus remarks in the eighth book of his *Digesta*, when it is arranged that the seller shall collect all past-due rents and pay them to the purchaser, he must answer for fault as well as fraud.

17. Celsus also deals with the following case in the same book: you sold your share of an estate belonging to Titius and you jointly, but before giving delivery you are compelled to become a party to an action for division of the common property. If the estate is adjudged to your co-owner, he holds you are liable to the purchaser only for what you received from Titius for your share: but if the whole of the land is awarded to you, you must convey the whole of it to the purchaser, on condition that he pays you the sum you were adjudged to pay to Titius for his share. But while you are bound to answer for eviction as regards the part which you sold, you need only give an undertaking against fraud with respect to the other part, for it is equitable that the position of the purchaser should be the same as it would have been if the action for division had been directed against him. If the judge divides the land between Titius and you in definite portions, you are certainly bound to deliver to the purchaser the part which is adjudged to you.

18. Any gift made to a slave by the seller before delivery must also be handed over; as also rights of succession acquired through the slave, and all legacies without looking to the person

---

has an action for partition raised against him before delivery, his obligation to deliver is extinguished if the whole property is adjudged to the other party or parties to the action. Cp. D. 10. 3. 7, 13. The principle in all the cases is that the profit and the risk pass to the buyer on the completion of the contract.

§ **18.** Compare D. 28. 5. 38, §§ 5 and 39,—*lucrum facere eius serui iure, quem uendidit, non debet.*

quisitae et legata omnia, nec distinguendum, cuius respectu ista sint relicta. item quod ex operis seruus praestitit uenditori, emptori restituendum est, nisi ideo dies traditionis ex pacto prorogatus est, ut ad uenditorem operae pertinerent.

19. Ex uendito actio uenditori competit ad ea consequenda, quae ei ab emptore praestari oportet.

20. Ueniunt autem in hoc iudicium infra scripta. in primis pretium, quanti res uenit. item usurae pretii post diem traditionis : nam cum re emptor fruatur, acquissimum est eum usuras pretii pendere.

21. Possessionem autem traditam accipere debemus et si precaria sit possessio : hoc enim solum spectare debemus, an habeat facultatem fructus percipiendi.

22. Praeterea ex uendito agendo consequetur etiam sumptus qui facti sunt in re distracta, ut puta si quid in aedificia distracta erogatum est : scribit enim Labeo et Trebatius esse ex uendito hoc nomine actionem. idem et si in aegri serui curationem impensum est ante traditionem aut si quid in disciplinas, quas[1]

---

§§ **20, 21.** The general rule was that the price was due as soon as delivery of possession was given, and that the buyer must pay interest on the price from that date if nothing was set out to the contrary. *Usuras emptor, cui possessio rei tradita est, si pretium uenditori non obtulerit, quamuis pecuniam obsignatam in depositi causa habuerit, aequitatis ratione praestare cogitur* (C. iv. 32. 2 ; cp. C. iv. 49. 5 ; D. 22. 1. 18, 1 ; Paul, *Sent.* ii. 17. 9). It was thought equitable that the buyer should pay interest in lieu of the natural or civil fruits of the thing sold from the time when he had the power to reap them ; hence interest was due even where he held merely on sufferance during the seller's pleasure (*precario*), because that tenure was protected by the possessory interdicts against all the world, except the granter (see Hunter, *Roman Law*, p. 380, where a parallel is drawn with the copyhold tenure of English law). It was illegal to stipulate for more than the legal rate of interest in name of damages for delay in paying the price (§ 26 *infra*) ; see also p. 222 *infra*, and Pothier, §§ 283-289.

[1] quae? (*Basil.*)

out of regard for whom they have been left. Likewise all the profit derived by the seller from the slave's labour must be accounted for to the purchaser, unless the time for delivery was postponed by arrangement to let the seller have the advantage of the slave's services till then.

19. The action on sale is open to the seller for the enforcement of the obligations incumbent on the purchaser towards him.

20. The things which may be sued for in this action are as follows: First, the price for which the thing was sold, and also interest on the price from the date of delivery; for as the purchaser enjoys the use of the article, it is quite fair that he should pay interest on the price.

21. Delivery of possession must be understood to have taken place, though it is granted only at will: for the sole criterion is whether the buyer has the power to take the fruits.

22. The action on sale, moreover, enables the seller to recover any expenses incurred in respect of the thing, for example any outlays on a house he has sold; for according to Labeo and Trebatius an action on sale will lie for that: the same is true of money spent in curing a sick slave before delivery, or in giving a course of instruction such as the buyer himself would probably

---

In Scotland 'interest is also due *ex lege*. Thus, in a sale of lands, the purchaser is, by an act of the law itself, bound to pay interest for the price of the subject bought, from the term at which he enters into possession as long as he retains the price; for the price becomes a *surrogatum*, or thing substituted in place of the subject sold; and, therefore, the interest of the price must be given in consideration of the fruits of that subject' (Ersk. iii. 3. 79). So, in the case of goods also, the seller has the right to sue for the price and interest, whether the goods sold are specific or not, provided goods according to the contract have been tendered.

In England, on the other hand, in an action for the price of goods, nothing more than the sum due can be recovered, unless there was an express promise to pay interest. In general, interest by way of damages for the detention of a debt is not allowed. Accordingly in S. G. B. § 50 there is no mention of interest.

§ 22. See Pothier, *Vente*, § 291; *Code* iv. 49. 13 and 16.

uerisimile erat etiam emptorem uelle impendi. hoc amplius Labeo ait et si quid in funus mortui serui impensum sit, ex uendito consequi oportere, si modo sine culpa uenditoris mortem obierit.

23. Item si conuenerit, cum res ueniret, ut locuples ab emptore reus detur, ex uendito agi posse, ut id fiat.

24. Si inter emptorem praediorum et uenditorem conuenisset, ut, si ea praedia emptor heresue eius pluris uendidisset, eius partem dimidiam uenditori praestaret et heres emptoris pluris ea praedia uendidisset, uenditorem et uendito agendo partem eius, quo pluris uendidisset, consecuturum.

25. Si procurator uendiderit et cauerit emptori, quaeritur, an domino uel aduersus dominum actio dari debeat. et Papinianus libro tertio responsorum putat cum domino ex empto agi posse utili actione ad exemplum institoriae actionis, si modo rem uendendam mandauit: ergo et per contrarium dicendum est utilem ex empto actionem domino competere.

26. Ibidem Papinianus respondisse se refert, si conuenerit, ut ad diem pretio non soluto uenditori duplum praestaretur, in fraudem constitutionum uideri adiectum, quod usuram legitimam excedit: diuersamque causam commissoriae esse ait, cum ea specie, inquit, non faenus illicitum contrahatur, sed lex contractui non improbata dicatur.

---

§ 24. Cp. D. 18. 1. 7, 2, *supra* p. 23.

§ 25. As to the *actio institoria*, see *Inst*. iv. 7, §§ 2, 5-8. The exigencies of commerce led to a limited recognition of the agency of free persons in the later law. A shipmaster (*magister nauis*) could enter into contracts for behoof of the vessel so as to bind the owner or charterer, and a manager in charge of a shop or other business (*institor*) was an agent within the line of the business; the parties with whom they contracted could sue their principals directly. It appears from a few texts such as this that action by and against the principal was allowed in some other cases on the analogy of the two above-mentioned. There has been much controversy as to the exact nature and limits of the system of free agency developed from this germ. In the circum-

have been willing to pay for. Labeo goes so far as to say that the seller should recover by this action the expense of the funeral of a slave who has died, provided he came by his death through no fault on the seller's part.

23. Again, this action will lie for the enforcement of an agreement made at the time of the sale that the buyer should find a person of means to be surety.

24. If the buyer and seller of certain properties agree that if the purchaser or his heir shall sell the same for a higher price, they shall hand over to the seller one-half of the profit, and if the purchaser's heir does sell them for a higher price, the seller can recover his half of the profit by bringing the action on sale.

25. If an agent of the owner sells and gives security to the purchaser, the question arises whether the owner is the party to sue or be sued on the contract. Papinian expresses an opinion, in the third book of his *Responsa*, that the owner can be sued by a modified form of the action on purchase, on the analogy of the *actio institoria*, provided he gave authority to sell: whence it follows, conversely, that a modified form of the action on sale is competent to the owner.

26. In the same place, Papinian says he gave an opinion that an agreement to pay double the price in the event of failure to pay by the appointed term appeared to be in contravention of the imperial constitutions, in so far as it stipulates for more than the legal rate of interest; and he adds, that the *lex commissoria* is in a different position, for it does not stipulate for an illegal rate of interest, but attaches a perfectly proper condition to the contract.

---

stances here figured, it appears from D. 3. 3. 67 that the *procurator* was liable to the buyer under his warranty against eviction, even after he had given up the agency.

§ 26. As to the *lex commissoria*, see notes on D. 18. 1. 6, 1, *supra* p. 16 sq.

After many fluctuations in the legal rate of interest, Justinian fixed differential rates, ranging from 12 per cent. on maritime risks to 4 per cent. on agricultural loans (C. iv. 32. 26, 1). The covenant would be bad in the case here put, in so far as it

27. Si quis colludente procuratore meo ab eo emerit, an possit agere ex empto? et puto hactenus, ut aut stetur emptioni aut discedatur.

28. Sed et si quis minorem uiginti quinque annis circumuenerit, et huic hactenus dabimus actionem ex empto, ut diximus in superiore casu.

29. Si quis a pupillo sine tutoris auctoritate emerit, ex uno latere constat contractus: nam qui emit, obligatus est pupillo, pupillum sibi non obligat.

30. Si uenditor habitationem exceperit, ut inquilino liceat habitare, uel colono ut perfrui liceat ad certum tempus, magis esse Seruius putabat ex uendito esse actionem: denique Tubero ait, si iste colonus damnum dederit, emptorem ex empto agentem cogere posse uenditorem, ut ex locato cum colono experiatur, ut quidquid fuerit consecutus, emptori reddat.

31. Aedibus distractis uel legatis ea esse aedium solemus dicere, quae quasi pars aedium uel propter aedes habentur, ut puta putealia

---

stipulates for more than 12 per cent. *Uenditori si emptor in pretio soluendo moram fecerit, usuras dumtaxat praestabit, non omne omnino, quod uenditor mora non facta consequi potuit, ucluti si negotiator fuit, et pretio soluto ex mercibus plus quam ex usuris quaerere potuit* (D. 18. 6. 20); see note, p. 192 *post*.

§§ **27, 28**. The party using the fraud is bound by the contract, if the party defrauded decides that it is his interest to affirm it.

§ **29**. Ulpian may only mean that the buyer does not take the pupil bound in an actionable sense. The general opinion is that a contract made by a pupil without the concurrence of his tutor is a *negotium claudicans*, which the pupil can affirm or disaffirm at his option (p. 62). But it is contended by other writers that this view is not supported by the texts and is not in harmony with the spirit of Roman law, *nam iniquum est non esse mihi cum illo actionem, si nolit, illi uero, si uelit, mecum* (D. 17. 1. 3, 2). They hold that the effect of a contract between a pupil at his own hand and another person, is that the pupil is bound *naturaliter* to the full extent, but *ciuiliter* only so far as he has been enriched by it, while the other contractor is liable in the fullest

27. If a man buys from my agent in collusion with him, can he bring an action on purchase? I think he can, to the effect of compelling me to hold or reject the sale.

28. Also, if a man defrauds a minor, under twenty-five years of age, we will give him an action on purchase to the same effect as in the preceding case.

29. If a person buys from a pupil without the concurrence of his tutor, the contract is binding only on the one side: the buyer is under obligation to the pupil, but the pupil is under no obligation to him.

30. If the seller reserves a right of habitation for a tenant, or liberty to take the fruits up to a certain period in favour of a lessee, Servius held the more correct opinion to be, that an action on sale was competent: Tubero adds that if the tenant does any damage the buyer can bring the action on purchase to compel the seller to proceed against the tenant by the action on hire, and to hand over to him what he recovers.

31. When a house is sold or bequeathed as a legacy, the practice is to count as accessories of the building all that is possessed as part of or for the purposes of the house, for example, the case enclosing a well,

---

sense for everything he undertook: *pupillus vendendo sine tutoris auctoritate non obligetur, sed nec in emendo, nisi in quantum locupletior factus est* (D. 26. 8. 5, 1): *idem potest quaeri, si sine tutoris auctoritate pactus fuerit, ut discedatur ab emptione, an perinde sit, atque si ab initio sine tutoris auctoritate emisset, ut scilicet ipse non teneatur, sed agente eo retentiones competant?* (D. 18. 5. 7, 1; cp. D. 3. 5. 3, 4; *Inst.* i. 21 pr.). The other contractor thus acquires a counter-claim against the pupil, which he can make effectual by putting in a plea of compensation or retention in respect of the full sum, when the pupil brings his action against him. See Vangerow, § 279.

§ 30. For other examples of action at the instance of A against B to compel him to sue C, and to hand over what was recovered, see D. 19. 2. 60, 5; D. 47. 2. 52, 8.

§ 31. *Putealia* means the case or enclosure protecting the mouth of a well.

14. Pomponius libro XXXI ad Quintum Mucium.

(id est quo puteum operitur),

15. Ulpianus libro XXXII ad edictum.

lines[1] et labra, salientes; fistulae quoque, quae salientibus iunguntur, quamuis longe excurrant extra aedificium, aedium sunt: item canales: pisces autem qui sunt in piscina non sunt aedium nec fundi,

16. Pomponius libro XXXI ad Quintum Mucium.

non magis quam pulli aut cetera animalia, quae in fundo sunt.

17. Ulpianus libro XXXII ad edictum.

Fundi nihil est, nisi quod terra se tenet: aedium autem multa esse, quae aedibus adfixa non sunt, ignorari non oportet, ut puta seras claues claustra: multa etiam defossa esse neque tamen fundi aut uillae haberi, ut puta uasa uinaria torcularia, quoniam haec instrumenti magis sunt, etiamsi aedificio cohaerent.

1. Sed et uinum et fructus perceptos uillae non esse constat.

2. Fundo uendito uel legato sterculinum et stramenta emptoris et[2] legatarii sunt, ligna autem uenditoris uel heredis, quia non sunt fundi, tametsi ad eam rem comparata sunt. in sterculino autem distinctio Trebatii probanda est, ut, si quidem stercorandi agri causa comparatum sit, emptorem sequatur, si uendendi, uenditorem, nisi si aliud actum est: nec interest, in stabulo iaceat an aceruus sit.

L. 15.—*Lines* is the reading of F; *lacus* (after δεξαμεναί of *Basil.*) and *funes* are suggested emendations. Some kind of vessel is meant in any case. *Salientes* means springs or fountains (cp. D. 33. 7. 12, 24). As to *fistulae*, see p. 128 *ante*. As to possession of fish in a pond, see D. 41. 2. 3, 14; fish kept alive in a tank or aquarium till wanted are in possession, but fish in a pond having their natural liberty are not.

L. 17 pr.—*Instrumentum* differs from *pars fundi* in not being

[1] lenes? (*Mom.*, cp. D. S. 5. 17, 1). [2] uel?

14. POMPONIUS.

(that is, what covers a well),

15. ULPIAN.

water troughs and reservoirs, fountains; the pipes connected with fountains, although they project far beyond the buildings, are also accessories of a house: so are conduits: but the fish in a fish-pond do not pertain to the house or lands,

16. POMPONIUS.

any more than the young fowls or other animals on an estate.

17. ULPIAN.

Every accessory of land must be attached to the soil, but it should be known that many things may form accessories of a house without being fixed to it, *e.g.* locks, keys, bolts; there are many things, again, which are sunk in the earth, and yet are not considered pertinents of land or a country-house, *e.g.* wine-vats and wine-presses, because these rather belong to the head of plenishing, even though they are attached to the building.

1. It is settled that wine and fruits ingathered do not pass to the buyer of a country-house.

2. When land is sold or left as a legacy, the dung and straw belong to the purchaser or legatee, but the stock of wood belongs to the seller or heir, because it is not a part of the land although provided for its behoof. In regard to dung, however, the distinction drawn by Trebatius commends itself, that if meant to manure the land it goes to the purchaser, but if meant to sell it falls to the vendor, provided there is no arrangement to the contrary; and it makes no difference whether it lies in the stalls or has been made into a heap.

---

affixed to the soil. In the case of a farm, it includes all implements and appliances necessary for preparing and preserving the produce; in the case of a house, it is opposed to *ornamentum*, and includes in particular the means of protection from fire and storms: see for details D. 33 tit. 7, and D. 19. 2. 19, 2.

3. Quae tabulae pictae pro tectorio includuntur itemque crustae marmoreae aedium sunt.

4. Reticuli circa columnas, plutei circa parietes, item cilicia uela aedium non sunt.

5. Item quod insulae causa paratum est, si nondum perfectum est, quamuis positum in aedificio sit, non tamen uidetur aedium esse.

6. Si ruta et caesa excipiantur in uenditione, ea placuit esse ruta, quae eruta sunt, ut harena creta et similia : caesa ea esse, ut arbores caesas et carbones et his similia. Gallus autem Aquilius, cuius Mela refert opinionem, recte ait frustra in lege uenditionis de rutis et caesis contineri,[1] quia si non specialiter uenierunt, ad exhibendum de his agi potest neque enim magis de materia caesa aut de caementis aut de harena cauendum est uenditori quam de ceteris quae sunt pretiosiora.

7. Labeo generaliter scribit ea quae perpetui usus causa in aedificiis sunt aedificii esse, quae uero ad praesens, non esse aedificii, ut puta fistulae temporis quidem causa positae, non sunt aedium, uerum tamen si perpetuo fuerint positae, aedium sunt.

8. Castella plumbea, putea,[2] opercula puteorum, epitonia fistulis adplumbata (aut quae terra continentur quamuis non sint adfixa) aedium esse constat.

9. Item constat sigilla, columnas quoque et personas, ex quorum rostris aqua salire solet, uillae esse.

10. Ea quae ex aedificio detracta sunt ut reponantur aedificii sunt : at quae parata sunt ut imponantur, non sunt aedificii.

---

§ 3. *Tectorio sc. opere*, i.e. mural paintings instead of the ordinary chalk or gypsum covering on the walls.

§ 4. *Reticuli*, draperies of fine net-work. *Plutei* are probably cupboards or bookshelves set against the wall.

§ 6. Compare D. 18. 1. 66, 2, *supra* p. 114, and L. 38, 2 *infra*. *Ruta-caesa* is often used in a general sense to embrace everything that does not pass to the purchaser as part or pertinent of the thing sold, and may sometimes be rendered 'moveables' as opposed to fixtures; it covered all stock and

[1] caveri ?   [2] putea *del.*

3. Frescoes on the walls in place of plaster-work, as also marble plaques, are accessories of a house.

4. The draperies on the pillars, the brackets on the walls, and hangings of goats' hair do not belong to the house.

5. Again, anything procured for use in a building, although placed in its position, is not held to be part of the house, until it is permanently attached.

6. If things that may be dug up or cut are reserved in the contract, it is settled that 'things dug up' mean things dug from the soil, as sand, chalk, and the like, while 'things cut down' include trees that have been cut, charcoal, and the like. Gallus Aquilius, however, as reported by Mela, observes truly that a clause in the contract relative to things dug and cut is useless, because, unless they are expressly sold, an action by the seller claiming production is competent; for it is no more necessary for him to make a reservation of timber cut down, or of rubble or sand, than of other things of greater value.

7. Labeo states, as a general rule, that things placed in a building for the permanent better enjoyment of it are pertinents, but not what is there for a temporary purpose; for example, pipes laid down for temporary use do not belong to a house, but those which are to remain permanently do.

8. Lead reservoirs, wells, and well-covers, stop-cocks soldered on to water-pipes (or anything driven into the ground without being fastened), are admitted to be accessories of a house.

9. It is also settled that statuettes, as also columns and figures with water spouting from their jaws, are accessories of a country-house.

10. Anything removed from a building, if meant to be replaced, is a pertinent of the building; but things provided for incorporation in it are not pertinents.

---

furnishings, supplies of corn, fruits ingathered, firewood, building materials on the spot, and the like.

§ **10.** Things detached from a building when it is sold may yet be appurtenances, *e.g.* if removed for repairs, or if in use during only a portion of the year and put away for the rest.

11. Pali qui uineae causa parati sunt, antequam collocentur, fundi non sunt, sed qui exempti sunt hac mente ut collocentur, fundi sunt.

18. IAUOLENUS libro VII ex Cassio.

Granaria quae ex tabulis fieri solent ita aedium sunt, si stipites eorum in terra defossi sunt: quod si supra terram sunt, rutis et caesis cedunt.

1. Tegulae quae nondum aedificiis impositae sunt, quamuis tegendi gratia allatae sunt, in rutis et caesis habentur: aliud iuris est in his quae detractae sunt ut reponerentur: aedibus enim accedunt.

19. GAIUS ad edictum praetoris titulo de publicanis.

Ueteres in emptione uenditioneque appellationibus promiscue utebantur.

20. GAIUS libro XXI ad edictum prouinciale.

Idem est et in locatione et conductione.

21. PAULUS libro XXXIII ad edictum.

Si sterilis ancilla sit, cuius partus uenit, uel maior annis quinquaginta, cum id emptor ignorauerit, ex empto tenetur uenditor.

1. Si praedii uenditor non dicat de tributo sciens, tenetur ex empto: quod si ignorans non praedixerit, quod forte hereditarium praedium erat, non tenetur.

LL. 19, 20.—The meaning may be either (1) that, in speaking of the contract of sale or location, the usage was to use either of the correlative expressions (*emptio-uenditio, locatio-conductio*) indifferently to denote the transaction as a whole; or (2) 'that in the contracts of sale and location terms were formerly used indiscriminately,' which Cujas explains by the hypothesis that the terms denoting sale and location were originally used synonymously (*e.g.* '*uendere*' and '*locare*' in the lex agraria of 643), these contracts not having been discriminated sharply in early times.

L. 21 pr.—Here the thing sold is a non-existing and impossible object, and the sale is therefore a nullity. Besides,

11. Props made ready for use in a vineyard do not belong to the land till they are driven into their places; but if they have been sorted out for the purpose of being set up, they belong to the land.

18. JAVOLEN.

Grain-stores made of planks in the ordinary way are pertinents of a house when the posts are sunk into the ground, but if they rest on the surface they count as moveables.

1. Tiles not yet fixed on a building, though they have been brought there for the purpose of roofing it, are reckoned in the class of moveables; but it is different with those that have been taken off the roof and are to be put on again, for they cede to the building.

19. GAIUS.

The older jurists used the names *emptio* and *venditio* for the contract indifferently.

20. GAIUS.

The same is true of the words *locatio* and *conductio*.

21. PAUL.

If a man sells the unborn child of a female slave who is barren, or upwards of fifty years of age, he is liable under the action on purchase if the buyer was unaware of the fact.

1. If the seller of real estate knows it to be subject to land-tax, and does not inform the purchaser, he is liable under the contract: but if the failure to give notice was due to ignorance, the property having come to him say by succession, he is not liable.

---

it lets in a claim for damages, like the sale of a non-existent inheritance (D. 18. 4. 8, 9). The ground of the claim we may assume to be that the transaction in question infers fraud, or at least inexcusable error amounting to gross carelessness on the part of the seller, and the measure of damages would be the same as is indicated in D. 18. 1. 62, 1, *supra* p. 111.

§ 1. If the property came by succession, he might fairly plead ignorance of the taxes on it (D. 50. 17. 42). But the plea will

2. Quamuis supra diximus, cum in corpore consentiamus, de qualitate autem dissentiamus, emptionem esse, tamen uenditor teneri debet, quanti interest non esse deceptum, etsi uenditor quoque nesciet: ueluti si mensas quasi citreas emat, quae non sunt.

3. Cum per uenditorem steterit, quo minus rem tradat, omnis utilitas emptoris in aestimationem uenit, quae modo circa ipsam rem consistit: neque enim si potuit ex uino puta negotiari et lucrum facere, id aestimandum est, non magis quam si triticum emerit et ob eam rem, quod non sit traditum, familia eius fame laborauerit: nam pretium tritici, non seruorum fame necatorum consequitur. nec maior fit obligatio, quod tardius agitur, quamuis crescat, si uinum hodie pluris sit, merito, quia siue datum esset, haberem emptor, siue non, quoniam [1] saltem hodie dandum est quod iam olim dari oportuit.

---

not be good if he made any declaration about burdens at the time of sale; if he said there were no charges of this kind, or that they were of less amount, he is bound as if he had given a guarantee.

§ 2. All the good MSS. except F read '*emptionem non esse*,' which would mean that the mistake is essential, and annuls the contract; but this compels us to give *qualitas* the sense of *materia* or *substantia*, and does not suit the context in other respects.

Taking the Florentine reading, Savigny explains the validity of the contract on the ground that it is not essential error to mistake the kind of wood of which a piece of furniture is made, its form and purpose being the primary consideration, and there being no such difference in kind between citron and common wood as there is between a precious and a base metal (D. 18. 1. 9, 2 and note). He accounts for the indemnity which Paul says the seller is bound to pay, by assuming that he expressly or tacitly promised to give a citron table, just as in D. 18. 1. 45, *supra* p. 94. The assumption of a warranty he holds to be necessary, because an action for damages is allowed even though the seller has not misled the buyer fraudulently, being himself in error, and the only possible ground for holding a seller in

[1] quoniam *del.*

2. Although we have laid down the principle that a sale is valid when the parties are agreed upon the specific object, notwithstanding a difference about its quality, still the seller, even though himself in ignorance, must indemnify the buyer for what he has lost by being misled; for instance where a man buys a table, thinking it is made of citron-wood when it is not.

3. Where non-delivery is attributable to the fault of the seller, all the advantage the buyer might have gained is to be taken into account, provided it is directly connected with the default: for though he could have made a profit by trading say with wine bought by him, that does not enter into the calculation; just as a man whose slaves are famine-stricken, through failure to deliver wheat purchased by him, cannot recover the value of the slaves killed by starvation, but only the price of the wheat. Delay in bringing the action cannot make the obligation more onerous, although its amount will be larger if the article has meantime risen in price; and rightly so, because if it had been delivered I should have it as purchaser, and, failing delivery, it must be handed over now at least, seeing it should have been delivered long ago.

---

good faith liable to compensate the buyer is on account of a breach of a warranty of quality. See Sav. *Syst.* iii. p. 287. It must be allowed, however, that there is some difficulty in assuming an express warranty here in face of the words *de qualitate dissentiamus*, and the result reached after all is somewhat commonplace. Others explain it as a case of implied warranty, the circumstances being such as to lead the buyer to expect a table of citron.

§ 3. The expression here used, *utilitas quae circa ipsam rem consistit*, has been made the foundation for a distinction between *damnum circa rem* and *damnum extra rem*, as though Paul had meant to suggest these as suitable technical terms for damage which does, and damage which does not, entitle to compensation. In all probability no such distinction was intended, and the use of these terms is now given up by the best writers, as it has led to much confusion. *Circa ipsam rem* is either (1) 'attaching to the thing owing,' which is put shortly for 'due to the non-prestation of the thing owing,' or (2) 'connected with the matter

4. Si tibi fundum uendidero, ut eum conductum certa summa haberem, ex uendito eo nomine mihi actio est, quasi in partem pretii ea res sit.

5. Sed et si ita fundum tibi uendidero, ut nulli alii eum quam mihi uenderes, actio eo nomine ex uendito est, si alii uendideris.

6. Qui domum uendebat excepit sibi habitationem, donec uiueret, aut in singulos annos decem : emptor primo anno maluit decem praestare, secundo anno habitationem praestare. Trebatius ait mutandae uoluntatis potestatem eum habere singulisque annis alterutrum praestare posse, et quamdiu paratus sit alterutrum praestare petitionem non esse.

---

in question,' referring generally to the act or default which grounds the claim. Paul wishes to limit the generality of *omnis utilitas* by a qualifying clause : the debtor in case of *mora* must make up the full *interesse*, but that includes only the damage *circa rem*, *i.e.* such as can be shown to stand related as effect to the ground of obligation as a cause ; if the damage is too remote to allow of this connection being proved, no compensation is due. The profits which the buyer might possibly have made by trading with the goods, had they been delivered in time, are of this latter sort, and so do not form an element in the claim against the seller ; just as it is laid down in D. 18. 6. 20 that no damages can be demanded for delay in paying the price beyond the legal interest on it, though the seller might possibly have made large gains by the use of the money. These passages do not absolutely negative the right to indemnification for profits missed (*lucrum cessans*) as well as for loss sustained (*damnum emergens*) ; they simply point out that the party claiming on account of loss of profit must demonstrate that the loss was the actual and natural result of the delay complained of. For instance, damages for the detention of a debt could be claimed ' *ultra legitimum modum usurarum*,' where the creditor could point to loss sustained in the actual circumstances of the case, *e.g.* if he had, in reliance on his debtor's promise to pay at a certain place, bound himself under a penalty to advance the amount of the debt to a third party there, the debtor must indemnify him for the penalty incurred ; and if the creditor's uniform practice was to expend moneys payable to him in the

4. If I have sold you a farm with a condition that I am to get a lease of it at a specified rent, the action on sale lies to enforce the condition, as though it were part of the price.

5. So if I have sold you a farm with a condition that you are not to sell it to anyone except me, the action on sale is competent if you sell it to another.

6. The seller of a house stipulated for the right to dwell in it during his lifetime, or for ten *aurei* a year instead: the purchaser preferred the first year to pay the ten *aurei*, but the second year to give the occupancy. Trebatius holds that he has the right to change his mind, and may give whichever he pleases each year, and that no action will lie so long as he is prepared to give the one or the other.

---

purchase of goods, he can claim for loss of profit (D. 13. 4. 2, 8). These texts, rightly understood, do not conflict with the general principles as to compensation; the most that can be said is that the difficulty of connecting the loss of profit with the default of the debtor is somewhat too sharply expressed.

As to the measure of damages for the seller's delay in delivery, see L. 3, § 3 *supra*.

The illustration of the famine-stricken slave establishment points to this proposition, that compensation is due only for such losses as the party in default foresaw, or might by the exercise of reasonable prudence have anticipated as the direct result of his delay. Granting that the slaves would not have died had the corn been sent in time, that does not establish the necessary causal connection; many other circumstances would require to be taken into consideration, *e.g.* whether it was impossible to procure other means of sustenance, whether the buyer had not been negligent in letting his supplies run so low, etc. In a certain state of the facts the seller might no doubt be responsible, say if the contract had been made with express reference to the victualling of the buyer's establishment. Vangerow, § 571.

§§ **4, 5.** See D. 18. 1. 75; ib. 79.

§ **6.** The obligation on the buyer is alternative, to give the right of habitation, or a yearly sum instead, and where there is an alternative annual prestation due, the debtor has an annual right of election.

22. IULIANUS libro VII digestorum.

Si in qualitate fundi uenditor mentitus sit, non in modo eius, tamen tenetur emptori: pone enim dixisse eum quinquaginta iugera esse uineae et quinguaginta prati et in prato plus inueniri, esse tamen omnia centum iugera.

23. IULIANUS libro XIII digestorum.

Si quis seruum, quem cum peculio uendiderat, manumiserit, non solum peculii nomine, quod seruus habuit tempore quo manumittebatur, sed et eorum quae postea adquirit tenetur, et praeterea cauere debet, quidquid ex hereditate liberti ad eum peruenerit, restitutu iri. MARCELLUS notat: illa praestare uenditor ex empto debet, quae haberet emptor, si homo manumissus non esset: non continebuntur igitur quae, si manumissus non fuit, adquisiturus non esset.

24. IULIANUS libro XV digestorum.

Si seruus, in quo usus fructus tuus erat, fundum emerit et antequam pecunia numeraretur, capite minutus fueris, quamuis pretium solueris, actionem ex empto non habebis propter talem capitis deminutionem, sed indebiti actionem aduersus uenditorem habebis. ante capitis autem minutionem nihil interest, tu soluas an seruus ex eo peculio quod ad te pertinet: nam utroque casu actionem ex empto habebis.

1. Seruum tuum imprudens a fure bona fide emi: is ex

In singulos annos decem has been taken to mean a right of habitation for ten separate years as opposed to a liferent right, but it seems better to take it of a money alternative in the shape of a ground rent. Cp. D. 44. 7. 44, 3: *modus obligationis est, cum stipulamur decem aut hominem: nam alterius solutio totam obligationem interemit nec alter peti potest, utique quamdiu utrumque est.*
As to *habitatio*, see *Inst.* ii. 5. 5; D. 7. 8. 10.

L. 23.—Julian is obviously wrong, for he first allows the buyer compensation for what he has lost through non-implement of the contract, viz. the *peculium* of the slave and all subsequent additions to it, and then secures him an interest in the *hereditas;* but there would have been no *hereditas* if the slave had remained

22. JULIAN.

If the seller of an estate has made false statements about its condition, though not about the total contents, still he is responsible to the purchaser; *e.g.* suppose he said there were 50 acres of vineyard and 50 of meadow, and it turns out there is more of meadow, though the total is 100 acres.

23. JULIAN.

If a master manumits a slave whom he has sold along with his *peculium*, he is liable not only for the *peculium* which the slave had at the time of manumission, but for all he acquires subsequently, and he must besides give security that he will hand over any part of the freedman's succession which may come to him [as patron]. MARCELLUS makes this correction: the action on purchase obliges the seller to make good to the buyer all that he would have got if the slave had not been manumitted; it will therefore not include what the slave would not have acquired unless he had been manumitted.

24. JULIAN.

If a slave in whom you had a usufruct has bought an estate, and you undergo a change of status before payment of the price, such a change bars you from suing on the contract in spite of subsequent payment, but you can competently bring a *condictio indebiti* against the seller. But if payment be made before the change of status, it is immaterial whether it is made by you or by the slave out of a *peculium* belonging to you; for in either case you can maintain an action on purchase.

1. I bought a slave belonging to you in good faith, not know-

---

a slave. The same thing is twice assessed, for the *hereditas* consists of the acquisitions subsequent to manumission.

L. 24 pr.—The usufructuary of a slave was owner of all the slave acquired by his labour or *ex re fructuarii*; any other acquisitions, such as gifts and legacies, belonged to the owner of the slave. *Inst.* ii. 9. 4.

§ 1. The rights of a *bonâ fide* possessor of a slave in his

peculio quod ad te pertinebat hominem parauit, qui mihi traditus est. posse te eum hominem mihi condicere Sabinus dixit, sed si quid mihi abesset ex negotio quod is gessisset, inuicem me tecum acturum de peculio. Cassius ueram opinionem Sabini rettulit, in qua ego quoque sum.

2. Seruo uendente hominem fideiussor uenditionis omnia praestare debet in quae obligaretur si pro libero fideiussisset: nam et in dominum actio sic datur, ut emptor eadem consequatur quae libero uendente consequi debuisset, sed ultra peculii taxationem dominus non condemnatur.

25. IULIANUS libro LIV digestorum.

Qui pendentem uindemiam emit si uuam legere prohibeatur a uenditore, aduersus eum petentem pretium exceptione uti poterit 'si ea pecunia, qua de agitur, non pro ea re petitur, quae uenit neque tradita est.' ceterum post traditionem siue lectam uuam calcare siue mustum euehere prohibeatur, ad exhibendum uel iniuriarum agere poterit, quemadmodum si aliam quamlibet rem suam tollere prohibeatur.

26. ALFENUS UARUS libro II digestorum.

Si quis, cum fundum uenderet, dolia centum, quae in fundo

---

acquisitions were the same as those of a fructuary (Gaius ii. 92, *Inst*. ii. 9. 4); all the slave acquires by administering the possessor's property or by his own labour goes to the possessor, all he acquires on any other title forms a *peculium* belonging to the true owner. In the case figured, the *seruus ordinarius* purchased a *seruus uicarius*, paying for him out of this latter fund; delivery was given to the possessor, who thus acquired the slave *sine causa*, and is therefore liable to a *condictio*. The possessor, however, is entitled, when sued for the *uicarius*, to claim as a set-off all expenses he has paid out of his own funds (including the *peculium* of the *ordinarius* so far as it belongs to him), such as commission charges on the sale, cost of keep, and the like. If he inadvertently delivered the slave without enforcing the set-off, a *condictio incerti* would lie at his instance to recover his outlay (D. 12. 6. 40, 1). The above case is stated in almost the same terms in D. 12. 1. 31, 1.

ing that the seller had stolen him, and he purchased out of his *peculium* belonging to you a slave who is delivered to me. Sabinus held that you could bring a condiction against me for that slave, but that I would have a counter claim against you by the *actio de peculio* for any expense I have been put to in the course of the transaction. Cassius confirms the correctness of this opinion, and I concur.

2. When a slave sells another slave, the surety for the seller must undertake exactly the same obligations as if he were surety for a free man: for action is competent against his owner as well, so that the buyer can recover all that he would have been entitled to recover had the seller been free, only decree against the owner must be limited to the amount of the *peculium*.

25. Julian.

The buyer of a ripe vintage, if prevented by the seller from gathering the grapes, can plead this defence to an action for the price: 'the sum sued for is claimed in respect of a thing which was sold but not delivered.' If, however, after delivery has been given, he is prevented from pressing the grapes or from removing the must, he can bring the action for production of property or for injury done, just as if he were hindered from taking away any other kind of property belonging to him.

26. Alfenus Verus.

If a person has promised, when selling a piece of land, that a

---

Had the *vicarius* been delivered to the *ordinarius* direct, he would have been acquired for the true proprietor immediately. Cp. D. 41. 1. 21 pr.; ib. 54, 4.

L. 25.—The equitable plea which the defender could urge, viz. that he had an unsatisfied claim against the pursuer, arising out of the same contract, is variously designated in the texts, see note on p. 130 *ante*.

As to the *actio iniuriarum*, see *Inst.* iv. tit. 4.

L. 26.—See D. 18. 1. 34 pr., and L. 11, § 17 *supra*.

esse adfirmabat, accessura dixisset, quamuis ibi nullum dolium fuisset, tamen dolia emptori debebit.

27. Paulus libro III epitomarum Alfeni.

Quidquid uenditor accessurum dixerit, id integrum ac sanum tradi oportet: ueluti si fundo dolia accessura dixisset, non quassa, sed integra dare debet.

28. Iulianus libro III ad Urscium Ferocem.

Praedia mihi uendidisti, et conuenit ut aliquid facerem, quod si non fecissem, poenam promisi. respondit, uenditor antequam poenam ex stipulatu petat, ex uendito agere potest: si[1] consecutus fuerit, quantum poenae nomine stipulatus esset, agentem ex stipulatu doli mali exceptio summouebit: si ex stipulatu poenam consecutus fueris, ipso iure ex uendito agere non poteris nisi in id quod pluris eius interfuerit id fieri.

29. Iulianus libro IV ex Minicio.

Cui res sub condicione legata erat, is eam imprudens ab herede emit: actione ex empto poterit consequi emptor pretium, quia non[2] ex causa legati rem habet.

L. 27—The rules of the edict as to defects apply to accessories expressly promised in the contract, D. 21. 1. 32 and 33.

L. 28.—It was common to fix conventional or penal damages against the person making default in doing some act which he had engaged to do. In such a case the creditor may avail himself either of the action on the contract or of the action on the stipulation. But the penalty was not absolutely conclusive as the measure of damages; if it fell short of full compensation for the damage actually sustained, the creditor could bring the contractual action for the deficiency in supplement of the other. For a similar relation between concurrent actions, see D. 13. 6. 7, 1 ; D. 47. 7. 1 ; D. 44. 7. 41, 1.

[1] sic *ins.*   [2] quando ?

hundred vats which he stated to be on it should pass as a pertinent, he will be bound to the purchaser for the vats, though there were none at all on the land.

27. PAUL.

Anything promised by the seller as an accessory must be delivered sound and whole: for instance, if he has promised vats as an accessory, he must give whole ones without flaw.

28. JULIAN.

You have sold me lands, and it has been agreed I am to do some act, or in default I have engaged to pay a penalty. Urseius gave this opinion: 'the seller, before suing on the stipulation for the penalty, can bring the action on sale; and if he recovers as much as he stipulated for by way of penalty, he will be repelled by the plea of fraud if he sues on the stipulation: if on the other hand one recovers the penalty in an action on the stipulation, he is barred by mere force of law from suing on the contract except for any further interest he had in its fulfilment.

29. JULIAN.

A conditional legatee, in ignorance of his right, bought the subject of his legacy from the heir: he can recover the purchase-price in an action on the contract, because he does not possess the subject on his title as legatee.

Ipso iure means directly or immediately by the civil law, without the aid of the praetor or recourse to an exception.

Probably *fueris* and *poteris* are corruptions for *fuerit* and *poterit*.

L. 29.—*Quia non* seems to be wrong; the reason given does not account for the *actio ex empto*, but rather points to the legatee's right to an *actio ex testamento*. Mommsen suggests *quando*.

The hypothesis is that the legatee, knowing nothing of his right, buys the thing *pendente condicione*. The sale is effectual, because the thing is not his but the heir's. But when the con-

30. AFRICANUS libro VIII quaestionum.

Seruus, quem de me cum peculio emisti, priusquam tibi traderetur, furtum mihi fecit. quamuis ea res quam subripuit interierit, nihilo minus retentionem eo nomine ex peculio me habiturum ait, id est ipso iure ob id factum minutum esse peculium, eo scilicet, quod debitor meus ex causa condictionis sit factus. nam licet, si iam traditus furtum mihi fecisset, aut omnino condictionem eo nomine de peculio non haberem aut eatenus haberem, quatenus ex re furtiua auctum peculium fuisset, tamen in proposito et retentionem me habiturum et, si omne peculium penes te sit, uel quasi plus debito soluerim posse me condicere. secundum quae dicendum: si nummos, quos seruus iste mihi subripuerat, tu ignorans furtiuos esse quasi peculiares ademeris et consumpseris, condictio eo nomine mihi aduersus te competet, quasi res mea ad te sine causa peruenerit.

1. Si sciens alienam rem ignoranti mihi uendideris, etiam priusquam euincatur utiliter me ex empto acturum putauit in id quanti mea intersit meam esse factam: quamuis enim alioquin uerum sit uenditorem hactenus teneri, ut rem emptori habere

---

dition arrives he can recover the price by the *actio empti*, because he is entitled under the will to have the thing *gratis*. The heir's right in the thing was defeasible from the first, and he could give no better title to a purchaser. The legatee has the right, on the arrival of the condition, to claim the thing as his, wherever it is found; he may be said, in the case here supposed, to suffer eviction at his own hands, and so he can competently bring the *actio empti*. Under Justinian the legatee could sue for return of the price, even if he knew that the thing had been conditionally bequeathed to him (C. vi. 43. 3, 4).

L. 30 pr.—A slave who committed a theft of his master's property became indebted *naturaliter* to his master, who could deduct the true value of the stolen property from the *peculium* before handing it over to the purchaser (D. 15. 1. 9, 6), or could bring a *condictio* if he had already transferred the *peculium*. The natural obligation between the slave and his owner was not strong enough to sustain an action (*Inst.* iv. 8. 6), but the law recog-

30. AFRICANUS.

I have sold you a slave with his *peculium*, and prior to delivery he steals something from me. Even though the stolen property has perished, I have notwithstanding, according to this jurist's opinion, a right to retain the value of it out of the *peculium*,— that is to say, the slave's *peculium* is legally subject to a deduction on account of his act, simply because he has become my debtor in respect of the *condictio* I can bring against him. For granted that, if he had stolen from me after being delivered to you, I should either have had no claim at all against the *peculium*, or one limited to the additional value it derived from the stolen property, yet in the case figured I have the right of retention; and moreover, if the whole of his *peculium* is already in your hands, I can bring a *condictio* just as if I had paid you more than I was owing. It follows from this that if you have appropriated and spent moneys stolen from me by this slave of yours, believing they formed part of the *peculium*, and not knowing they were stolen, I can bring a *condictio* to recover them from you on the ground that property of mine has come into your hands without valuable consideration.

1. If you sell me something which you know, and I do not know, to belong to another, the opinion of counsel was that, without waiting for eviction, I could bring an equitable action on purchase for the interest I had in being made owner: for although it is true, on the other hand, that the seller is only

---

nised it as a sufficient ground for retention or deduction by the owner, when creditors sought to enforce their claims by the *actio de peculio*. The use of *ait* shows that Africanus is quoting the opinion of some other jurist.

For the *condictio sine causa* mentioned in the last sentence, compare D. 12. 1. 32.

§ 1. The *actio ex empto* on the ground of the fraud here involved has this advantage over the *actio ex stipulatu* that the latter is not competent till eviction has ensued (L. 4 *supra*).

On this section see notes, pp. 50, 55 *ante*.

liceat, non etiam ut eius faciat, quia tamen dolum malum abesse
praestare debeat, teneri eum, qui sciens alienam, non suam
ignoranti uendidit: id est[1] maxime, si manumissuro uel pignori
daturo uendiderit.

31. Neratius libro III membranarum.

Se ea res quam ex empto praestare debebam ui mihi adempta
fuerit: quamuis eam custodire debuerim, tamen propius est ut
nihil amplius quam actiones persequendae eius praestari a me
emptori oporteat, quia custodia aduersus uim parum proficit.
actiones autem eas non solum arbitrio, sed etiam periculo tuo
tibi praestare debebo, ut omne lucrum ac dispendium te sequatur.

1. Et non solum quod ipse per eum adquisii praestare debeo,
sed et id quod emptor iam tunc sibi tradito seruo adquisiturus
fuisset.

2. Uterque nostrum eandem rem emit a non domino, cum
emptio uenditioque sine dolo malo fieret, traditaque[2] est: siue
ab eodem emimus siue ab alio atque alio, is ex nobis tuendus est
qui prior ius eius[3] adprehendit, hoc est, cui primum tradita est.
si alter ex nobis a domino emisset, is omnimodo tuendus est.

32. Ulpianus libro XI ad edictum.

Si quis a me oleum quod emisset adhibitis iniquis ponderibus
accepisset, ut in modo me falleret, uel emptor circumscriptus
sit a uenditore ponderibus minoribus, Pomponius ait posse

L. 31 pr.—As to the *custodia* required of the seller, see
D. 18. 1. 35, 4; as to his duty to assign actions, *Inst.* iii.
23. 3.

§ 1. This text is to be understood of the case where there has
been delay in giving delivery, and some editors insert words to
that effect. Cp. L. 13, § 18 *supra*.

§ 2. Julian states the rule thus: *ut, si quidem ab eodem non
domino emerint, potior sit, cui priori res tradita est, quod si a
diuersis non dominis, melior causa sit possidentis quam petentis*
(D. 6. 2. 9, 4); cp. D. 20. 4. 14: *Si non dominus duobus eandem*

---

[1] [id est] et? (*Mom.*)   [2] utrique *ins.*   [3] iusto?

bound to answer to the buyer for quiet possession of the subject, and not to make him owner of it also, yet a seller who knows that the right of property is in a third person and not in himself is responsible to a purchaser ignorant of that fact, because he is bound to warrant the absence of fraud: this is especially true of the sale of a slave to one who intended to manumit him, or to give him in pledge.

31. Neratius.

If I am forcibly deprived of a thing which I am bound to deliver under a contract of sale, although the duty of taking care of it lay upon me, yet it may readily be assumed that I satisfy that duty by transferring to the purchaser the actions for its recovery, because careful keeping does not avail against violence. As regards the rights of action, my duty will be to cede them to you, subject to your discretion and also at your peril, so that the gain and the loss may alike be yours.

1. [In the case of non-delivery of a slave] I am bound to account not only for all that I have acquired by means of him [since the delay], but also for all that the purchaser would have acquired if he had been delivered at the proper time.

2. Suppose we have both purchased the same thing from one not the true owner, and, on the completion of the contract in good faith, the thing has been delivered: then, whether we have bought from the same person or from different persons, he who was first seised of his right, that is, who first got delivery, must be protected in his possession. But if one of us purchased from the true owner, he has a paramount claim to the possession.

32. Ulpian.

If a man who bought oil from me has had it weighed at delivery with false weights, in order to deceive me as to the quantity, or if the buyer is overreached by the seller by the use

---

rem diuersis temporibus pigneraucrit, prior potior est, quamuis, si a diuersis non dominis pignus accipiamus, possessor melior sit.

L. 32.—See D. 4. 3. 18, 3; D. 18. 1. 71.

dici[1] uenditorem sibi dare oportere quod plus est petere: quod habet rationem: ergo et emptor ex empto habebit actionem, qua contentus esse possit.

33.   ULPIANUS libro XXIII ad edictum.

Et si uno pretio plures res emptae sint [et quaedam earum uel omnes euictae sint], de singulis ex empto et uendito agi potest.

34.   ULPIANUS libro XVIII ad edictum.

Si fundo uendito in qualitate iugerum captio est, ex empto erit actio.

35.   ULPIANUS libro LXX ad edictum.

Si quis fundum emerit, quasi per eum fundum eundi agendi ius non esset, et interdicto de itinere actuque uictus sit, ex empto habebit actionem: licet enim stipulatio de euictione non committatur, quia non est de iure seruitutis in rem actione pronuntiatum, tamen dicendum est ex empto actionem competere.

L. 33.—The words in brackets are inserted on the authority of the *Basilika*.

L. 35.—A person who could claim a positive servitude on the ground of use, *i.e.* who had in fact done the act or acts constituting the servitude, was entitled to protection by means of interdict in order to secure him in the continued enjoyment of the right. This remedy did not directly raise the question of the right to the servitude; there were declaratory actions *in rem* for that purpose (*actio confessoria, actio negatoria*, see *Inst.* iv. 6. 2 sq.): the procedure by interdict was based on the quasi-possession of the right, and was intended to prevent violent interference on the part of the owner of the servient tenement, leaving it open to the latter to disprove the existence of the pretended right if he could. The interdict dealing with a servitude road (*de itinere actuque priuato*) was available to any one who had used it during 30 days in one year, provided his

[1] dici *del.*

of light weights, Pomponius says that in the first case the seller can sue for the return of the surplus; which is reasonable: and it follows that in the other case the buyer will have the action on purchase for the satisfaction of his claim.

33. ULPIAN.

If several things have been bought together for a lump price [and all or some of them have been evicted], the actions on purchase and on sale are competent in regard to any one of them.

34. ULPIAN.

An action on purchase will lie for any deception in regard to the condition of the ground in a sale of land.

35. ULPIAN.

If a man has bought a piece of land in the belief that no one has right to a footpath or driving road through it, and if he fails to obtain interdict against a party claiming such right, he is entitled to the action on purchase: for though the stipulation against eviction does not come into play, there having been no judgment in a real action regarding the servitude right, still it must be held there is room for the action on purchase.

---

possession had not been violent, clandestine, or on sufferance. *Praetor ait: 'Quo itinere actuque privato quo de agitur, uel uia hoc anno nec ui nec clam nec precario ab illo usus es, quominus ita utaris, uim fieri ueto'* (D. 43. 19. 1 pr.).

For the decision that there is nothing in the case here put involving an infringement of the stipulation against eviction, compare D. 21. 2. 75: *Quod ad seruitutes praediorum attinet, si tacite secutae sunt et uindicentur ab alio, Quintus Mucius et Sabinus existimant uenditorem ob euictionem teneri non posse: nec enim euictionis nomine quemquam teneri in eo iure, quod tacite soleat accedere: nisi ut optimus maximusque esset traditus fuerit fundus.* Cp. D. 18. 1. 59 *supra*.

36. PAULUS libro VII ad Plautium.

Uenditor domus antequam eam tradat, damni infecti stipulationem interponere debet, quia, antequam uacuam possessionem tradat, custodiam et diligentiam praestare debet et pars est custodiae diligentiaeque hanc interponere stipulationem: et ideo si id neglexerit, tenebitur emptori.

37. PAULUS libro XIV ad Plautium.

Sicut aequum est bonae fidei emptori alterius dolum non nocere, ita non est aequum eidem personae uenditoris sui dolum prodesse.

38. CELSUS libro VIII digestorum.

Si uenditor hominis dixit peculium eum habere decem nec quemquam[1] adempturum, et[2] si plus habet, totum praestet, nisi hoc actum est, ut dumtaxat decem praestaret, si minus est, praestet esse decem et talem seruum esse, ut tantum peculii habeat.

1. Si per emptorem steterit, quo minus ei mancipium traderetur, pro cibariis per arbitrium indemnitatem posse seruari Sextus Aelius, Drusus dixerunt, quorum et mihi iustissima uidetur esse sententia.

2. Firmus a Proculo quaesiit, si de plumbeo castello fistulae sub terram missae aquam ducerent in aenum lateribus circumstructum, an hae aedium essent, an ut ruta caesa uincta fixaque,

---

L. 36.—When a house was in a ruinous condition, the owner of it could be compelled to give caution to the owner of the next property that he would make good any damage caused by its fall. As to the seller's duty of *custodia* until delivery was given, see D. 18. 1. 35, 4 *supra*. The risk of the anticipated damage did not pass to the buyer because the seller alone up to the time of delivery had the title to exact the security.

L. 38, § 1.—Cp. D. 13. 6. 18, 2: the expense of the maintenance of a slave falls on the borrower (*commodatarius*), but serious charges incurred, say for curing him or in recovering him when he has run away, must be borne by the *commodans*.

§ 2. The correctness of the text is doubted by most editors.

[1] quicquam?   [2] esse?

36. PAUL.

As regards the period before delivery, the seller of a house ought to require [from the owner of the adjoining house] a stipulatory promise to pay for threatened damage, because he is bound to bestow due care and watchfulness until he delivers the full possession, and it falls within his obligation to exact this stipulation: accordingly he must answer to the purchaser for default in doing so.

37. PAUL.

While it is equitable that a purchaser in good faith should not suffer by the bad faith of another, it would be inequitable that he should profit by the bad faith of the seller.

38. CELSUS.

If the seller of a slave gave out that he had a *peculium* of ten *aurei*, and that there are no deductions to be made from it, then, if it amounts to more, the master must hand over the whole, unless the actual arrangement was that he should give no more than ten *aurei*; but if it comes to less, he is responsible for ten *aurei*, and for the slave being valuable enough to possess a *peculium* of that amount.

1. Where non-delivery of a slave has been due to fault on the part of the buyer, Sextus Aelius and Drusus hold that the seller has a right to be reimbursed for the expense of his maintenance as fixed by an arbiter, a view which appears to me very reasonable.

2. Firmus put this query to Proculus: where pipes carried underground convey water from a lead reservoir to a copper cauldron built in all round, are they pertinents of the house or are they like things dug and cut or fastened and fixed which are

---

Pothier and Glück would transpose the order thus, *an hae aedium essent ut nineta fixaque, an ut ruta caesaque aedium non essent*—whether the pipes in question are to be classed among fixtures belonging to the house, or among moveables which are not attached to the *solum*, and therefore are not appurtenances of the house.

quae[1] aedium non essent ille rescripsit referre, quid acti esset. quid ergo si nihil de ea re neque emptor neque uenditor cogitauerunt, ut plerumque in eiusmodi rebus euenisse solet, nonne propius est, ut inserta et inclusa aedificio partem eius esse existimemus?

39. MODESTINUS libro V responsorum.

Quaero, si quis ita fundum uendiderit, ut id uenum datum esse uideatur, quod intra terminos ipse possedit, sciens tamen aliquam partem certam se non possidere non certiorauerit emptorem, an ex empto iudicio teneatur, cum haec generalis adiectio ad ea, quae specialiter nouit qui uendidit nec excepit, pertinere non debeat, ne alioquin emptor capiatur, qui fortasse, si hoc cognouisset, uel empturus non esset uel minoris empturus esset, [si certioratus de loco certo fuisset][2]: cum hoc et apud ueteres sit relatum in eius persona, qui sic exceperat: 'scruitutes si quae debentur, debebuntur:' etenim iuris auctores responderunt, si certus uenditor quibusdam personis certas scruitutes debere non admonuisset emptorem, ex empto eum teneri debere, quando haec generalis exceptio non ad ea pertinere debeat, quae uenditor nouit quaeque specialiter excipere et potuit et debuit, sed ad ea quae ignorauit et de quibus emptorem certiorare nequiuit. Herennius Modestinus respondit, si quid circumueniendi emptoris causa uenditor in specie de qua quaeritur fecit, ex empto actione conueniri posse.

40. POMPONIUS libro XXXI ad Quintum Mucium.

Quintus Mucius scribit: dominus fundi de praedio arbores stantes uendiderat et pro his rebus[3] pecuniam accepit et tradere nolebat: emptor quaerebat, quid se facere oporteret, et uerebatur,

L. 40.—Compare L. 50 pr. *De rei uindicatione, Digest* 6. 1: *si ager ex emptionis causa ad aliquem pertineat, non recte hac actione agi poterit, antequam traditus sit ager tuncque possessio amissa sit.*

If something growing on an estate is sold by itself, the property in it does not pass till it is separated.

[1] quae *del.* [2] *del.* [3] arboribus? (*Mom.*)

not pertinents of a house? He answered that it was important to know what the parties actually agreed on. But suppose neither party gave a thought to the matter, as constantly happens in such cases, it is surely the more reasonable view that a thing attached to and enclosed within a building forms a part of it.

39. MODESTINE.

Suppose a man in selling land adds the condition, that only so much as he himself has possessed within the boundaries is to be taken as offered for sale, and though aware that he does not possess a particular portion yet gives no information to the purchaser,—the query is put, is he liable to an action on purchase, seeing that this general clause should not cover what was particularly known to the seller unless he expressly reserved it, otherwise the purchaser would be imposed upon; for had he known this he would perhaps not have bought at all, or would have given a lower price [if he had been informed that a certain part did not belong to the seller]: especially as it is reported in the old writers, that in a case where a man had stipulated that 'any servitudes affecting the lands shall remain a burden on them,' the authorised jurists were of opinion that if the seller knew and did not give notice to the purchaser that certain persons possessed servitude rights he must answer for it in the action on purchase, because this general proviso ought not to cover what the seller knew, and might and should have reserved by express words, but only what he did not know and could not therefore disclose to the purchaser. Herennius Modestinus gave it as his opinion, that if the seller did anything in the premises for the purpose of overreaching the buyer, he was amenable to the action on purchase.

40. POMPONIUS.

Quintus Mucius reports this case: The owner of lands sold timber growing on the estate, and received payment, but refused to give delivery: the vendee asked what he was to do, as he feared that the trees would be held not to have become his.

ne hae arbores eius non uiderentur factae. POMPONIUS: arborum, quae in fundo continentur, non est separatum corpus a fundo et ideo ut dominus suas specialiter arbores uindicare emptor non poterit: sed ex empto habet actionem.

41. PAPINIANUS libro III responsorum.

In uenditione super annua pensitatione pro aquae ductu infra [1] domum Romae constitutum [2] nihil commemoratum est. deceptus ob eam rem ex empto actionem habebit: itaque, si conueniatur ob pretium ex uendito, ratio improuisi oneris habetur.

42. PAULUS libro II quaestionum.

Si duorum fundorum uenditor separatim de modo cuiusque pronuntiauerit et ita utrumque uno pretio tradiderit, et alteri aliquid desit, quamuis in altero exsuperet, forte si dixit unum centum iugera, alterum ducenta habere, non proderit ei, quod in altero ducenta decem inueniuntur, si in altero decem desint. et de his ita apud Labeonem relatum est. sed an exceptio doli mali uenditori profutura sit, potest dubitari, utique si exiguus modus siluae desit et plus in uineis habeat, quam repromissum est. an non facit dolo, qui iure perpetuo utitur? nec enim hic quod amplius in modo inuenitur, quam alioquin dictum est, ad

---

L. 41.—For water-rate, or rather payment for way-leave (*pro aquae forma*), cp. D. 7. 1. 27, 3. As to the duty of the seller to disclose extraordinary liabilities which the buyer has not the means of discovering for himself (*improvisi oneris*), see L. 21, 1 *supra*.

L. 42.—The conclusion come to is, that when one and the same contract embraces several things, and there is more of one and less of another than was promised, compensation comes into play. Labeo, going by the letter of the agreement and applying strict legal rules, holds that the excess in the one piece of land is a windfall to the buyer (L. 38), and therefore cannot be set off against a deficiency in the other piece. Paul recognises this as

[1] intra? (*Mom.*)   [2] constituto?

POMPONIUS' opinion was: trees growing on a piece of land have no separate existence; the vendee therefore cannot bring a real action for his specific trees as their owner; but an action on purchase is competent.

41. PAPINIAN.

In a contract of sale no mention was made of an annual payment for liberty to conduct water under a house situated in Rome. The party deceived thereby is entitled to an action on purchase; and therefore, if he is sued by the action on sale for the price, this unforeseen burden is taken into account.

42. PAUL.

If a person, when selling two pieces of ground, states the contents of each separately, and then hands over both for a slump price, and if the one is found to be short of the measurement while the other is in excess of it,—say he stated that the one contained 100 acres and the other 200, it will not avail him that there are 210 acres in the one if there are 10 wanting in the other. An opinion to that effect is reported by Labeo. But there is room for doubt whether a plea of fraud would not avail the seller, suppose there was a slight deficiency of woodland, but a surplus of vineyard as compared with what was guaranteed. Is it not fraud to exact one's utmost legal rights? For here when it

a hardship, and admits the principle of compensation; he holds that the seller can plead the *exceptio doli* against the buyer suing for indemnification, on the ground that his demand is inequitable, because he suffers no prejudice, for what he loses on the one hand he gains on the other. There could not in equity be any question of compensation in a case where the quality of the soils differs, and there is an excess of the more valuable (*uinea*) and a deficiency of the less valuable (*pratum*); but in the converse case it would only be fair that the buyer should be indemnified, for he is entitled to demand at least as favourable a proportion between the more and the less valuable constituents of the land as the seller indicated. Cp. L. 13, § 14, *supra* p. 175; Pothier, *Vente*, § 256.

compendium uenditoris, sed ad emptoris pertinet: et tunc tenetur uenditor, cum minor modus inuenitur. uideamus tamen, ne nulla querella sit emptoris in eodem fundo, si plus inueniat in uinea quam [1] in prato, cum uniuersus modus constat. similis quaestio esse potest ei, quae in duobus fundis agitata est et si quis duos statuliberos uno pretio uendat et dicat unum decem dare iussum, qui quindecim dare debebat [alterum item decem, qui quinque dare debebat]: nam et hic tenebitur ex empto actione, quamuis emptor a duobus uiginti accepturus sit. sed rectius est in omnibus supra scriptis casibus lucrum cum damno compensari et si quid deest emptori siue pro modo siue pro qualitate loci, hoc ei resarciri.

43. PAULUS libro V quaestionum.

Titius cum decederet, Seiae Stichum Pamphilum Arescusam per fideicommissum reliquit eiusque fidei commisit, ut omnes ad libertatem post annum perduceret. cum legataria fideicommissum ad se pertinere noluisset nec tamen heredem a sua petitione liberasset, heres eadem mancipia Sempronio uendidit nulla commemoratione fideicommissae libertatis facta: emptor cum pluribus annis mancipia supra scripta sibi seruissent, Arescusam manumisit, et cum ceteri quoque serui cognita uoluntate defuncti fideicommissam libertatem petissent et heredem ad praetorem perduxissent, iussu praetoris ab herede sunt manumissi. Arescusa quoque nolle se emptorem patronum habere responderat.

Jus perpetuum should mean 'law always in force'; some take it to refer to public law, others to action under the *edictum perpetuum*.

Where a slave received by his master's will a conditional bequest of freedom, say on his paying a certain sum or on the lapse of a certain time, he was described as *statu liber*, and the heir was his master, so long as the condition was unpurified or pendent. See *Digest* 40, tit. 7, *De Statuliberis*.

LL. 43, 44.—Seia's repudiation of the legacy was not allowed to prejudice the trust-gift of freedom to the slaves

[1] uel.

turns out that there is an excess over the measurement promised it is the buyer who reaps the profit; and still the seller is bound in case of a deficiency to make it good. But in the case of a single piece of land I think that no action is competent to the purchaser, although he finds more vineyard and less meadow, if the total measurement is correct. A point analogous to that which has been discussed in regard to the two pieces of land, may be raised where a man sells for a slump price two slaves who have been promised their freedom, declaring that the one was enjoined to pay 10 aurei, whereas the real sum was 15 (and the other to pay 10, the real sum being 5), for in this case also an action on purchase will lie, although the purchaser is to get 20 aurei from the pair. But it is fairer in all the above-mentioned cases to set off the loss and gain against each other, and if the buyer suffers either as regards the extent or the quality of the land to give him compensation.

43. PAUL.

Titius at his death left the slaves Stichus, Pamphilus, and Arescusa to Seia, by a testamentary trust, under the trust condition that she should make them all free after a year. Seia, the legatee, having refused the trust, without exonerating the heir from his suit, the heir sold the said slaves to Sempronius without making any reference to the trust grant of freedom: after the vendee had held them as slaves for several years, he manumitted Arescusa; and then the other two, becoming aware of the intentions of their late master, claimed their freedom in pursuance of the trust, and summoned the heir before the praetor, by whose orders they were set free. Moreover, Arescusa had now declared that she declined to have the vendee as her patron.

(D. 40. 5. 33, 2); neither did the fact that the heir sold them without informing the purchaser that they were *statu liberi* prevent them from claiming their freedom at the expiry of the year, or as soon after as they became aware of their rights, *si sub condicione fuit ei libertas relicta et pendente condicione alienatus sit, attamen cum sua causa alienatur* (D. ib. 24, 21). The con-

cum emptor pretium a uenditore empti iudicio Arescusae quoque nomine repeteret, lectum est responsum Domitii Ulpiani, quo continebatur Arescusam pertinere ad rescriptum sacrarum constitutionum, si nollet emptorem patronum habere: emptorem tamen nihil posse post manumissionem a uenditore consequi. ego cum meminissem et Iulianum in ea sententia esse, ut existimaret post manumissionem quoque empti actionem durare, quaero, quae sententia uera est. illud etiam in eadem cognitione nomine emptoris desiderabatur, ut sumptus, quos in unum ex his quem erudierat fecerat, ei restituerentur. idem quaero, Arescusa, quae recusauit emptorem patronum habere, cuius set liberta constituta? an possit uel legatariam quae non liberauit uel heredem patronum habere? nam ceteri duo ab herede manumissi sunt. respondi: semper probaui Iuliani sententiam putantis manumissione non [amitti actionem: itaque quod ius habuit emptor aduersus heredem Arescusae nomine, etsi manumisit eam, non] amittitur eo modo. de sumptibus uero, quos in erudiendum hominem emptor fecit, uidendum est: nam empti iudicium ad eam quoque speciem sufficere existimo: non enim pretium continet tantum, sed omne quod interest emptoris seruum non

stitutions referred to gave a slave who had been alienated the right to say whether he preferred to have the heir or the purchaser as patron: the object was to prevent him being obliged to take a patron, whom the testator did not mean to give him (*ne contra uoluntatem defuncti durior eius condicio constituatur*, Digest, *loc. cit.*).

The words in brackets are those suggested by Mommsen to fill up what is obviously a lacuna between *non* and *amittitur*. *Quod ius habuit:* the claim in question is founded on the fact that the purchaser has lost the right of patronage over Arescusa as she preferred to have the heir for patron. Paul, differing from Ulpian, and agreeing with Julian, holds that, though he has manumitted her, he still has a sufficient interest to support the *actio empti* either for return of the price or, more probably, to the effect of recovering damages for the loss of the *patronatus*. The next question is, What are the purchaser's rights in regard to the other two slaves, whom he has been obliged to hand over

The vendee having brought an action on purchase against the vendor for repayment of the price of Arescusa as well as the other two, an opinion obtained from Ulpian was read, which was to the effect that the case of Arescusa fell to be decided by the rescript in the imperial constitutions, if she refused to have the purchaser as her patron, and the vendee on the other hand, after having given her her freedom, had no claim against the vendor. But as I remembered that Julian was of opinion that the action on purchase was equally competent after enfranchisement, the question arises, Which view is correct? In the same action there was also a conclusion at the instance of the purchaser for reimbursement of the expenses he had been put to in training one of the slaves. In short, the question with regard to Arescusa is, Whose freedwoman has she become, seeing she would not accept the vendee as her patron? Could she choose the legatee, although she did not release her or the heir as patron? There is no question as to the other two, for the heir actually enfranchised them. I give this opinion: I have always concurred in the view of Julian that action on the contract does not fall by manumission; consequently the fact that the vendee has released Arescusa does not extinguish the claim competent to him against the heir on her account. Coming to the question of the expenses incurred in training the slave, I think that the action on purchase covers that point also, for it is not limited to the price, but includes all the interest the vendee had in being maintained in possession of

---

to the heir for enfranchisement, on the hypothesis that their value has been considerably increased in the meanwhile by outlays for training? Paul says he can recover his outlay by the *actio empti*, which covers *omne quod interest* as well as the purchase money; but he adds that it is equitable that the vendor's liability for eviction should be limited to such increase in value as he might reasonably have had in view at the time of the sale. In L. 44 Africanus suggests the double of the price as a reasonable limitation. Justinian (C. vii. 47 pr. 1) fixed the highest measure of damages in contractual obligations for a specific object at the double, in order to expedite legal

euinci. plane si in tantum excedisse proponas, ut non sit cogitatum a uenditore de tanta summa (ueluti si ponas agitatorem postea factum uel pantomimum euictum esse eum, qui minimo ueniit pretio), iniquum uidetur in magnam quantitatem obligari uenditorem,

44. AFRICANUS libro VIII quaestionum.

(cum et forte idem mediocrium facultatium sit: et non ultra duplum periculum subire eum oportet)

45. PAULUS libro V quaestionum.

idque et Iulianum agitasse Africanus refert: quod iustum est: sicut minuitur praestatio, si seruus deterior apud emptorem effectus sit, cum euincitur.

1. Illud expeditius uidebatur, si mihi alienam aream uendideris et in eam ego aedificauero atque ita eam dominus euincit: nam

proccedings: *Sancimus itaque in omnibus casibus, qui certam habent quantitatem uel naturam, ueluti in uenditionibus et locationibus et omnibus contractibus, hoc quod interest dupli quantitatem minime excedere.* There is some doubt as to what *simplum* Justinian had in view when he fixed the *duplum* as the limit of damages; he may either have meant what Africanus seems to indicate here, that the purchaser was in no case to recover more than double the purchase money, or possibly that the claim must not exceed the double of the market value. If he intended the latter, the enactment is singularly vague, for it leaves open all questions as to the time and place to be looked at in fixing the value.

L. 45 pr.—In this passage and in D. 21. 2. 70 it is clearly stated that, if the property has fallen in value between the date of the contract and the time of eviction, the seller is not bound to repay the actual amount of the purchase money, but only the diminished value: *euicta re ex empto actio non ad pretium duntaxat recipiendum, sed ad id, quod interest, competit: ergo et si minor esse coepit, damnum emptoris erit.*

Pothier contends that the purchaser is always entitled in case of eviction to recover the price in full, even though the article

the slave. No doubt in cases where the value has risen so far above the purchase price that the vendor cannot have contemplated so large a sum (suppose, for instance, that the property in a slave who was sold for a trifle is carried off after he has been trained as a charioteer or a stage-player), it does not seem equitable that the vendor should be liable for so considerable a sum,

44. AFRICANUS.

(for he may be a person of slender means: and his liability should be limited to double the price)

45. PAUL.

Africanus reports that Julian came to the same conclusion; and it is the correct view: similarly the compensation payable on eviction diminishes if the slave has fallen in value in the purchaser's hands.

1. There seemed less room for doubt in the following case: you sold me a building site belonging to another person, and

---

has meanwhile deteriorated, because the obligations of the buyer and seller are reciprocal, and it would be inequitable that the seller who is in default in not making a good title should be allowed to pocket part of the price. He explains the texts above cited as referring not to the price which is a constant quantity, but to the buyer's interest in the maintenance of his possession, which rises and falls according as the value of the article is enhanced or diminished. *Vente,* §§ 69, 130 sq. The French Code faithfully reproduces the view of Pothier in art. 1631: the seller must restore the entire price, whether the loss of value or deterioration is due to the fault of the purchaser or to inevitable accident. But there is no warrant in the texts for separating the buyer's *interesse* from his claim for return of the price as if they were subject to different rules; on the contrary, it is laid down repeatedly that the *quod interest* is the true and only measure of the indemnity which the evicted purchaser can claim by the *actio empti, e.g.* C. viii. 44. 23; D. 21. 2. 8; ib. 15; ib. 60.

§ 1. This section contains a qualification of the rule that the seller is liable to the evicted purchaser in full damages, including

quia possim petentem dominum, nisi impensam aedificiorum soluat, doli mali exceptione summouere, magis est, ut ea res ad periculum uenditoris non pertineat. quod et in seruo dicendum est, si in seruitutem, non in libertatem cuinceretur, ut dominus mercedes et impensas praestare debeat. quod si emptor non possideat aedificium uel seruum, ex empto habebit actionem. in omnibus tamen his casibus, si sciens quis alienum uendiderit, omnimodo teneri debet.

2. Superest tertia deliberatio, cuius debet esse liberta Arescusa, quae recusat emptorem. et non sine ratione dicetur eius debere effici libertam, a quo uendita est, id est heredis, quia et ipse ex empto actione tenetur: sed hoc ita, si non Arescusa elegerit emptoris patronatum: tunc etenim et illius remanet liberta et ille ex empto actionem non habet, quia nihil eius interest, cum eam libertam habet.

46. PAULUS libro XXVI quaestionum.

Si quis alienam rem uendiderit et medio tempore heres domino rei exstiterit, cogetur implere uenditionem.

compensation for the outlays. If the purchaser was in possession *bonâ fide* when the true owner raised his *vindicatio*, he could claim repayment of any necessary or beneficial expenditure on the subject as a condition of yielding up the possession, and make the claim effectual by retention, cp. *Inst.* ii. 1. 30. If he neglected to do so, he had no recourse against the vendor, who could defeat his claim by an *exceptio doli*. But he might be unable for various reasons to make any demand upon the evicting owner, *e.g.* because he had never obtained possession, or where he bought a putative slave and was ousted from the possession, not at the suit of a third person, but through the supposed slave proving his freedom (*si in libertatem cuinceretur*); in such cases his remedy is against the seller as his author. And finally, if the seller acted in bad faith by selling in the knowledge that he had no title, he is liable *omnimodo* (*i.e.* ' whether there is a right of retention against the party evicting or not,' or possibly ' without any restriction of the liability '). See C. viii. 44. 9; ib. 16; Pothier, *Vente*, §§ 133–137.

after building on it I am evicted by the true owner; now, as I am in a position to make an effectual answer to his demand by pleading bad faith, unless he offers to pay my outlay on the buildings, it seems reasonable that the risk of the outlay should not fall upon the vendor. In the same way, when I am deprived of the possession of a slave, not by his establishing his freedom but because he is claimed by the rightful owner, the latter is bound to indemnify me for advances and outlays. But if the vendee is not in possession of the house or slave, he will be allowed an action on purchase. Yet in all these cases, if the vendor knew that he was selling what belonged to another, he must be held liable in every event.

2. There remains the third question, under whose patronage is Arescusa to be since she will not acknowledge the purchaser as patron? The most reasonable view is that she should become the freedwoman of the man who sold her, that is to say of the heir, because he is responsible under the action on purchase: provided always Arescusa does not choose to have the purchaser for patron: for if she does, she remains his freedwoman, and he cannot maintain the action on purchase, because he has no interest now that he has the rights of a patron over Arescusa.

46. Paul.

A person who has sold a thing belonging to another, and has subsequently succeeded as heir to the owner, will be compelled to fulfil the contract of sale.

§ 2. It might be contended that the heir had renounced the rights of *patronatus* by selling Arescusa and allowing the buyer to manumit her. The answer (says Pothier) is that he has not surrendered the right absolutely, but only in favour of a particular person. If Arescusa declines to have the purchaser as patron, the rights in question are held to revert to the seller, who is now liable to the purchaser in respect of their loss. Cp. D. 21. 2. 26.

L. 46. — See *Digest* 21, tit. 3, *De exceptione rei uenditae et traditae*, L. 1. pr. § 1, *Marcellus scribit, si alienum fundum*

47. PAULUS libro VI responsorum.

Lucius Titius accepta pecunia ad materias uendendas sub poena certa, ita ut, si non integras repraestauerit[1] intra statuta tempora, poena conueniatur,[2] partim datis materiis decessit: cum igitur testator in poenam commiserit neque heres eius reliquam materiam exhibuerit, an et in poenam et in usuras conueniri possit, praesertim cum emptor mutuatus pecuniam usuras grauissimas expendit ? Paulus respondit ex contractu, de quo quaeritur, etiam heredem uenditoris in poenam conueniri posse. in actione quoque ex empto officio iudicis post moram intercedentem usurarum pretii rationem haberi oportere.

48. SCAEUOLA libro II responsorum.

Titius heres Sempronii fundum Septicio uendidit ita: 'fundus Sempronianus, quidquid Sempronii iuris fuit, erit tibi emptus tot nummis' uacuamque possessionem tradidit neque fines eius demonstrauit : quaeritur, an empti iudicio cogendus sit ostendere ex instrumentis hereditariis, quid iuris defunctus habuerit et fines ostendere. respondi id ex ea scriptura praestandum, quod

---

uendideris et tuum postea factum petas, huc te exceptione recte repellendum. Sed et si dominus fundi heres uenditori exsistat idem erit dicendum.

L. 47.—On receiving the price, Titius bound himself to pay a stipulated penalty in case of failure to deliver the materials by a certain date, not in lieu of his obligation but to corroborate it. Could his heir be sued, if default were made, both for the penalty and for interest on the price ? The answer is : he can be sued for the penalty *ex contractu de quo quaeritur, i.e.* in virtue of the stipulation for the penalty above mentioned ; and, moreover, when the *actio ex empto* is raised, the judge will take into account the interest on the purchase-money from the date when delivery should have been given. These are separate claims, and are enforceable by separate actions; there is therefore no question of *consumptio actionis.* Observe that the expiry of the period

[1] repraesentauerit? (*Cuj.*) [2] committatur?

47. Paul.

Lucius Titius received payment for building material sold subject to a certain penalty, which was to be incurred in case he did not deliver the whole quantity within a fixed period, and he died after delivering only part of it: seeing that the deceased has incurred the stipulated penalty, and his heir has failed to supply the rest of the material, can the heir be sued both for the penalty and interest on the price, especially if the buyer borrowed the money and has to pay heavy interest? Paul's opinion was that the heir also could be competently sued for the penalty under the agreement in question; and further, in the action on purchase, it was the duty of the judge to allow interest on the price from the date when the delay began.

48. Scaevola.

Titius, the heir of Sempronius, sold a piece of land to Septicius on these terms, 'The estate of Sempronius, with all such rights as he enjoyed, shall be yours by purchase for so much,' and gave him full possession without pointing out its boundaries: the question was put whether Titius can be compelled by the action on purchase to show from the title deeds the extent of the deceased's right and to point out the boundaries. I answered that under such a clause the parties were bound to give effect to

---

appointed for the execution of the contract is here treated as equivalent to a formal demand for payment, according to the maxim *dies interpellat pro homine*. It is disputed whether, in all cases where the date of payment was definitely fixed, the debtor was held to be in *mora* as soon as it passed without payment. Where the sum or the date was uncertain, the creditor was bound as a rule to make a demand at a suitable time and place (D. 22. 1. 32 pr.).

Benjamin remarks on the resemblance between the civil law and the common law rules as to payment and tender. *Sale*, p. 571.

L. 48.—See D. 18. 1. 63, 1.

sensisse intelleguntur: quod si non appareat, debere uenditorem et instrumenta fundi et fines ostendere: hoc etenim contractui bonae fidei consonat.

49. Hermogenianus libro ii iuris epitomarum.

Qui per collusionem imaginarium colonum circumueniendi emptoris causa subposuit, ex empto tenetur nec defenditur, si, quo facilius excogitata fraus occultetur, colonum et quinquennii pensiones in fidem suam recipiat.

1. Pretii, sorte licet post moram soluta, usurae peti non possunt, cum hae non sint in obligatione, sed officio iudicis praestentur.

50. Labeo libro iv posteriorum a Iauoleno epitomatorum.

Bona fides non patitur, ut, cum emptor alicuius legis beneficio pecuniam rei uenditae debere desisset antequam res ei tradatur, uenditor tradere compelletur[1] et re sua careret.[2] possessione autem tradita futurum est, ut rem[3] uenditor neque amitteret, utpote cum petenti eam rem [emptor exceptionem rei uenditae et traditae opponere possit nec perinde sit, quasi eam rem] petitor ei neque uendidisset neque tradidisset.

L. 49 pr.—Five years was a common period for a lease of lands.

§ 1. Interest was generally due on the unpaid price from the date of delivery (see L. 13, § 20 *supra* p. 178), although no demand for payment had been made by the seller; for the obligation to pay interest is not a result of *mora* in the technical sense (that is to say, of formal *interpellatio*), but is grounded on equity. Pothier draws this distinction: if the thing sold produces fruits natural or civil, interest is due from the time of delivery; if it does not, interest is due only from the date of the formal demand for payment (§ 283 sq.): and the French Civil Code, art. 1652, has adopted his view, but it is doubtful if the rules there stated are in harmony with the authorities as a whole, though they receive some support from this text and from C. iv. 49. 13,

---

[1] compellatur.   [2] carere.   [3] et pecuniam *ins.*

what may be inferred to have been their intention: but, if that cannot be made out, the seller ought to exhibit the titles and point out the boundaries, these being natural incidents of a contract of good faith.

49. Hermogenian.

A seller is liable by the action on purchase for falsely putting forward as tenant a person with whom he has an arrangement in order to defraud the purchaser, and it does not shield him if, the better to conceal the fraudulent scheme, he becomes surety for the tenant and his rent for five years.

1. No action will lie for interest on the price, if the principal sum has once been paid although after some delay, because interest is not a ground of action in itself, but is awarded at the discretion of the judge.

50. Labeo.

It is inconsistent with good faith that, where the purchaser's obligation to pay the price of the subject is extinguished by force of statute before delivery is made, the seller should be compelled to deliver and so to sacrifice his property. But if the possession has been transferred, the consequence is that the seller loses both the subject and its price, because if he sues for the subject the purchaser can meet him with the equitable plea that it was sold and delivered, and this case is not the same as where the pursuer has not sold and given delivery.

---

and iv. 54. 5. It is laid down here that, if the seller has once accepted payment of the price without interest for the period subsequent to delivery, he cannot bring a special action to recover the interest, because it is payable not on any special ground of obligation, but in the ordinary action for the price, as the judge in the exercise of his equitable discretion may direct. Cp. D. 16. 3. 24.

L. 50.—This lex refers to the case where a statute in favour of debtors relieves the buyer of his obligation to pay the price; it is generally thought the allusion is to *novae tabulae*. Labeo observes that in such an event the seller is entitled on equitable

51. Labeo libro v. posteriorum a Iauoleno epitomatorum.

Si et per emptorem et uenditorem mora fuisset, quo minus uinum praeberetur[1] et traderetur, perinde esse ait, quasi si per emptorem solum stetisset: non enim potest uideri mora per uenditorem emptori facta esse ipso moram faciente emptore.

1. Quod si fundum emisti ea lege, uti des pecuniam kalendis Iuliis, et si ipsis calendis per uenditorem esset factum, quo minus pecunia ei solueretur, deinde per te staret quo minus solueres, uti posse aduersus te lege sua uenditorem dixi, quia in uendendo hoc ageretur, ut, quandoque per emptorem factum sit, quo minus pecuniam soluat, legis poenam patiatur. hoc ita uerum puto, nisi si quid in ea re uenditor dolo fecit.

---

grounds to retain the subject sold, if it has not been delivered, and to resist an action for delivery; but he has no remedy, if he has already given delivery: in fact, he applies the maxim *in pari causa melior est condicio possidentis*. The reading in the text is that proposed by Mommsen: he supplies '*et pecuniam*' on the authority of the *Basil.* in order to explain '*acque*,' and in the clause within brackets (which has long been adopted by most editors to supply an obvious lacuna in the MSS.) he alters the traditional reading by putting '*nec perinde sit*' for '*ut perinde habeatur*.' Some writers, retaining the traditional text, maintain that Labeo meant to decide both cases in the same way from the standpoint of *bona fides*. The connection of ideas is then as follows: where delivery has been made, the strict legal effect would be (*futurum est*) that the seller would lose his property without getting an equivalent, because the buyer could meet his *actio Publiciana* with the *exceptio rei uenditae et traditae*; hence, to avoid this inequitable result, the case is to be dealt with as if there had been no sale and no delivery, that is to say, the buyer is not to be allowed the *exceptio* as an answer to the seller claiming the property as his. This explanation requires us to give a conditional (not a future) sense to *futurum est*, and to make the *ut*-clause a consequence depending upon these words. But the grammar is not easy, and there appears to be no authority for the conclusion reached. See Bechmann, *Kauf* i. p. 598 sq.

[1] probaretur? (*Faber*).

51. Labeo.

If the vendor and vendee are jointly responsible for delay in supplying and delivering wine, the case is dealt with as if the delay had been due to the vendee solely; for it cannot be held that the vendee has been prejudiced by the vendor's delay when he has himself contributed to the delay.

1. If you bought a piece of ground on the condition that you should pay the price on the 1st of July, and if payment was rendered impossible on that date by the vendor's fault and on a subsequent date by your default, the vendor can in my opinion put the condition in force against you, because the bargain made at the time of the sale was that as soon as the vendee was in default in paying the price he should incur the stipulated penalty. I take for granted, of course, that the vendor has not acted fraudulently in the premises.

L. 51 pr.—The true principle, as stated by Pomponius, is that, where there is delay by the creditor and the debtor successively, the party who is last in delay must bear the consequences. Suppose the buyer has made a requisition for delivery, and so put the seller in *mora*, and thereafter, when the seller tenders the article, the buyer refuses to accept delivery; the result is that the seller's *mora* is purged, *post moram offerendo purgat moram* (D. 45. 1. 73, 2), and the buyer being now in *mora* must bear all risk. On the other hand, *si per emptorem mora fuisset, deinde, cum omnia in integro essent, venditor moram adhibuerit, cum posset se exsolvere aequum est, posteriorem moram venditori nocere* (D. 18. 6. 18).

§ 1. The case figured is of this kind: the buyer engages to pay on 1st July, but cannot find the seller or any authorised agent to whom he can make payment, or his tender of payment is refused for some reason; subsequently, when the seller has returned, or has waived his objection, the buyer is out of the way, or for some other reason fails to pay: Labeo holds that the buyer has lost his rights under the contract. His only safety, it would appear, is to hold himself in readiness to pay whenever payment becomes possible. The last sentence qualifies the decision: the seller is guilty of fraud if he purposely kept out of

52. SCAEVOLA libro VII digestorum.

Creditor fundum sibi obligatum, cuius chirographa tributorum a debitore retro solutorum apud se deposita habebat, uendidit Maeuio ea lege, ut, si quid tributorum nomine debitum esset, emptor solueret: idem fundus ob causam eorum tributorum, quae iam soluta erant, a conductore saltus, in quo idem fundus est, uenit cumque idem Maeuius emit et pretium soluit: quaesitum est, an empti iudicio uel aliqua[1] actione emptor a uenditore consequi possit, ut solutionum supra scriptarum chirographa ei dentur. respondit posse emptorem empti iudicio consequi, ut instrumenta de quibus quaereretur exhibeantur.

1. Praedium aestimatum in dotem a patre filiae suae nomine datum obligatum creditori deprehenditur: quaesitum est, an filius, qui hereditatem patris retinet, cum ab ea se filia abstinuisset dote contenta, actione ex empto teneatur, ut a creditore lueret et marito liberum praestaret. respondit teneri.

2. Inter uenditorem et emptorem militiae ita conuenit, ut salarium, quod debeatur ab illa persona, emptori cederet: quaesitum est, emptor militiae quam quantitatem a quo exigere debet et quid ex eiusmodi pacto uenditor emptori praestare debeat. respondit uenditorem actiones extraordinarias eo nomine quas haberet praestare debere.

---

the way on the 1st with the intention of demanding payment at a time when he knew the buyer would be unable to meet his demand.

L. 52 pr.—The tax-farmer of the district (*conductor saltus sc. publici, i.e. publicanus*) sold the lands for alleged arrears of land-tax; and Maevius requires the receipts which are in the mortgagee's possession to disprove the allegation.

§ 1. Cp. D. 23. 3. 10, 5, *aestimatio enim pro uenditione est*: the husband to whom property is conveyed at a valuation in name of dowry is in the position of a purchaser. The heir

[1] alia qua? (*Mom.*)

52.   Scaevola.

A creditor, who held a mortgage over certain lands and had in his keeping the receipts for former payments of land-tax by the debtor, sold the lands to Maevius, under the condition that the purchaser should pay the arrears of land-tax, if any. The same lands were thereafter put up for sale by the tax-farmer of the district within which they lay on account of the taxes already paid, and Maevius purchased them and paid the price. The question was asked, Can the purchaser by an action on purchase or other proceeding compel the seller to give up to him the vouchers for payments above mentioned? The answer was that the purchaser can obtain exhibition of the documents in question by the action on purchase.

1. It is found that a subject which was valued and conveyed by a father as part of his daughter's dowry is burdened with a mortgage. The query was put whether a son who has entered into possession as his father's heir—while the daughter, satisfied with her dowry, renounced her rights—can be compelled by the action on purchase to redeem the subject from the creditor and convey it unencumbered to her husband. The answer was in the affirmative.

2. The seller and purchaser of the profits of an office having agreed that the pay due to the holder should pass to the purchaser, the question was raised how much the purchaser could exact and from whom, and what the obligations of the seller to the purchaser were in virtue of such an agreement. The opinion given was that the seller is bound to assign the special actions to which he has right.

---

must therefore discharge the burden. See note on p. 144 ante.

§ 2. *Militia* (*i.e.* a service, post, or office in the imperial court) could be the subject of sale, legacy, or pledge, or, more correctly, the interest in it could be assigned; *militia quae uendi uel ad heredes transmitti potest* (C. viii. 14. 27). The sale of the higher offices

3. Ante domum mari iunctam molibus iactis ripam constituit, et uti ab eo possessa domus fuit Gaio Seio uendidit: quaero, an ripa, quae ab auctore domui coniuncta erat, ad emptorem quoque iure emptionis pertineat. respondit eodem iure fore uenditam domum, quo fuisset priusquam ueniret.

53. LABEO libro I pithanon.

Si mercedem insulae accessuram esse emptori dictum est, quanti insula locata est, tantum emptori praestetur. PAULUS: immo si insulam totam uno nomine locaueris et amplioris conductor locauerit et in uendenda insula mercedem emptori cessuram esse dixeris, id accedet, quod tibi totius insulae conductor debebit.

1. Si eum fundum uendidisti, in quo sepulcrum habuisti, nec nominatim tibi sepulcrum excepisti, parum habes eo nomine cautum. PAULUS: minime, si modo in sepulcrum iter publicum transit.

2. Si habitatoribus habitatio lege uenditionis recepta est, omnibus in ea habitantibus praeter dominum recte recepta habitatio est. PAULUS: immo si cui in ea insula, quam uendideris, gratis habitationem dederis et sic receperis: 'habitatoribus aut [1] quam quisque diem conductum habet,' parum caueris (nominatim enim de his recipi oportuit) itaque eos habitatores emptor insulae habitatione impune prohibebit.

---

was prohibited (C. ix. 27. 6). *Extraordinariae actiones* under the formulary system were not competent to an ordinary *iudex*; the jurisdiction was confined entirely to the magistrates.

L. 53, § 2.—Compare D. 19. 2. 25, 1. For the servitude of *habitatio* see *Inst.* ii. 5. 5, and *Digest* 7. 8. 10 sq.: it was similar to the privilege now sometimes granted to persons in reduced circumstances of occupying a suite of apartments or a house; it was of an alimentary character, and was not lost by non-usage or *capitis deminutio minima*. Justinian first raised it to the rank of a proper servitude (C. iii. 33. 13). He allowed the *habitator* to let the house.

[1] ad? (*Husch.*)

3. A man built an embankment with a foundation of masonry in front of his house, close to the sea; he then sold the house to Gaius Seius 'as it had been possessed by him': I put the question, Does the embankment, which was connected with the house by the seller, also pass to the purchaser in virtue of the sale? The answer was: the sale will carry all the appurtenances that belonged to the house before it was sold.

53. LABEO.

If the buyer has got an assurance that the rents of a block of houses shall pass as an accessory, the whole of the rents must be handed over. PAUL remarks: if, however, you have let the whole block to one tenant, who has sublet for a higher rent, and you have promised the rent as an accessory when selling the block, the amount of the accessory will only be the sum payable by the lessee of the whole block.

1. If you have sold a piece of ground which contains your burial-place, without expressly reserving your right of burial, you have failed to preserve your right. 'Not at all,' says PAUL, 'provided a public road leads to the burial-ground.'

2. If by the contract of sale a right of habitation is reserved for the occupants, it is sufficiently secured for all who dwell in the block except the owner. But, according to PAUL, if you have given a man a gratuitous grant of the right to dwell in the block you have sold, and have made a reservation in these terms 'in favour of the occupants or till the expiry of each man's lease,' the reservation is ineffectual (for they should have been designated by name), and so they may be deprived of their right by the purchaser without redress.

If the conjecture *ad* be adopted, the reason why the gratuitous grantees of the right are not protected by the special clause of reservation is that they have no lease for a fixed term. But the MSS. reading *aut* is supported by the *Basil.*, and is probably right.

54. Labeo libro II pithanon.

Si seruus quem uendideras iussu tuo aliquid fecit et ex eo crus fregit, ita demum ea res tuo periculo non est, si id imperasti, quod solebat ante uenditionem facere, et si id imperasti, quod etiam non uendito seruo imperaturus eras. Paulus: minime: nam si periculosam rem ante uenditionem facere solitus est, culpa tua id factum esse uidebitur: puta enim cum fuisse seruum, qui per catadromum descendere aut in cloacam demitti solitus esset. idem iuris erit, si eam rem imperare solitus fueris, quam prudens et diligens pater familias imperaturus ei seruo non fuerit. quid si hoc exceptum fuerit? tamen potest ei seruo nouam rem imperare,[1] quam imperaturus non fuisset, si non uenisset: ueluti si ei imperasti, ut ad emptorem iret, qui peregre esset: nam certe ea res tuo periculo esse non debet. itaque tota ea res ad dolum malum dumtaxat et culpam uenditoris dirigenda est.

1. Si dolia octoginta accedere fundo, quae infossa essent, dictum erit, et plura erunt quam ad eum numerum, dabit emptori ex omnibus quae uult, dum integra det: si sola octoginta sunt, qualiacumque emptorem sequentur nec pro non integris quicquam ei uenditor praestabit.

55. Pomponius libro X epistularum.

Si seruus, qui emeretur uel promitteretur, in hostium potestate sit, Octauenus magis putabat ualere emptionem et stipulationem, quia inter ementem et uendentem esset commercium: potius

---

L. 54 pr.—As to *custodia* by the seller pending delivery, see p. 72 *ante*. The real question always is, as Paul observes, Was the work so dangerous that no man of ordinary prudence would have set his slave to do it?

§ 1. In the first case the seller engages to furnish 80 out of a larger number; it is the sale of indeterminate *corpora*, and therefore it is an implied condition that the vats actually delivered shall be in good order. In the second case the vats are specific-

---

[1] quod si hoc exceptum fuerit, etiam potest ei seruo nouam rem imperare. item potest ei eam rem imperare? (*Mom.*)

54. Labeo.

If you order a slave whom you have sold [but not delivered] to do something, and he breaks his leg in doing it, the risk falls upon you unless the order be such as he was wont to carry out before the sale, and such as you would have given although you had not sold him. 'Not at all' says Paul; 'for if he was accustomed to do dangerous work before the sale, it will be held that you were in fault: if, for example, he was used to going on the tight-rope, or being let down into sewers. The same will apply if you have been in the habit of imposing tasks which a careful and circumspect master would not have set to that slave. But how if a reservation was made with reference to this? Still the master may order the slave some new duty which he would not have laid on him if he had not sold him, for instance, to go to the purchaser who is abroad: now, that should certainly not be at your peril. Thus the sole criterion in all such cases is whether there has been misconduct or fault on the part of the vendor.

1. If the vendor has promised to give along with the lands 80 vats which are sunk in the ground, and it is found there are more than that number, he may give the vendee any of the lot he pleases, so long as they are sound; but if there are exactly 80, they will pass to the vendee, let their condition be what it may, and the vendor will not be responsible for broken ones.

55. Pomponius.

If a slave, who has been taken captive by the enemy, is sold or promised by stipulation, Octavenus would hold the sale or stipulation valid, there being *commercium* between the buyer and seller; for the difficulty lies not so much in the nature

---

ally ascertained, and here the seller is not responsible for patent defects which the buyer's inspection should have revealed to him.

L. 55.—The circumstances which justify the judge in interposing to grant time or a stay of proceedings till performance

enim difficultatem in praestando eo inesse, quam in natura,[1] etiamsi officio iudicis sustinenda esset eius praestatio, donec praestari possit.

becomes possible are not detailed : it may, however, be assumed that it was essential that both parties should have been in excusable ignorance of the obstacle to performance when they

[1] quam eum non esse in rerum natura ? (*Mom.*)

as in the performance of the obligation, although the judge ought, in the exercise of his discretion, to grant delay of performance till it becomes possible.

entered into the contract. The phrase *difficultas in praestando* shows that the case stated was not regarded as one of absolute but only of relative impossibility. Cp. D. 45. 1. 73.

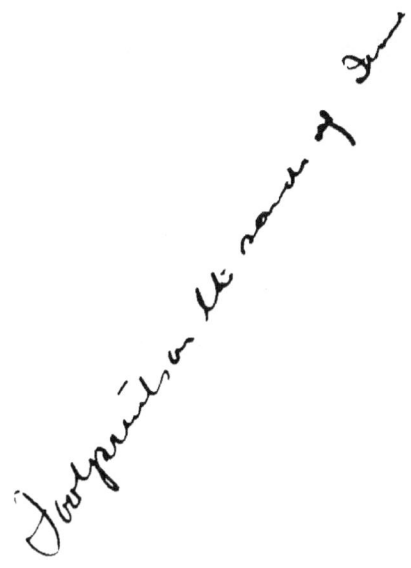

APPENDIX.

APPENDIX.

SALE OF GOODS BILL.

MEMORANDUM.

1. THIS Bill is drafted on the same lines as the Bills of Exchange Act, 1882. It endeavours to reproduce as exactly as possible the statutory and common law rules relating to the sale of goods, leaving any amendments that may seem desirable to be introduced at a later stage.

2. The Bill is almost entirely a reproduction of the common law. With the exception of the Statute of Frauds, the legislative enactments relating to the sale of goods deal only with isolated points of not much general importance. In so far as such enactments deal solely with the law of sale they have been reproduced in the Bill; but where they relate mainly to some different subject-matter, and deal only incidentally with the law of sale, or where they affect only certain specified classes of goods, they have been covered by saving clauses. If the whole law of contract was codified the present Bill would form a single chapter in the Code. In accordance with this principle, no attempt is made to reproduce the effect of cases, which, though arising out of sales, merely illustrate principles common to the whole law of simple contracts. A similar course was observed with regard to the Bills of Exchange Act, 1882.

3. The Bill does not extend to Scotland. The law of Scotland with respect to the sale of goods differs in many important respects from the law of England. Hence a merely codifying Bill could not extend to both countries. For example—

(a.) The Statute of Frauds (29 Car. 2. c. 3, s. 17, as amended by the 9 Geo. 4. c. 14, s. 7) does not extend to Scotland.

(b.) In England the property in goods passes under a contract of sale as soon as the parties intend it to pass, whether the goods be delivered or not. In Scotland the rule of the civil law prevails, and the property in goods sold does not pass until delivery. It has, however, been pointed out by Lord Blackburn that since the 19 & 20 Vict. c. 60, s. 1, this distinction is of not much importance, for whenever the property would pass in England, the buyer in Scotland acquires a *jus ad rem*, though not a *jus in rem*. The goods are at the buyer's risk, and the seller's creditors cannot attach them; see *M'Bain* v. *Wallace*, 6 App. Cas. 888.

(c.) Certain stipulations which in England would only be treated as warranties are treated in Scotland as conditions, so that where an English buyer could only treat the breach of the stipulation as a ground of damages, a Scotch buyer might be entitled to rescind the contract; *Couston* v. *Chapman*, L. R. 2 Sc. App. 250.

(d.) In England when goods are ordered from a manufacturer, as such, there is an implied warranty that the goods supplied shall be of his own make. In Scotland there is no such warranty; *Johnson* v. *Railton*, 7 Q. B. D. at pp. 445, 455.

(e.) The English rule as to sales in market overt does not apply in Scotland.

(f.) The seller's lien in Scotland is regulated by the Statute 19 & 20 Vict. c. 60, ss. 2 and 3.

4. The Bills of Exchange Bill, as originally drafted, did not apply to Scotland, but after consultation with Scotch legal authorities it was thought desirable to lay down uniform rules for both countries, and this was effected by amendments in committee, in some cases the Scotch, and in others the English, rule being adopted. Possibly a similar course might be found feasible in the case of the present measure. The Bills of Exchange Act, 1882, has worked smoothly, and has already been adopted by Canada and by six of the Australian Colonies.

5. As regards terminology, it is to be noted that the terms 'seller' and 'buyer' are used uniformly throughout the Bill to the exclusion of the synonymous terms 'vendor and purchaser' and 'vendor' and 'vendee,' and the terms 'sale' and 'agreement to sell' are used to the exclusion of the terms 'executed and executory contract of sale.'

March 1892.

APPENDIX.

ARRANGEMENT OF CLAUSES.

PART I.

FORMATION OF THE CONTRACT.

Contract of Sale.

Clause
1. Sale and agreement to sell.
2. Capacity to buy and sell.

Formalities of the Contract.

3. Contract of sale, how made.
4. Contract of sale for ten pounds and upwards.

Subject-Matter of Contract.

5. Existing or future goods.
6. Goods which have ceased to exist.
7. Goods perishing before sale but after agreement to sell.

The Price.

8. Ascertainment of price.

Clause
9. Agreement to sell at valuation.

Conditions and Warranties.

10. Exclusion of implied terms and conditions.
11. Stipulations as to time.
12. Warranty after sale completed.
13. When condition to be treated as warranty.
14. Implied undertaking as to title, etc.
15. Sale by description.
16. Rule of *caveat emptor.* Implied undertakings as to quality, fitness, or condition.

Sale by Sample.

17. Sale by sample.

PART II.

EFFECTS OF THE CONTRACT.

Transfer of Property as between Seller and Buyer.

Clause
18. Goods must be ascertained.
19. Property passes when intended to pass.
20. Rules for ascertaining intention.
21. Reservation of right of disposal.
22. Risk *primâ facie* passes with property.

Transfer of Title.

Clause
23. Sale by person not the owner.
24. Market overt.
25. Sale under voidable title.
26. Revesting of property in stolen goods on conviction of offender.
27. Seller or buyer in possession after sale.
28. Effect of writs of execution.

PART III.

PERFORMANCE OF THE CONTRACT.

Clause
29. Duties of seller and buyer.
30. Payment and delivery are concurrent conditions.
31. Rules as to delivery.
32. Delivery of wrong quantity.
33. Instalment deliveries.
34. Delivery to carrier.

Clause
35. Risk where goods are delivered at distant place.
36. Buyer's right of examining the goods.
37. Acceptance.
38. Buyer not bound to return rejected goods.
39. Liability of buyer for neglecting or refusing delivery of goods.

PART IV.

RIGHTS OF UNPAID SELLER AGAINST THE GOODS.

Clause
40. Unpaid seller defined.
41. Unpaid seller's rights.

Unpaid Seller's Lien.

42. Seller's lien.
43. Part delivery.
44. Termination of lien.

Stoppage in transitu.

45. Right of stoppage *in transitu*.

Clause
46. Duration of transit.
47. How stoppage *in transitu* is effected.

Re-sale by Buyer or Seller.

48. Effect of sub-sale or pledge by buyer.
49. Sale not generally rescinded by lien or stoppage *in transitu*.

PART V.

ACTIONS FOR BREACH OF THE CONTRACT.

Remedies of the Seller.

Clause
50. Action for price.
51. Damages for non-acceptance.

Remedy of the Buyer.

52. Damages for non-delivery.

Clause
53. Specific performance may be decreed.
54. Breach of warranty of quality, fitness, or condition.
55. Interest and special damages.

PART VI.

SUPPLEMENTARY.

Clause
56. Contract of exchange of goods.
57. Rights and duties under Act enforceable by action.
58. Auction sales.
59. Sale of horses.
60. Repeals.

Clause
61. Savings.
62. Interpretation of terms.
63. Commencement.
64. Extent.
65. Short title.
  SCHEDULES.

APPENDIX.

A Bill intituled an Act for Codifying the Law relating to the Sale of Goods.

Be it enacted by the Queen's most Excellent Majesty, by and with the advice and consent of the Lords Spiritual and Temporal, and Commons, in this present Parliament assembled, and by the authority of the same, as follows :—

PART I.

Formation of the Contract.

Contract of Sale.

I. *Sale and agreement to sell.*—(1.) A contract of sale of goods is a contract whereby the seller transfers or agrees to transfer the property in goods to the buyer for a money consideration, called the price. There may be a contract of sale between one part owner and another.

(2.) A contract of sale may be absolute or conditional.

(3.) Where under a contract of sale the property in the goods is transferred from the seller to the buyer the contract is called a sale ; but where the transfer of property in the goods is to take place at a future time or subject to some condition thereafter to be fulfilled the contract is called an 'agreement to sell.'

(4.) An agreement to sell becomes a sale when the time elapses or the conditions are fulfilled subject to which the property in the goods is to be transferred.

II. *Capacity to buy and sell.*—Capacity to buy and sell is regulated by the general law concerning capacity to contract, and to transfer and acquire property.

Provided that where necessaries are sold and delivered to an infant or to a person who by reason of mental incapacity or drunkenness is incompetent to contract, he must pay a reasonable price therefor.

'Necessaries' in this section mean goods suitable to the condition in life of such infant or other person, and to his actual requirements at the time of the sale and delivery.

Formalities of the Contract.

III. *Contract of sale, how made.*—Subject to the provisions of this Act and of any statute in that behalf, a contract of sale may be made in writing (either with or without seal), or by word of mouth, or partly in writing and partly by word of mouth, or may be implied from the conduct of the parties.

Provided that nothing in this section shall affect the law relating to corporations.

IV. *Contract of sale for ten pounds and upwards.*—(1.) A contract for the sale of any goods of the value of ten pounds or upwards shall not be allowed to be good unless the buyer shall accept part of the goods so sold, and actually receive the same, or give something in earnest to bind the contract, or in part payment, or unless some note or memorandum in writing of the contract be made and signed by the party to be charged or his agent in that behalf.[1]

(2.) The provisions of this section apply to every such contract, notwithstanding that the goods may be intended to be delivered at some future time, or may not at the time of such contract be actually made, procured, or provided, or fit or ready for delivery, or some act may be requisite for the making or completing thereof, or rendering the same fit for delivery.[2]

(3.) There is an acceptance of goods within the meaning of this section when the buyer does any act in relation to the goods which recognises a pre-existing contract of sale whether there be an acceptance in performance of the contract or not.

(4.) The provisions of this section do not apply to a contract of exchange of goods.

Subject-Matter of Contract.

V. *Existing or future goods.*—(1.) The goods which form the subject of a contract of sale may be either existing goods or goods to be manufactured or acquired by the seller after the making of the contract of sale, in this Act called 'future goods.'

(2.) There may be a contract for the sale of goods, the acquisition of which by the seller depends upon a contingency which may or may not happen.

(3.) Where by a contract of sale the seller purports to effect a present sale of future goods, the contract operates as an agreement to sell the goods.

VI. *Goods which have ceased to exist.*—Where there is a contract for the sale of specific goods, and the goods without the knowledge of the seller have ceased to exist at the time of the contract, the contract is void.

VII. *Goods perishing before sale but after agreement to sell.*—Where there is an agreement to sell specific goods, and subsequently the goods, without any fault on the part of the seller or buyer, perish before the risk passes to the buyer, the agreement is thereby avoided.

The Price.

VIII. *Ascertainment of price.*—(1.) The price in a contract of sale may be fixed by the contract, or may be left to be fixed in manner thereby agreed.

(2.) When the price is not determined in accordance with the foregoing provisions the buyer must pay a reasonable price. What is a reasonable price is a question of fact dependent on the circumstances of each particular case.

IX. *Agreement to sell at valuation.*—(1.) Where there is an agreement to sell goods on the terms that the price is to be fixed by the valuation of a third party, and such third party cannot or does not make such valuation, the agreement is avoided; provided that if the goods or any

---

[1] 29 Car. 2. c. 3, s. 17, and 9 Geo. 4. c. 14, s. 7.
[2] 9 Geo. 4. c. 14, s. 7.

part thereof have been delivered to and appropriated by the buyer he must pay a reasonable price therefor.

(2.) Where such third party is prevented from making the valuation by the fault of the seller or buyer, the party not in fault may maintain an action for damages against the party in fault.

Conditions and Warranties.

X. *Exclusion of implied terms and conditions.*—Where any right, duty, or liability would arise under a contract of sale, by implication of law, it may be negatived or varied by express agreement or by the course of dealing between the parties, or by usage, if the usage be such as to bind both parties to the contract.

XI. *Stipulations as to time.*—(1.) Unless a different intention appears from the terms of the contract, stipulations as to time of payment are not deemed to be of the essence of a contract of sale. Whether any other stipulation as to time is of the essence of the contract or not depends in each case on the construction of the contract.

(2.) In a contract of sale 'month' means *primâ facie* calendar month.

XII. *Warranty after sale completed.*—Where a warranty is given after the contract of sale is completed, it must be supported by fresh consideration.

XIII. *When condition to be treated as warranty.*—(1.) Where a contract of sale is subject to any condition to be fulfilled by the seller, the buyer may waive the condition, or may elect to treat the breach of such condition as a breach of warranty, and not as a ground for treating the contract as repudiated.

(2.) Whether a stipulation in a contract of sale is a condition, the breach of which may give rise to a right to treat the contract as repudiated, or a warranty, the breach of which may give rise to a claim for damages, but not to a right to treat the contract as repudiated, depends in each case on the construction of the contract.

(3.) Where a contract of sale is not severable, and the buyer has accepted the goods, or part thereof, or the contract was for specific goods, the property in which has passed to the buyer, the breach of any condition to be fulfilled by the seller can only be treated as a breach of warranty, and not as a ground for treating the contract as repudiated, unless there be a condition in the contract to that effect.

(4.) Nothing in this section shall affect the case of any condition or warranty, fulfilment of which is excused by law by reason of impossibility or otherwise.

XIV. *Implied undertaking as to title, etc.*—In a contract of sale, unless the circumstances of the contract are such as to show a different intention, there is—

- (1.) An implied condition on the part of the seller that he has a right to sell the goods.
- (2.) An implied warranty that the buyer shall have and enjoy quiet possession of the goods.
- (3.) An implied warranty that the goods are free from any charge or lien thereon not declared at the time of sale.

XV. *Sale by description.*—Where there is a contract for the sale of goods by description, there is an implied condition that the goods shall correspond with the description; and if the sale be by sample, it is not sufficient that the bulk of the goods corresponds with the sample if the goods do not also correspond with the description.

XVI. *Rule of caveat emptor.*—*Implied conditions as to quality or fitness.*—Subject to the provisions of this Act and of any statute in that behalf, there is no implied undertaking as to the quality or fitness of goods supplied under a contract of sale, except as follows:—

(1.) An implied undertaking as to quality or fitness may be annexed by the usage of trade.

(2.) Where the buyer, expressly or by implication makes known to the seller the particular purpose for which the goods are required, so as to show that the buyer relies on the seller's skill or judgment and the goods are of a description which it is in the course of the seller's business to supply (whether he be the manufacturer or not), there is an implied undertaking that the goods shall be reasonably fit for such purpose, provided that in the case of a contract for the sale of a specified article under its patent or other trade name, there is no implied undertaking as to its fitness for any particular purpose.

(3.) Where goods are bought by description from a seller who deals in goods of that description (whether he be the manufacturer or not) and the buyer has no opportunity of examining the goods, there is an implied undertaking that the goods shall be of merchantable quality.

(4.) An express condition or warranty does not negative a condition or warranty implied by this Act unless inconsistent therewith.

Sale by Sample.

XVII. *Sale by sample.*—(1.) A contract of sale is a contract for sale by sample when there is a term in the contract, express or implied, to that effect. The exhibition of a sample during the making of the contract does not of itself make it a contract for sale by sample.

(2.) In the case of a contract for sale by sample—

(a.) There is an implied undertaking that the bulk shall correspond with the sample in quality.

(b.) There is an implied undertaking that the buyer shall have a reasonable opportunity of comparing the bulk with the sample.

(c.) There is an implied undertaking that the goods shall be free from any defect, rendering them unmerchantable, which would not be apparent on reasonable examination of the sample.

PART II.

Effects of the Contract.

Transfer of Property as between Seller and Buyer.

XVIII. *Goods must be ascertained.*—Where there is a contract for the sale of unascertained goods no property in the goods is transferred to the buyer unless and until the goods are ascertained.

XIX. *Property passes when intended to pass.*—(1.) Where there is a contract for the sale of specific or ascertained goods, the property in them is transferred to the buyer at such time as the parties to the contract intend it to be transferred.

(2.) For the purpose of ascertaining the intention of the parties regard shall be had to the terms of the contract, the conduct of the parties, and the circumstances of the case.

XX. *Rules for ascertaining intention.*—Unless a different intention appears, the following are rules for ascertaining the intention of the parties as to the time at which the property in the goods is to pass to the buyer:—

Rule 1.—Where there is an unconditional contract for the sale of specific goods, in a deliverable state, the property in the goods passes to the buyer when the contract is made, and it is immaterial whether the time of payment or the time of delivery, or both, be postponed.

Rule 2.—Where there is a contract for the sale of specific goods, and the seller is bound to do something to the goods, for the purpose of putting them into a deliverable state, the property does not pass until such thing be done.

Rule 3.—Where there is a contract for the sale of specific goods in a deliverable state, but the seller is bound to weigh, measure, test, or do some other act or thing with reference to the goods for the purpose of ascertaining the price, the property does not pass until such act or thing be done.

Rule 4.—When goods are delivered to the buyer on approval or on 'sale or return,' or other similar terms, the property therein passes to the buyer—

(*a.*) When he signifies his approval or acceptance to the seller, or does any other act adopting the transaction.

(*b.*) If he does not signify his approval or acceptance to the seller, but retains the goods without giving notice of rejection, then, if a time has been fixed for the return of the goods, on the expiration of such time, and, if no time has been fixed, on the expiration of a reasonable time. What is a reasonable time is a question of fact.

Rule 5.—(1.) Where there is a contract for sale of unascertained or future goods by description, and goods of that description and in a deliverable state are unconditionally appropriated to the contract, either by the seller with the assent of the buyer, or by the buyer with the assent of the seller, the property in the goods thereupon passes to the buyer. Such assent may be express or implied, and may be given either before or after the appropriation is made.

(2.) Where, in pursuance of the contract, the seller delivers the goods to the buyer or to a carrier or other bailee (whether named by the buyer or not) for the purpose of transmission to the buyer, and does not reserve the right of disposal, he is deemed to have unconditionally appropriated the goods to the contract.

XXI. *Reservation of right of disposal.*—(1.) Where there is a contract for the sale of specific goods or where goods are subsequently appropriated to the contract, the seller may, by the terms of the contract or appropriation, reserve the right of disposal of the goods until certain conditions are fulfilled. In such case, notwithstanding the delivery of the goods to the buyer, or to a carrier or other bailee for the purpose of transmission to the buyer, the property in the goods does not pass to the buyer until the conditions imposed by the seller are fulfilled.

(2.) Where goods are shipped, and by the bill of lading the goods are deliverable to the order of the seller or his agent, the seller is *primâ facie* deemed to reserve the right of disposal.

(3.) Where the seller of goods draws on the buyer for the price, and transmits the bill of exchange and bill of lading to the buyer together to secure acceptance or payment of the bill of exchange, the buyer is bound to return the bill of lading if he does not honour the bill of exchange, and if he wrongfully retains the bill of lading, the property in the goods does not pass to him.

XXII. *Risk* primâ facie *passes with property.*—Unless otherwise agreed, the goods remain at the seller's risk until the property therein is transferred to the buyer, but when the property therein is transferred to the buyer, the goods are at the buyer's risk whether delivery has been made or not.

Provided that where delivery has been delayed through the fault of either buyer or seller, the goods are at the risk of the party in fault as regards any loss which would not have occurred but for such fault.

Provided also that nothing in this section shall affect the duties or liabilities of either seller or buyer as a bailee of the goods of the other party.

Transfer of Title.

XXIII. *Sale by person not the owner.*—(1.) Subject to the provisions of this Act, where goods are sold by a person who is not the owner thereof, and who does not sell them under the authority or with the consent of the owner, the buyer acquires no better title to the goods than the seller had, unless the owner of the goods is by his conduct precluded from denying the seller's authority to sell.

(2.) Provided also that nothing in this Act shall affect—
- (*a.*) The provisions of the Factors Acts, or any enactment enabling the apparent owner of goods to dispose of them as if he were the true owner thereof;
- (*b.*) The validity of any contract of sale under any special common law, or statutory power of sale, as in the case of a sale by a

pawnee, distrainor, sheriff, master of a ship, or person selling under the order of a court of competent jurisdiction.

XXIV. *Market overt.*—(1.) Where goods are sold in market overt, according to the usage of the market, the buyer acquires a good title to the goods, provided he buys them in good faith and without notice of any defect or want of title on the part of the seller.

(2.) Nothing in this section shall affect the provision of this Act relating to the sale of horses.

XXV. *Sale under voidable title.*—When the seller of goods has a voidable title thereto, but his title has not been avoided at the time of the sale, the buyer acquires a good title to the goods, provided he buys them in good faith and without notice of the seller's defect of title.

XXVI. *Revesting of property in stolen goods on conviction of offender.*— (1.) Where goods have been stolen and the offender is prosecuted to conviction, the property in the goods so stolen revests in the person who was the owner of the goods, or his personal representative, notwithstanding any intermediate dealing with them, whether by sale in market overt or otherwise.[1]

(2.) Notwithstanding any enactment to the contrary, where goods have been obtained by fraud or other wrongful means not amounting to larceny, the property in such goods shall not revest in the person who was the owner of the goods, or his personal representative, by reason of the conviction of the offender.

XXVII. *Seller or buyer in possession after sale.*—(1.) Where a person having sold goods continues, or is in possession of the goods, or of the documents of title to the goods, the delivery or transfer by that person, or by a mercantile agent acting for him, of the goods or documents of title under any sale, pledge, or other disposition thereof, to any person receiving the same in good faith and without notice of the previous sale, shall have the same effect as if the person making the delivery or transfer were expressly authorised by the owner of the goods to make the same.[2]

(2.) Where a person having bought or agreed to buy goods obtains, with the consent of the seller, possession of the goods or the documents of title to the goods, the delivery or transfer by that person, or by a mercantile agent acting for him, of the goods or documents of title, under any sale, pledge, or other disposition thereof, to any person receiving the same in good faith and without notice of any lien or other right of the original seller in respect of the goods, shall have the same effect as if the person making the delivery or transfer were a mercantile agent in possession of the goods or documents of title, with the consent of the owner.[3]

(3.) In this section the term 'mercantile agent' has the same meaning as in the Factors Acts.

XXVIII. *Effect of writs of execution.*—(1.) A writ of *fieri facias* or other writ of execution against goods shall bind the property in the goods of the execution debtor as from the time when the writ is delivered to the sheriff to be executed; and, for the better manifestation of such time,

---

[1] Cf. 24 & 25 Vict. c. 96, s. 100.   [2] 52 & 53 Vict. c. 45, s. 8.
[3] 52 & 53 Vict. c. 45, s. 9.

it shall be the duty of the sheriff, without fee, upon the receipt of any such writ to endorse upon the back thereof the day, month, and year when he received the same.[1]

Provided that no such writ shall prejudice the title to such goods acquired by any person in good faith and for valuable consideration, unless such person had at the time when he acquired his title notice that such writ or any other writ by virtue of which the goods of the execution debtor might be seized or attached had been delivered to and remained unexecuted in the hands of the sheriff.[2]

(1.) In this section the term 'sheriff' includes an under sheriff, coroner, and the deputy, or agent of any such officer.

PART III.

Performance of the Contract.

XXIX. *Duties of seller and buyer.*—It is the duty of the seller to deliver the goods, and of the buyer to accept and pay for them, in accordance with the terms of the contract of sale.

XXX. *Payment and delivery are concurrent conditions.*—Unless otherwise agreed, delivery of the goods and payment of the price are concurrent conditions, that is to say, the seller must be ready and willing to give possession of the goods to the buyer in exchange for the price, and the buyer must be ready and willing to pay the price in exchange for possession of the goods.

XXXI. *Rules as to delivery.*—(1.) Whether it is for the buyer to take possession of the goods or for the seller to send them to the buyer is a question depending in each case on the contract, express or implied, between the parties.

(2.) Where under the contract of sale the seller is bound to send the goods to the buyer, but no time for sending them is fixed, the seller is bound to send them within a reasonable time. What is a reasonable time is a question of fact.

(3.) Where the goods at the time of sale are in the possession of a third person, there is no delivery by seller to buyer unless and until such third person acknowledges to the buyer that he holds the goods on his behalf; provided that nothing in this section shall affect the operation of the issue or transfer of any document of title to goods.

(4.) Demand or tender of delivery may be treated as ineffectual unless made at a reasonable hour. What is a reasonable hour is a question of fact.

(5.) Unless otherwise agreed, the expenses of and incidental to putting the goods into a deliverable state must be borne by the seller.

XXXII. *Delivery of wrong quantity.*—(1.) Where the seller delivers to the buyer a quantity of goods less than he contracted to sell, the buyer may reject them, but if the buyer accepts the goods so delivered he must pay for them at the contract rate.

(2.) Where the seller delivers to the buyer a quantity of goods larger than he contracted to sell, the buyer may accept the goods included in

[1] 29 Car. 2. c. 3, s. 15. [2] 19 & 20 Vict. c. 97, s. 1.

the contract and reject the rest, or he may reject the whole. If the buyer accepts the whole of the goods so delivered he must pay for them at the contract rate.

(3.) Where the seller delivers to the buyer the goods he contracted to sell mixed with goods of a different description not included in the contract, and the buyer cannot sever the goods included in the contract from the other goods without incurring trouble or expense, he may reject the whole.

XXXIII. *Instalment deliveries.*—(1.) Unless otherwise agreed, the buyer of goods is not bound to accept delivery thereof by instalments.

(2.) Where there is a contract for the sale of goods to be delivered by stated instalments, which are to be separately paid for, and the seller makes defective deliveries in respect of one or more instalments, or the buyer neglects or refuses to take delivery of or pay for one or more instalments, it is a question in each case depending on the terms of the contract and the circumstances of the case, whether the breach of contract is a repudiation of the whole contract, or whether it is a severable breach giving rise to a claim for compensation, but not to a right to treat the whole contract as repudiated.

XXXIV. *Delivery to carrier.*—(1.) Where, in pursuance of a contract of sale, the seller is authorised or required to send the goods to the buyer, delivery of the goods to a carrier, whether named by the buyer or not, for the purpose of transmission to the buyer is *primâ facie* deemed to be a delivery of the goods to the buyer.

(2.) Unless otherwise authorised by the buyer, the seller must make such contract with the carrier on behalf of the buyer as may be reasonable, having regard to the nature of the goods and the other circumstances of the case. If the seller omit so to do, and the goods are lost or damaged in course of transit, the buyer may decline to treat the delivery to the carrier as a delivery to himself, or may hold the seller responsible in damages.

XXXV. *Risk where goods are delivered at distant place.*—Where the seller of goods agrees to deliver them at a place other than that where they are when sold, the buyer must, unless otherwise agreed, take any risk of deterioration in the goods necessarily incident to the course of transit.

XXXVI. *Buyer's right of examining the goods.*—(1.) Where goods are delivered to the buyer, which he has not previously examined, he is not deemed to have accepted them unless and until he has had a reasonable opportunity of examining them for the purpose of ascertaining whether they are in conformity with the contract.

(2.) Unless otherwise agreed, when the seller tenders delivery of goods to the buyer, he is bound, on request, to afford the buyer a reasonable opportunity of examining the goods for the purpose of ascertaining whether they are in conformity with the contract.

XXXVII. *Acceptance.*—The buyer is deemed to have accepted the goods when he intimates to the seller that he has accepted them, or when the goods have been delivered to him, and he does any act in relation to them which is inconsistent with the ownership of the seller, or when after the lapse of a reasonable time he retains the goods without intimating to the seller that he has rejected them.

XXXVIII. *Buyer not bound to return rejected goods.*—Unless otherwise agreed, where goods are delivered to the buyer, and he refuses to accept them, having the right so to do, he is not bound to return them to the seller, but it is sufficient if he gives notice to the seller that he refuses to accept them.

XXXIX. *Liability of buyer for neglecting or refusing delivery of goods.*—When the seller is ready and willing to deliver the goods, and requests the buyer to take delivery, and the buyer does not within a reasonable time after such request take delivery of the goods, he is liable to the seller for any loss occasioned by his neglect or refusal to take delivery, and also for a reasonable charge for the care and custody of the goods. Provided that nothing in this section shall affect the rights of the seller where the neglect or refusal of the buyer to take delivery amounts to a repudiation of the contract.

PART IV.

Rights of Unpaid Seller against the Goods.

XL. *Unpaid seller defined.*—(1.) The seller of goods is deemed to be an 'unpaid seller' within the meaning of this Act—
(*a.*) When the whole of the price has not been paid or tendered;
(*b.*) When a bill of exchange or other negotiable instrument has been received as conditional payment, and the condition on which it was received has not been fulfilled by reason of the dishonour of the instrument or otherwise.

(2.) In this part of this Act the term 'seller' includes any person who is in the position of a seller, as, for instance, an agent of the seller to whom the bill of lading has been endorsed, or a consignor or agent who has himself paid, or is directly responsible for, the price.

XLI. *Unpaid seller's rights.*—(1.) Subject to the provisions of this Act, and of any Statute in that behalf, notwithstanding that the property in the goods may have passed to the buyer, the unpaid seller of goods, as such, has by implication of law—
(*a.*) A lien on the goods for the price while he is in possession of them;
(*b.*) In case of the insolvency of the buyer, a right of stopping the goods *in transitu* after he has parted with the possession of them;
(*c.*) A right of re-sale as limited by this Act.

(2.) Where the property in goods has not passed to the buyer, the unpaid seller has, in addition to his other remedies, a right of withholding delivery similar to and co-extensive with his rights of lien and stoppage *in transitu* where the property has passed to the buyer.

Unpaid Seller's Lien.

XLII. *Seller's lien.*—(1.) Subject to the provisions of this Act, the unpaid seller of goods who is in possession of them is entitled to retain

possession of them until payment or tender of the price in the following cases, namely:—
- (*a.*) Where the goods have been sold without any stipulation as to credit;
- (*b.*) Where the goods have been sold on credit, but the term of credit has expired;
- (*c.*) Where the buyer becomes insolvent.

(2.) The seller may exercise his right of lien notwithstanding that he is in possession of the goods as agent or bailee for the buyer.

XLIII. *Part delivery.*—(1.) Where an unpaid seller has made part delivery of the goods, he may exercise his right of lien on the remainder, unless such part delivery has been made under such circumstances as to show an agreement to waive the lien.

XLIV. *Termination of lien.*—(1.) The unpaid seller of goods loses his lien thereon—
- (*a.*) When he delivers the goods to a carrier or other person for the purpose of transmission to the buyer without reserving the right of disposal of the goods;
- (*b.*) When the buyer or his agent lawfully obtains possession of the goods;
- (*c.*) By waiver thereof.

(2.) The unpaid seller of goods, having a lien thereon, does not lose his lien by reason only that he has obtained judgment for the price of the goods.

Stoppage in transitu.

XLV. *Right of stoppage* in transitu.—Subject to the provisions of this Act, when the buyer of goods becomes insolvent, the unpaid seller who has parted with the possession of the goods has the right of stopping them *in transitu*, that is to say, he may resume possession of the goods as long as they are in course of transit, and may retain them until payment or tender of the price.

XLVI. *Duration of transit.*—(1.) Goods are deemed to be in course of transit from the time when they are delivered to a carrier by land or water, or other bailee, for the purpose of transmission to the buyer, until the buyer, or his agent in that behalf, takes delivery of them from such carrier or other bailee.

(2.) If the buyer or his agent in that behalf obtains delivery of the goods before their arrival at the appointed destination, the transit is at an end.

(3.) If, after the arrival of the goods at the appointed destination, the carrier or other bailee acknowledges to the buyer, or his agent, that he holds the goods on his behalf and continues in possession of them as bailee for the buyer, or his agent, the transit is at an end, and it is immaterial that a further destination for the goods may have been indicated by the buyer.

(4.) If the goods are rejected by the buyer, and the carrier or other bailee continues in possession of them, the transit is not deemed to be at an end, even if the seller has refused to receive them back.

(5.) When goods are delivered to a ship chartered by the buyer, it is a question depending on the circumstances of the particular case, whether they are in the possession of the master as a carrier, or as agent to the buyer.

(6.) Where the carrier or other bailee wrongfully refuses to deliver the goods to the buyer, or his agent in that behalf, the transit is deemed to be at an end.

(7.) Where part delivery of the goods has been made to the buyer, or his agent in that behalf, the remainder of the goods may be stopped *in transitu*, unless such part delivery has been made under such circumstances as to show an agreement to give up possession of the whole of the goods.

XLVII. *How stoppage* in transitu *is effected.*—(1.) The unpaid seller may exercise his right of stoppage *in transitu* either by taking actual possession of the goods, or by giving notice of his claim to the carrier or other bailee in whose possession the goods are. Such notice may be given either to the person in actual possession of the goods or to his principal. In the latter case the notice, to be effectual, must be given at such time and under such circumstances that the principal, by the exercise of reasonable diligence, may communicate it to his servant or agent in time to prevent a delivery to the buyer.

(2.) When notice of stoppage *in transitu* is given by the seller to the carrier, or other bailee in possession of the goods, he must re-deliver the goods to, or according to the directions of the seller. The expenses of such re-delivery must be borne by the seller.

Re-sale by Buyer or Seller.

XLVIII. *Effect of sub-sale or pledge by buyer.*—Subject to the provisions of this Act, the unpaid seller's right of lien or stoppage *in transitu* is not effected by any sale, pledge, or other disposition of the goods which the buyer may have made, unless the seller has assented thereto.

Provided that where a document of title to goods has been lawfully transferred to any person as buyer or owner of the goods, and that person transfers the document to a person who takes the document in good faith and for valuable consideration, then, if such last-mentioned transfer was by way of sale, the unpaid seller's right of lien or stoppage *in transitu* is defeated, and if such last-mentioned transfer was by way of pledge or other disposition for value, the unpaid seller's right of lien or stoppage *in transitu* can only be exercised subject to the rights of the transferee.

XLIX. *Sale not generally rescinded by lien or stoppage* in transitu.—(1.) Subject to the provisions of this section, a contract of sale is not rescinded by the mere exercise by an unpaid seller of his right of lien or stoppage *in transitu*.

(2.) Where an unpaid seller who has exercised his right of lien or stoppage *in transitu* re-sells the goods, the buyer acquires a good title thereto as against the original buyer.

(3.) Where the goods are of a perishable nature, or where the unpaid seller gives notice to the buyer of his intention to re-sell, and the buyer does not within a reasonable time pay or tender the price, the unpaid seller may re-sell the goods and recover from the original buyer damages for any loss occasioned by his breach of contract.

(4.) Where the seller expressly reserves a right of re-sale in case the buyer should make default, and on the buyer making default re-sells the goods, the original contract of sale is thereby rescinded, but without prejudice to any claim the seller may have for damages.

PART V.

ACTIONS FOR BREACH OF THE CONTRACT.

Remedies of the Seller.

L. *Action for price.*—(1.) Where, under a contract of sale, the property in the goods has passed to the buyer, and the buyer wrongfully neglects or refuses to pay for the goods according to the terms of the contract, the seller may maintain an action against him for the price of the goods.

(2.) Where, under a contract of sale, the price is payable on a day certain irrespective of delivery, and the buyer wrongfully neglects or refuses to pay such price, the seller may maintain an action for the price, although the property in the goods has not passed, and the goods have not been appropriated to the contract.

LI. *Damages for non-acceptance.*—(1.) Where the buyer wrongfully neglects or refuses to accept and pay for the goods, the seller may maintain an action against him for damages for non-acceptance.

(2.) The measure of damages is the estimated loss directly and naturally resulting, in the ordinary course of events, from the buyer's breach of contract.

(3.) Where there is an available market for the goods in question, the measure of damages is *primâ facie* to be ascertained by the difference between the contract price and the market or current price at the time or times when the goods ought to have been accepted, or, if no time was fixed for acceptance, then at the time of the refusal to accept.

Remedies of the Buyer.

LII. *Damages for non-delivery.*—(1.) Where the seller wrongfully neglects or refuses to deliver the goods to the buyer, the buyer may maintain an action against the seller for damages for non-delivery.

(2.) The measure of damages is the estimated loss directly and naturally resulting, in the ordinary course of events, from the seller's breach of contract.

(3.) Where there is an available market for the goods in question the measure of damages is *primâ facie* to be ascertained by the difference between the contract price and the market or current price of the goods at the time or times when they ought to have been delivered, or, if no time was fixed, then at the time of the refusal to deliver.

LIII. *Specific performance may be decreed.*—In any action for breach of contract to deliver specific goods for a price in money, on application of the plaintiff, and by leave of the judge, before whom the action is tried, the jury shall, if they find the plaintiff entitled to recover, find by their verdict (or if there be no jury, then the judge shall find) what are the goods in respect of the non-delivery of which the plaintiff is entitled to recover, and which remain undelivered; what, if any, is the sum which the plaintiff would have been liable to pay for the delivery thereof; what damages, if any, the plaintiff would have sustained if the goods should be delivered under execution as hereinafter mentioned; and what damages if not so delivered; and thereupon if judgment shall be given for the plaintiff, the judge in his discretion, on the application of the plaintiff, shall have power to order execution to issue for the delivery, on payment of such sum, if any, as shall have been found to be payable by the plaintiff as aforesaid, of the said goods without giving the defendant the option of retaining the same upon paying the damages assessed.[1]

For the purposes of this section 'plaintiff' includes a defendant who counterclaims for delivery of the goods.

LIV. *Breach of warranty of quality, fitness, or condition.*—(1.) Where, under a contract of sale, there is an undertaking as to the quality or fitness of the goods, and the goods do not fulfil the undertaking, the buyer may reject the goods unless he has accepted them, or unless the contract was for the sale of specific goods, and the property in the goods has passed to the buyer.

(2.) Where the buyer has accepted the goods, or where the contract was for the sale of specific goods and the property therein has passed to the buyer, the buyer is not entitled to reject the goods unless there was a condition in the contract to that effect; but he may—

(*a.*) Set up against the seller the breach of warranty in diminution or extinction of the price; or

(*b.*) Maintain an action against the seller for damages for the breach of warranty.

(3.) The measure of damages for breach of warranty of quality or fitness is the estimated loss directly and naturally resulting, in the ordinary course of events, from the breach of warranty.

(4.) In the case of breach of warranty of quality such loss is *primâ facie* the difference between the value of the goods at the time of delivery to the buyer and the value they would have had if they had answered to the warranty.

(5.) The fact that the buyer has set up the breach of warranty in diminution or extinction of the price does not prevent him from maintaining an action for the same breach of warranty if he has suffered further damage.

LV. *Interest and special damages.*—Nothing in this Act shall affect the right of the buyer or the seller to recover interest or special damages in any case where by law interest or special damages may be recoverable, or to recover money paid where the consideration for the payment of it has failed.

[1] 19 & 20 Vict. c. 97, s. 2.

PART VI.

Supplementary.

LVI. *Contract of exchange of goods.*—(1.) Where the consideration for the transfer of the property in goods from one person to another consists of other goods, the contract is called a contract of exchange of goods.

(2.) Except as otherwise provided by this Act, the provisions of this Act relating to contracts of sale, apply, with any necessary modifications, to contracts of exchange of goods.

LVII. *Rights and duties under Act enforceable by action.*—Where any right, duty, or liability is declared by this Act, it may, unless otherwise by this Act provided, be enforced by action.

LVIII. *Auction sales.*—In the case of a sale by auction—

(1.) Where goods are put up for sale by auction in lots, each lot is *primâ facie* deemed to be the subject of a separate contract of sale:

(2.) A sale by auction is complete when the auctioneer announces its completion by the fall of the hammer, or in other customary manner. Until such announcement is made any bidder may retract his bid:

(3.) When a sale by auction is not notified to be subject to a reserved price, or right to bid on behalf of the seller, it shall not be lawful for the seller to bid himself or to employ any person to bid at such sale, or for the auctioneer knowingly to take any bid from the seller or any such person: Any sale contravening this rule may be treated as fraudulent by the buyer:[1]

(4.) A sale by auction may be notified to be subject to a reserved price, and a right to bid may also be reserved expressly by or on behalf of the seller.[2]

When a right to bid is expressly reserved, but not otherwise, the seller, or any one person on his behalf, may bid at the auction in such manner as he may think proper.

LIX. *Sale of horses.*—With respect to contracts for the sale of horses, the rules in the First Schedule to this Act shall be observed and shall have effect as being enacted by this Act.

LX. *Repeals.*—The enactments mentioned in the Second Schedule to this Act are hereby repealed as from the commencement of this Act to the extent in that schedule mentioned.

Provided that such repeal shall not affect anything done or suffered, or any right, title, or interest acquired or accrued before the commencement of this Act, or any legal proceeding or remedy in respect of any such thing, right, title, or interest.

LXI. *Savings.*—(1.) The rules in bankruptcy relating to contracts of sale shall continue to apply thereto, notwithstanding anything in this Act contained.

(2.) The rules of the common law, including the law merchant, save in so far as they are inconsistent with the express provisions of this Act, shall continue to apply to contracts for the sale of goods.

(3.) Nothing in this Act or in any repeal effected thereby shall affect

---

[1] Cf. 30 & 31 Vict. c. 48, s. 5.   [2] Cf. 30 & 31 Vict. c. 48, s. 6.

the enactments relating to bills of sale, or any enactment relating to the sale of goods which is not expressly repealed by this Act.

LXII. *Interpretation of terms.*—(1.) In this Act, unless the context or subject-matter otherwise requires—

'Action' includes counterclaim and set off.

'Buyer' means a person who buys or agrees to buy goods.

'Condition' means a condition precedent.

'Contract of sale' includes an agreement to sell as well as a sale.

'Delivery' means voluntary transfer of possession from one person to another. A person is deemed to be in possession of goods or of the documents of title to goods, where the goods or documents are in his actual custody or are held by any other person subject to his control, or for him or on his behalf.

'Document of title to goods' has the same meaning as it has in the Factors Acts.

'Factors Acts' mean the Factors Act, 1889, and any enactment amending or substituted for the same.

'Fault' means wrongful act or default.

'Future goods' mean goods to be manufactured or acquired by the seller after the making of the contract of sale.

'Goods' include all chattels personal other than things in action and money. The term also includes emblements and things attached to or forming part of the land which are agreed to be severed before sale or under the contract of sale.

'Property' means the general property in goods, and not merely a special property.

'Quality of goods' includes their state or condition.

'Sale' includes a bargain and sale, as well as a sale and delivery.

'Seller' means a person who sells or agrees to sell goods.

'Specific goods' mean goods identified and agreed upon at the time a contract of sale is made.

'Undertaking' includes a condition as well as a warranty.

'Warranty' means an agreement with reference to goods which are the subject of a contract of sale, but collateral to the main purpose of such contract, the breach of which gives rise to a claim for damages, but not to a right to treat the contract as repudiated.

(2.) A thing is deemed to be done in 'good faith' within the meaning of this Act when it is in fact done honestly, whether it be done negligently or not.

(3.) A person is deemed to be insolvent within the meaning of this Act who either has ceased to pay his debts in the ordinary course of business, or cannot pay his debts as they become due, whether he has committed an act of bankruptcy or not.

(4.) Goods are in a 'deliverable state' within the meaning of this Act when they are in such a state that the buyer would under the contract be bound to take delivery of them.

LXIII. *Commencement.*—This Act shall come into operation on the first day of November one thousand eight hundred and ninety-two.

LXIV. *Extent.*—This Act shall not extend to Scotland or Ireland.

LXV. *Short title.*—This Act may be cited as the Sale of Goods Act, 1892.

SCHEDULES.

FIRST SCHEDULE.

Rules as to the Sale of Horses.

1. The sale of any horse, whether in market overt or otherwise, shall be void as against the true owner thereof, unless such sale be made in accordance with the following rules.[1]

2. When a stolen horse has been sold in market overt, and in accordance with these rules, the true owner may recover the same, if he make claim thereto within six months of the theft, on tendering to any person who may have bought it in good faith the price which he gave for the same.[2]

3. The market authority in every horse fair or market shall cause a special open place to be marked out for the sale of horses.[3]

4. There shall be a toll-keeper appointed for such place, who shall take tolls and keep the place from ten before noon until sunset of each market day, and no tolls shall be taken except between the aforesaid hours.

5. No horse shall be sold or otherwise transferred, unless it has been exposed in the place of sale for one hour at least during the hours aforesaid.

6. When the toll is taken the parties to the sale or transfer shall be present before the toll-keeper, and the toll-keeper shall enter in a book, to be kept for that purpose, the names, surnames, and addresses of the parties, together with the colour and one special mark at least of the horse so sold or transferred.

7. The toll-keeper shall not enter the sale or transfer in his book, unless he will take upon himself perfect knowledge of the name, surname, and address of the person selling or transferring the horse, or unless the person so selling or transferring the horse is vouched for by a sufficient and credible person known to the toll-keeper, who is personally acquainted with him, and knows his name, surname, description, and address. In the latter case the toll-keeper shall enter in his book the name, address, and description of the seller or transferrer, and of the person who vouches for him, and also the price, if any, given for the horse.[4]

8. A note of the entry in the toll-keeper's book shall be given to the buyer, who shall pay the sum of twopence therefor.

9. Not later than the day after the conclusion of the fair or market the toll-keeper shall deliver his book to the market authority, who shall cause a note to be made of the true number of all horses sold at the said fair or market.[5]

10. In these rules the term 'horse' includes mare, gelding, colt, and

---

[1] 31 Eliz. c. 12, s. 2.　　　　[2] 31 Eliz. c. 12, s. 4.
[3] 2 & 3 Phil. & Mar. c. 7, ss. 2, 4.　　[4] 31 Eliz. c. 12.
[5] 2 & 3 Phil. & Mar. c. 7, s. 3.

filly; and 'toll-keeper' includes deputy toll-keeper, or book-keeper, when by usage no toll is taken.

11. When, according to the usage of the market no toll is taken, the book-keeper shall be entitled to one penny for each sale or transfer entered in his book.[1]

SECOND SCHEDULE.

This schedule is to be read as referring to the revised edition of the Statutes prepared under the direction of the Statute Law Committee.

ENACTMENTS REPEALED AS TO ENGLAND.

Session and Chapter.	Title of Act and Extent of Repeal.
2 & 3 Phil. & Mar. c. 7,	An Act against the buying of stolen horses. The whole Act.
31 Eliz. c. 12, .	An Act to avoid horse stealing. The whole Act.
1 Jac. 1. c. 21, . .	An Act against brokers. The whole Act.
29 Cha. 2. c. 3, . .	An Act for the prevention of frauds and perjuries. In part; that is to say, sections fifteen and sixteen.[2]
9 Geo. 4. c. 14, . .	An Act for rendering a written memorandum necessary to the validity of certain promises and engagements. In part; that is to say, section seven.
19 & 20 Vict. c. 97, .	The Mercantile Law Amendment Act, 1856. In part; that is to say, sections one and two.

[1] 2 & 3 Phil. & Mar. c. 7, s. 8.
[2] Commonly cited as sections sixteen and seventeen.

INDEX TO THE LATIN TEXT AND NOTES.

For Arrangement of Clauses in the Sale of Goods Bill, see pp. 239, 240.

	PAGE
Accessio temporis ad usucapionem,	127
Accessions belong to buyer from completion of sale,	116, 174, 177 sq.
Accessories, error as to,	60
things intended for permanent use on the property are,	184 sq., 186
and belongings of a house,	88, 128, 182 sq., 186, 206, 228
and appurtenances of land,	88, 97, 126, 151, 172-4, 184, 188, 230
standing crops are,	87, 172
praedial servitudes as,	96
all water-works, and right of aqueduct are,	88, 96, 128, 184, 206
roads, shores, and public places are not,	99
ruta-caesa are not,	114, 186, 206
peculia of slaves are not,	57
acquisitions through slaves after sale are,	176
liability for defects in,	198
effect of eviction from,	162
Accretion after sale,	174
ACTIO EMPTI is *bonae fidei*,	156
price must be tendered,	172
lies for all non-performance,	142, 156, 166, 198
„ for non-delivery,	143 sq., 160, 220
„ for short delivery,	143, 148, 212
„ for culpa,	24, 176, 206, 230
„ for dolus,	118, 152, 170, 182, 208, 222, 230
„ for fructus,	144
„ for return of arra,	158
„ alternatively with other actions,	148, 158
„ to enforce performance of a term in the contract,	88, 121
„ for reduction of the price,	170
might result in rescission,	156
propria et hereditaria,	154
where no stipulatio duplae,	160

260 INDEX TO THE LATIN TEXT AND NOTES.

	PAGE
ACTIO EMPTI, where vindicatio incompetent,	210
defences against,	146, 202
ACTIO VENDITI covers all the buyer's obligations,	178
" the price with interest from delivery,	178, 180, 222
" outlay on thing sold,	180
lies for share of profit on re-sale,	180
" for delay,	224
" for fraud of buyer,	170
" to compel removal of goods,	154
" to enforce a mixed covenant,	132, 148
" " lex commissoria,	18
Actio ad exhibendum,	58, 186, 196
aquae pluviae arcendae,	175
Aquilia,	175
communi dividundo,	176
confessoria, negatoria,	204
damni infecti,	175
extraordinaria,	228
injuriarum,	197
institoria,	180
noxalis,	146, 160
Pauliana,	53
praescriptis verbis,	19, 98
Publiciana,	224
quanti minoris,	157, 168
redhibitoria,	13, 157
Actions, concourse of,	154 sq., 160, 198, 220
duty to assign,	74, 202
Adjected pact. See *Pactum*.	
Aediles, edict of,	157, 167 sq.
Aestimatio in dotem,	226
Agency of free persons, limited recognition of,	82, 112, 180
agent buying with knowledge of defects,	34
seller's agent in collusion with buyer,	182
agent's fraud, effect of,	40, 110
Agreement to sell,	5
Alienatio,	9, 115
Alteration of contract by pact,	120
Alternative obligation,	50, 193
risk in,	66
Approval, sale on,	14, 22
Arbitrator, price referred to,	10
Arra,	68
Aversio, sale *en bloc*,	76, 110
Barter, distinguished from sale,	3 sq.
Bona fides, definition,	53
requires the obligations to be mutual in sale,	164, 222

INDEX TO THE LATIN TEXT AND NOTES.

	PAGE
Bonâ fide buyer, protection of,	15
must not profit by fraud of seller,	206
Bonus pater familias, what is,	23, 73
Bonus vir, what is,	23
Boundaries, seller's duty to point out,	111, 220
Burial-place, special property in,	50
free space round,	150
reservation of,	124, 228
Buyer must make seller owner of price,	156
„ pay interest on purchase money from delivery,	178
„ carry away or send for the goods,	145, 154
„ not be tutor of seller,	67, 97
rights of successor of,	126
Capacity of *filius familias* to contract,	10, 34, 151
of minor,	182
of pupil,	62, 172, 182
of slave,	34
Capitis deminutio,	194, 228
Casus, liability for,	73, 131
Causa rei,	116, 145
Causa lucrativa,	176
Charges on subject sold, recoverable by seller,	154, 178
„ when to be defrayed by seller,	144
„ non-disclosure of extraordinary,	188
Chirographa,	226
Commodum rei, like the risk, passes on completion of sale,	116, 174, 177 sq.
Concourse of actions,	154
Condictio causa data, causa non secuta,	5
incerti,	154
indebiti,	39, 148
sine causa,	69, 196, 200
Condition, suspensive (precedent) or resolutive (subsequent),	13
payment and delivery concurrent conditions,	131, 172, 196
left to discretion of the seller, effect of,	22
no action for non-fulfilment of,	88
not fulfilled through fault of the debtor,	98
in restraint of subsequent alienation,	126
conditional purchase,	39, 109
„ sales,	21 sq., 88 sq., 98, 126, 134
reference of price to arbitrator amounts to,	11
involved in *emptio ad gustum*,	66
Consent, nature of,	27
Construction. See *Interpretation*.	
Contract of Sale. See *Sale*.	
Correspondence, contract by,	9
Credit, sale on,	41 sq.
Crop, sale of future,	24, 27

262 INDEX TO THE LATIN TEXT AND NOTES.

                                                                                 PAGE

Crop, standing and future, risk of, ... 131
    ripe, passes to buyer, ... 173
    growing reserved, ... 86, 132
Culpa, seller responsible for, . . . 24, 176, 206, 230
Custodia, seller liable for, pending delivery, . . . 73
    seller not liable if property taken forcibly, . . . 202
    includes duty to exact *cautio damni infecti*, . . . 206
    seller orders slave to do dangerous work, . . . 230

Damages, conventional or penal, ... 198, 220
    measure of, ... 140 sq.
    „   terms used to express, . . . 95, 111, 169
    „   *lucrum cessans* and *damnum emergens*, . . 191 sq.
    „   where sale fraudulent, . . . 169, 202 sq.
    „   for breach of warranty, . . . 190 sq.
    „   for eviction, ... 194, 214 sq.
    See *Delivery, Dolus*.
Damnum fatale, ... 74, 103, 121
Damnum infectum, ... 175, 206
Defects. See *Warranty*.
Delay. See *Mora*.
Delivery passes property, if price paid or secured, . . 5, 42 sq.
    by instalments, ... 18
    thing stolen before, ... 73
    symbolical or fictitious, ... 125
    damages for non-delivery, . . 140, 160 sq., 190, 196
    „   for delay in, . . 140, 144, 190, 202, 206, 220
    question whether it can be enforced, . . . 141 sq.
    place of contract is place of, ... 145
    is primary obligation on seller, . . . 50, 156
    what it includes, ... 160
    gives title where two buy *a non domino*, . . . 202
Destruction of thing sold, ... 37, 103, 107
Distractio, ... 135
Dolium, ... 127
Dolus, definition of, ... 116
    causam dans and *incidens*, ... 117
    implied warranty against in *bonae fidei* contract, . 92, 152, 202
    non-disclosure of known burdens is, . 108, 114, 142, 188, 208, 210
    silence as to known defects is, ... 168
    false representations to affect the price are, . . 91, 170
    statements made in reckless ignorance of the facts are, . . 169
    in form of active concealment, ... 92
    misstatement as to extent or quality of land is, . 174, 204
    mere puffing, and statements as to patent defects are not, . 91
    sale of *res aliena* with knowledge is, . . 55, 152, 162, 200
    of freeman letting himself be sold as slave, . . 15
    practised to induce credit, ... 43

INDEX TO THE LATIN TEXT AND NOTES. 263

	PAGE
Dolus, upon creditors,	53
upon minor,	182
of tutor,	172
sundry cases of,	175, 176, 202, 222, 230
no remedy if no damage caused,	152
remedy by action on contract for rescission and damages,	158, 168, 182
„ „ „ or for damages only at party's option, or where fraud relates to a subsidiary matter,	80, 96, 114, 118, 146, 152, 170
of stranger to the contract, remedy by *actio doli*,	118
Donatio inter virum et uxorem,	82
Donation, distinguished from sale,	80, 81
Earnest,	18, 68, 158
Eavesdrop,	59
Edict. See *Aediles.*	
Emere,	9
Emphyteusis,	45
Emptio ad gustum,	66
ad mensuram,	67, 85
spei and rei speratæ,	24 sq., 83, 167
ENGLISH LAW: sale and exchange,	5
sale and contract for work and labour distinguished,	46
proof of sale,	12
earnest,	70
contract by correspondence,	8
ambiguity in contract,	49
implied warranty of title, and covenant for quiet possession,	53
sale by one not owner,	56
sale of stolen goods in market overt,	64
bonâ fide purchaser,	54
sale of future crop, and of a mere chance,	26
buying one's own property,	40
goods destroyed wholly or partially before contract completed,	37, 107
sale at a valuation,	11
reasonable price implied where no price fixed,	11
vendor's lien in sale of goods,	21
„ land,	42
stoppage *in transitu* does not rescind sale,	21
seller cannot rescind for default in payment,	20
theory of risk,	77 sq.
property and risk pass by same rules,	78
transfer of property in *corpus manufactum* in course of construction,	46 sq.
executory contracts of sale,	57
seller bailee for buyer pending delivery,	75

	PAGE
ENGLISH LAW: warranty in general,	92
„ of freedom from charges,	144
delivery and payment by instalments,	18
duty of buyer to carry away the goods,	154
sale and return, and sale on approval,	14
condition not fulfilled by fault of party,	99
mistake,	31–33
recovery of money paid in mistake,	38
ignorance of fact and law,	37
fraud,	54, 118
damages for non-delivery and delay,	140 sq.
interest not due, unless expressly promised,	179
actio quanti minoris allowed generally,	119
specific performance,	142
rules as to demand for payment and tender like those of civil law,	221
readiness to pay or deliver, proof required of,	131, 173
Erro,	158
Error in corpore is essential,	28
in substantia or materia, when essential,	30, 94
as to ownership of thing sold,	38
mutual error as to material properties,	35, 36
plated article bought for solid silver,	90
second-hand clothes bought for new,	95
as to wood of which furniture is made,	190
„ subject-matter being in commercio,	15 sq., 110
„ existence of subject-matter,	36, 103 sq.
„ as to accessory,	60
„ as to quantity, effects of,	87
of motive, effects of,	148
Eviction, no remedy for defect of title pending,	55
(except where sale is fraudulent),	201
implied warranty against,	114, 122
express warranty (stipulatio duplae),	15, 123
covenant not to answer for, effect of,	152, 164 sq.
on ground of adverse right of possession,	160
„ a personal servitude,	114
„ a noxal claim,	160
whether proof of servitude road over property amounts to,	204
no warranty against, in sale of pledge,	162
buyer need not cite his author, where claim indisputable,	160
from an accessory,	162
extent of claim for,	172, 176, 215 sq.
value at time of, is general measure of damages,	216
Exceptio doli,	35, 130, 172, 198, 210, 218
mercis non traditae,	130, 196
non adimpleti contractus,	130
rei venditae et traditae,	219, 222

	PAGE
Exchange, distinguished from sale,	6
Expectancy, sale of,	24, 26
Expromissor,	101
Fault. See *Culpa.*	
Faults, liability for secret, by the edict,	157, 167
Fidejussor, liability of, for sale by slave,	196
Filius familias. See *Capacity.*	
Fire, destruction of subject by,	103 sq.
Fixtures and moveables in question between buyer and seller,	184, 186, 188, 208
Flumen,	59
Fraud. See *Dolus.*	
Frauds, Statute of,	12, 46
Freemen, sale of,	15, 121
FRENCH LAW: as to ambiguity in contract,	49
effect of sale in passing title,	52
condition of tasting suspends sale,	67
as to earnest,	70
effect of partial destruction of subject,	107
delivery of key,	125
evicted purchaser can claim return of price in full,	217
rules as to interest on the price,	222
Fructus, interest due in consideration of,	178
buyer's action to recover,	145
if separated belong to the seller,	184
if not separated pass to the buyer,	174
See *Rents, Causa rei.*	
Fugitivus,	72, 158
Fungibles, risk in sale of,	75 sq.
Future goods,	26, 44, 112
Glans,	133
Good Faith. See *Bona fides.*	
Guarantee,	91
Habitatio, reservation of,	182, 193, 228
Hiring. See *Location.*	
Ignorance of law and of fact,	37
Impossibility of performance, absolute,	15, 37
„ relative,	54, 231
„ through destruction of thing sold,	36, 103 sq., 107
Innominate contract,	5, 11
Instrumentum,	184
Interdict, quod vi aut clam,	175
de itinere actuque privato,	204
Interdicted person, sale by,	53

266 INDEX TO THE LATIN TEXT AND NOTES.

	PAGE
Interesse. See *Damages.*	
Interest on price, when due,	178, 220, 222
legal rate of, is limit of damages for detention of price,	181
recoverable only in action for the price,	223
Interpretation: ambiguity construed against seller,	48
local custom to rule, where intention not expressed,	127
purchase *sibi et alii,*	112
examples of,	58, 84–88, 114, 126, 132
Ius gentium, sale an institution of,	7
Key, delivery of,	125
Laesio enormis,	5
Largess,	25
Legacy by way of sale,	146
conditional, purchase of by legatee,	200
Lex commissoria,	16, 18, 180
Lex contractus, emptionis, etc.,	9
Lien,	21, 42
Location, distinguished from sale,	45 sq., 113, 134
combined with sale,	132, 192
former loose use of terms denoting,	188
Locus poenitentiae,	12, 69
multa poenitentialis,	13
Mancipatio,	6, 42
Market overt,	56, 64
MAXIMS: Ambiguum pactum contra uenditorem interpretandum est,	48
Dies interpellat pro homine,	221
Falsa demonstratio non nocet dummodo constet de persona,	29
Ignorantia juris neminem excusat,	37
In contractibus in quibus utriusque contrahentis utilitas uersatur, levis culpa, non etiam levissima, praestatur,	73
Melior est causa possidentis quam petentis,	202, 224
Periculum rei uenditae nondum traditae est emptoris,	78
Res perit domino,	13, 77
Simplex commendatio non obligat,	93
Superficies solo cedit,	58
Uerba sunt interpretanda contra proferentem,	49
Mensura,	67, 85
Mercantile Law Amendment Act,	48, 92
Merx,	9
Militia, sale of,	227
Missilia,	25
Misrepresentations. See *Dolus, Warranty.*	
Mistake. See *Error.*	
Money, introduction of, and functions of,	2, 3
Mora, what constitutes,	220, 222, 225

	PAGE
Mora, of seller,	146
of buyer,	74, 144-6
of both parties successively,	225
Motive, error of,	148
Moveables,	186, 188

Negligence. See *Culpa*.
Negotium claudicans,	62
Nomen, sale of,	25, 61
Noxal action,	146, 160

Obligation defined,	22
Ornamenta,	56
Pactum adjectum, or conuentum, kinds and effects of,	121 sq.
de non praestanda euictione,	152, 162, 164
de retrouendendo,	126
displicentiae,	12
in diem addictio,	13
lex commissoria,	16 sq.
nudum grounds an exception but not an action,	121
protimeseos,	126
reservati dominii,	42

Parts and Pertinents. See *Accessories*.
Patent defects,	90
Patron's rights of succession,	214
Peculium castrense and quasi-castrense,	10

See also *Slave*.
Perfecta emptio,	76
Periculum, general principles as to,	75 sq., 110
in sale under resolutive condition,	13, 67
of thing stolen before delivery,	73
in *emptio ad gustum*,	67
in alternative obligations,	67, 77

Permutatio. See *Barter*.
Pledge, purchase of, by debtor from creditor,	83
agreement to sell to creditor,	134
seller of does not warrant against eviction,	162
Poison, sale of,	71
Possession, jural, may be subject of sale,	39, 64, 65, 144
undisturbed, must be given by seller,	65, 160
security for quiet, can be exacted,	158
adverse right of, as ground of eviction,	160
precarious,	178

See *Vacua Possessio*.
Precarium, as mode of tenure,	178
Pre-emption, right of,	126
PRICE: no price, no sale,	10, 80

INDEX TO THE LATIN TEXT AND NOTES.

	PAGE
PRICE: whether necessarily money,	3
must be *certum*,	22, 23
„ *verum*,	80
need not be *justum*,	82
cannot be left to the buyer,	22, 71
may be referred to the valuation of third party named,	10
„ made to depend on uncertain or unknown circumstance,	23, 80
„ supplemented by promise to do something, or to share profit on a re-sale,	132, 149, 180, 192
payable by instalments,	17
buyer's obligation to pay, with interest,	178
tender of, in *actio empti*,	129, 172, 196
may be in any currency agreed on,	120
unless paid or secured, or credit given, sale and delivery does not pass property,	41 sq.
alteration of, discharges the original contract,	122
Proculians and Sabinians,	4, 19, 112
Procurator. See *Agency*.	
Projectum,	133
Proof of the contract,	11
Property, sale not a transfer of, by the civil law,	50, 54
cannot be reserved in sale,	134
undertaking to transfer, is not sale,	51, 134
passes by delivery in credit sales, or where price paid or secured,	5, 41 sq., 100
passes by delivery of key,	124
Publicanus,	226
Puffery,	91
Pupilli. See *Capacity*.	
Purchaser. See *Buyer*.	
Quality, error as to,	31
of ground misstated,	146, 194, 204
Quantity, error as to,	87
less or more than stated,	143, 146, 175, 210
compensation between excess and defect of two things sold together,	210
Redhibitio,	13, 35, 157
Rents of property sold, whether accessions or not,	116, 174-6, 228
Representations (dicta). See *Warranty*.	
Res, jural sense of,	25
Res aliena, sale of,	54, 74, 152, 162, 176, 196, 200, 216 sq.
extra commercium,	15, 50, 60, 110
furtivae,	62 sq., 200
futurae,	24 sq., 62
obligata,	152
publicae,	16

INDEX TO THE LATIN TEXT AND NOTES. 269

	PAGE
Res religiosae et sacrae,	16, 49, 99, 110
sua, purchase of,	38 sq., 64, 82, 109
See also *Thing sold*.	
Rescission of contract,	13, 16
on ground of fraud,	158, 168, 182
for breach of condition *ne prostituatur*,	102
Reservation of right to take fruits,	88, 182
of minerals,	186
of quarries,	127
of right of *habitatio*,	182, 193, 228
of right of interment,	228
Resolutive conditions,	13, 20
Retention, unpaid seller's right of,	172
where obligation to pay price is extinguished by statute,	223
Revocation of contract *mutuo dissensu*,	20
Risk. See *Periculum*.	
Ruta-caesa,	114, 186, 206
SALE: origin in barter,	2
is a consensual and *bonae fidei* contract,	6, 7
is called 'emptio' or 'uenditio,' or both indifferently,	8, 188
distinguished from exchange,	5
„ location,	45 sq., 113, 134
„ donation,	80 sq.
proof of,	11
essentials of,	10 sq., 27
of moveables and unmoveables, same rules for,	12, 42
whether price in money essential,	5
when complete,	10, 70, 75 sq.
on approval,	14, 22
by instalments,	17
of an expectancy,	24, 26, 83, 167
under essential error,	28
of subject which has ceased to exist before contract complete,	37
by person interdicted,	53
of slave with his *peculium*,	57
„ wine *ad gustum*,	66
„ option,	67
„ of poison,	71
„ runaway slave,	73
„ fungibles,	75
„ thing impignorated,	82
„ standing crops,	87
„ burdened estate, whether release of burdens is a condition or a term in the contract,	89
„ material of standing houses,	100
„ free man,	121
„ office of profit (militia),	227

SALE, 'to Titius and myself,' effect of, ... 113
    at nominal price, ... 81
    as vehicle of legacy, ... 146
    if 'imaginaria,' is null, ... 101
    'uti optimus maximusque,' 108
    of several things for one price, ... 92, 204
    must not be of thing prohibited by law or contrary to morality, 16, 61, 71, 96, 99, 108
    See also under *Res, Thing sold, Price, Condition, Buyer.*

SCOTS LAW: sale and exchange of heritage, distinction between, . 6
    sale distinguished from hiring, ... 46
    contract merely gives *jus ad rem specificam,* . . 78
    in sale of heritage, the property must be passed, . 52
    question as to title to be given in sale of moveables, . 52
    contract by correspondence, ... 8
    proof of sale of goods, ... 12
    bargain of 'sale or return,' 14
    effect of resolutive condition where default in payment, 20
    seller's right of retention, ... 21
    „ stoppage *in transitu,* . . . 21
    question whether essential error of one party, not induced by the other, annuls consent, . . . 33
    as to property in manufactured article in course of making, 47
    buying one's own property, ... 41
    sale of what does not belong to the seller, . . 56
    sale of a chance, *e.g.* expected inheritance, . . 26
    eavesdrop, ... 60
    sale of stolen goods, ... 65
    earnest, ... 71
    price referred to one of the parties, . . . 71
    custody and precautions required of seller pending delivery, ... 74
    theory of risk, ... 77–80
    error in quantity, ... 87
    warranty, ... 93
    actio quanti minoris allowed only where fraud, . 119
    delivery by giving key of warehouse, . . . 125
    damages for non-delivery and delay, . . . 141
    specific implement, ... 142
    no legal hypothec for price over goods delivered, . 44
    insolvent buyer's right of rejection, . . . 44
    restitution granted where delivery induced by fraud, . 45
    implied grant of necessary ways, . . . 86
    duty of seller to purge incumbrances and charges, . 144
    performance by parties to be concurrent, . . 131
    interest due *ex lege* from date of delivery, . . 178

Secret faults. See *Aediles, Warranty.*

SELLER, obligations of, by the nature of the contract, . 50 sq., 156 sq.

INDEX TO THE LATIN TEXT AND NOTES. 271

	PAGE
SELLER, duty of custody till delivery,	74, 202, 206, 230
duty to deliver. See *Delivery*.	
„ discharge mortgage or pledge,	144, 226
„ give *vacua possessio*,	50, 118, 143 sq.
„ warrant against eviction,	114
„ point out defects and vices,	157
„ disclose extraordinary liabilities,	189, 210
cannot contract out of responsibility for fraud,	93, 116
if unpaid, has right of retention,	172
must point out boundaries,	111, 120
must exhibit vouchers for taxes paid,	226
can enforce buyer's duties by *actio uenditi*,	178
See also under *Sale*.	
Servitude, sale of,	83, 133, 144, 150
distinct from obligation,	136
question whether freedom from, implied,	109, 205
of *aquaeductus* passes by implication,	96
praedial could be sold only to adjacent owner,	151
omitted or imposed by mistake,	154
right, how protected,	204
effect of concealment of,	208
See also *Usufruct*.	
Ship, sale of, in course of construction,	47
Silva caedua,	88, 133
Slave, contractual capacity of,	35
accessions through,	176 sq., 202
rights of usufructuary and *bonâ fide* possessor,	195, 196
sale of, does not carry *peculium*,	56 sq.
maintenance of, after sale and before delivery,	206
theft by, „	200
sale of, if accounts satisfactory,	21
„ with special term *ne prostituatur*,	102
ordinarius and *vicarius*,	58, 196
sale of fugitive,	72, 158
sale of free man as,	15
Spes, sale of,	24 sq.
Statu liber,	212
Stillicidium,	59
Stipulatio duplae,	123, 158
Stolen property. See *Res furtiva*.	
Stoppage in transitu,	21
Superficies,	45, 58
Support, sale of right to,	132
Suspensive condition,	13
Terminology,	8
Tender of price necessary in *actio empti*,	129, 172, 196
Theft, a delict not a crime,	65

	PAGE
THING SOLD: no sale *sine re*,	24
must not have ceased to exist,	36, 103
may be any alienable property,	60
must be ascertained to complete the contract,	27 sq., 66, 74 sq.
may be a debt or other incorporeal,	25, 61
,, a *jus in re aliena*,	83, 132
,, a chance,	24 sq.
,, a right of possession,	39, 64, 83
,, a plurality of things sold *en bloc*,	76, 110
,, profits of an office,	227
See also under *Res, Sale*.	
Traditio. See *Delivery*.	
Tribonianisms,	42, 106
Tutor cannot purchase ward's property,	67, 97
Twelve Tables,	42
Usage determines *naturalia* of the contract,	156
Usucapio did not apply to stolen property,	63
accessio temporis in,	127
Usufruct, owner of, may purchase subject,	40
how constituted by reservation,	152
lapsed by *capitis deminutio*,	153, 195
bequest of,	128
Vacua possessio,	50, 119, 143 sq.
Variation of contract by *pactum adjectum*,	120 sq.
Venditio gratiosa,	81
Vendor. See *Seller*.	
Vendee. See *Buyer*.	
Vindicatio rei,	19, 42, 210
Vitia, seller liable for, by the edict,	157
Warrandice, absolute and from fact and deed,	163 sq.
WARRANTY and representation (*dictum promissumve*) treated alike,	88, 90 sq., 170
express, seller liable by the civil law for breach of, and for fraud,	168
implied by the edict, of sound quality,	150, 166–8, 230
latter covered all defects not pointed out, if serious enough to impair the use,	156–8
unless patent on inspection, or known to the buyer,	92, 93
implied in regard to accessories,	198, 230
liability for reckless statements,	168, 169
of undisturbed possession,	160
of quantity,	150
remedies for breach of,	168, 190
Writing not essential as evidence of consent,	12
agreement to reduce contract to,	12, 70

CATALOGUE OF LAW BOOKS
PUBLISHED BY

T. & T. CLARK,
38 GEORGE STREET, EDINBURGH.

INDEX.

	PAGE		PAGE
Adam's Acts of Sederunt,	12	Irons' Police Law,	10
Barclay's Digest,	5	Irons' Public-Houses Acts,	13
—— Public-Houses Acts,	13	Irvine's Game Laws,	13
—— Law of Highways,	14	Johnston's Crofters' Act,	3
Bell's Arbitration,	6	Journal of Jurisprudence,	16
—— Commentaries,	9	Kant's Philosophy of Law,	8
—— Principles,	1	Lorimer's Handbook,	5
Brunner's Law of England,	16	M'Glashan's Sheriff Court Practice,	14
Cabinet Library of Scarce Tracts,	15	Muirhead's Institutes of Gaius,	8
Campbell's Citation and Diligence,	15	Nasmyth's Public Health Manual,	4
Chisholm and Shennan's Local Government Act,	5	Neill's Maritime Causes,	10
		Patterson's Appeal Cases,	10
Clark on Partnership,	15	Puchta's Science of Jurisprudence,	8
Coldstream's Procedure,	7	Renton's Monomania,	14
Cook's Church Styles,	13	—— Criminal Procedure and Appeal,	7
Cowan's Land Rights,	14	Reports:—Court of Session, House of Lords, Justiciary, etc.,	12
Dickson on Evidence,	2		
Digest of Decisions, 1867-85,	11	Savigny's Private International Law,	6
Elliot's Erection of Parishes,	14	Shaw's Digest,	11
Fraser's Husband and Wife,	4	Shennan's Local Administration,	16
—— Master and Servant,	4	Smith's Law of Damages,	2
Goudy's Bankruptcy,	9	—— Poor Law,	11
Grierson on Evidence,	2	Steele on Landed Estates,	3
Guthrie's Select Cases,	6	Thomson on Bills,	14
Hay's Liability,	14	Whyte's Law Examination Manual,	9
—— Poor Law Decisions,	14	Wilson's Law of Sale,	16

NINTH EDITION.

Just published, in Two Volumes 8vo, price 47s. 6d.,

PRINCIPLES OF THE LAW OF SCOTLAND.

BY GEORGE JOSEPH BELL,
PROFESSOR OF THE LAW OF SCOTLAND IN THE UNIVERSITY OF EDINBURGH.

Ninth Edition, Revised and Enlarged
BY

WILLIAM GUTHRIE, Advocate, LL.D.,
SHERIFF-SUBSTITUTE OF LANARKSHIRE.

'"Bell's Principles" has long been the *vade mecum* of Scottish lawyers. No one who is engaged in professional practice can afford to do without it. . . . It meets the wants of the practising lawyer in a way that no other book can attempt to rival. For nearly half a century it has been recognised as a standard work, cited daily in the Courts, and accepted by the judges as possessing the highest authority. . . . No better editor than Sheriff Guthrie could be found anywhere. He has brought to his task not only thorough knowledge of the law, but great care and most conscientious industry. . . . The editorial work has indeed been a positive boon to the profession.'—*Juridical Review.*

'To every practising lawyer the work will be necessary, and perhaps more especially will it be found useful by the mercantile lawyer; while to the legal student it will still be the popular handbook of Scotch law, enhanced in value by Dr. Guthrie's labours.'—*Glasgow Herald.*

Just published, Second Edition, in demy 8vo, price 20s.,

THE LAW OF DAMAGES:

A Treatise on the Reparation of Injuries, as administered in Scotland.

By JOHN GUTHRIE SMITH,

SHERIFF OF ABERDEEN, KINCARDINE, AND BANFF.

CONTENTS.—CHAP. I. Grounds of Responsibility. II. Delict and Contract. III. The Limitations of Responsibility. IV. The Church and the Civil Law. V. Trespass to Person and Property. VI. Road and Railway Accidents. VII. Collisions at Sea. VIII. Fraud. IX. Injuries to Land. X. Defamation. XI. Abuse of Legal Process. XII. Infringement of Copyright, Patents, and Trade Marks. XIII. Master and Servant. XIV. The Measure of Damages. Appendix.

'Written with the same care and clearness that characterized the first edition, and kept it, even when beginning to get rather out of date, amongst the books that nearly every lawyer liked to have at hand for reference. The present edition will, we are convinced, more than preserve the old reputation, and take its place as a leading text-book.' —*Aberdeen Journal.*

'Mr. Guthrie Smith can claim for his treatise what another distinguished author asserted of his handiwork, that it "holds the field." The volume before us is the only work on the law of reparation as administered in Scotland, and the importance of that branch of the law to the practitioner, as well as the wide respect in which the author is held, will secure the book a place in every legal library.'—*Journal of Jurisprudence.*

'This work, touching every province of human life or experience, could have been written only by one who had pronounced many decisions and turned over many law books. It bears the stamp of long industry and wide erudition in domestic and foreign jurisprudence.'—*The Juridical Review.*

In Two Vols., royal 8vo, price 42s.,

A TREATISE

ON THE

LAW OF EVIDENCE IN SCOTLAND.

BY

WILLIAM GILLESPIE DICKSON, ADVOCATE.

Re-cast, Adapted to the Present State of the Law, and in part Re-written

BY

P. J. HAMILTON GRIERSON, B.A. OXON., ADVOCATE.

'The editorial work has been excellently done. . . . The highest praise that can be given to Mr. Grierson is that many, if not all, of his additions have so much the character and accurate induction of the original work that they cannot be distinguished from "Dickson" without looking at the older editions, or the date of the authority cited.'—*Glasgow Herald.*

'"Dickson on Evidence" has no rival.'—*Scottish Law Review.*

'The work of annotating, re-arranging, and in part re-writing the book has been carried through by Mr. P. J. H. Grierson, Advocate, and no more capable man could have been found to undertake the task. . . . The work is a most valuable addition to our law library, is certain to be of immense service to the legal practitioner, both in the Supreme and in the Inferior Courts, and even to the chamber lawyer; and does credit alike to the ability and the industry of the learned editor.'—*Journal of Jurisprudence.*

Just published, in demy 8vo (240 pages), price 6s.,

MANUAL OF THE
LOCAL GOVERNMENT (SCOTLAND) ACT, 1889.

By JOHN CHISHOLM AND HAY SHENNAN, Advocates.

CONTENTS.—Introduction.—Text of the Act, with Notes.—Appendices: *First*, Business and Powers of County Councils; *Second*, Statutory Dates for Business; *Third*, Registration and Election; *Fourth*, Effects of the Act in Burghs, with the last Census Returns; *Fifth*, County Councillors for Scotland.—Index.

'The introduction is a pattern of business-like brevity, orderliness, and accuracy; . . . and the same terseness and precision distinguish their commentary on the text, and their *résumés* in the appendices.'—*Scots Observer.*

'A most useful and meritorious work.'—*Scotsman.*

'The first place for good workmanship must certainly be given to the book of Messrs. Chisholm and Shennan.'—*The Juridical Review.*

Second Edition, in demy 8vo, price 5s.,

THE CROFTERS' HOLDINGS (SCOTLAND)
ACTS, 1886, 1887, AND 1888.

With an INTRODUCTION and NOTES, and an APPENDIX containing the Rules of Procedure, Forms for use under the Acts, the Table of Fees, etc.

By CHRISTOPHER N. JOHNSTON, M.A., Advocate.

'The book, which is well indexed, is altogether a very creditable piece of work, and thoroughly analyzes our latest "new departure" on the legislative line.'—*Scotsman.*

'For all who wish to be abreast of the times on the land question, the study of this statute is necessary, because it is an undeniable foreshadowing of the mode in which we may expect our legislators to deal with the land when the general land question comes before the country, and to those interested in that great question we heartily commend this work.'—*Aberdeen Journal.*

'Every one engaged in the Crofters' proceedings will readily find within the pages of this valuable compendium, the law and practice he requires with little trouble.'—*North British Agriculturist.*

In demy 8vo, price 5s.,

HANDBOOK ON THE MANAGEMENT OF
LANDED ESTATES
AND THE LAW RELATING THERETO.

With Appendix.

By W. H. STEELE, Solicitor.

'It will, without doubt, prove useful to factors, landlords, and tenants, as bringing them a plain definition of their position in law.'—*Scotsman.*

'There is a valuable appendix, including elaborate tables of scales of compensation for the unexhausted values of lime, manures, and feeding-stuffs, besides in a handy form the several Acts referred to in the text. . . It comes to fill an acknowledged want on popular lines, and will be of great service to factors and tenant-farmers.'—*Glasgow Herald.*

'In a concise and simple manner the author has produced a *vade mecum* for landlords, their agents and tenants, by the use of which they will be enabled to thoroughly comprehend the various clauses of an agricultural lease, and their respective rights and privileges under the same.'—*Estates Gazette.*

'We cannot commend this little volume too highly to all who are interested in its subject-matters.'—*Ayr Advertiser.*

Just published, in demy 8vo, price 7s. 6d.

A MANUAL OF PUBLIC HEALTH
AND SANITARY SCIENCE.

A Practical Guide to the Public Health (Scotland) Act, 1867, and the Local Government (Scotland) Act, 1889, for the use of

County Councillors, Members of District Committees and their Officers, under these Acts.

By T. G. NASMYTH, M.D., D.Sc. Ed.

'Dr. Nasmyth's *Manual* deserves a welcome from all who are practically concerned in the administration and carrying out of the Statutes regulating Public Health.'—*Scotsman.*

'In clearness, fulness, intelligibility, and point, no exposition could excel it.'—*Glasgow Herald.*

'Among practical manuals of sanitary science it has at present no competitor, and it will not easily find one worthy to be called or studied as a rival.'—*Scots Observer.*

'His book should be in the hands of every county councillor, of every magistrate, of every medical man, and of every intelligent citizen.'—*Health.*

In Two Volumes royal 8vo, Second Edition, price £4,

TREATISE ON
HUSBAND AND WIFE,
ACCORDING TO THE LAW OF SCOTLAND.

By PATRICK FRASER, LL.D.,
ONE OF THE SENATORS OF THE COLLEGE OF JUSTICE.

'Still more conspicuously in its new than in its old form, the book furnishes proof of the learning, the industry, and the expository power of its author, and it is not likely to lose its place among the very highest authorities on the vast and complex subject with which it deals.'—*Scotsman.*

'Of the book itself it would be difficult to speak in too high terms. Its merits as a legal text-book have been long ago recognised in the previous edition, and we have here the result of the author's matured reading and experience.'—*Courant.*

'It is a book that will be necessary to every practising lawyer, to every student of Scotch history, and to every one who attempts to meddle with the marriage laws of Scotland in Parliamentary or popular discussion.'—*Glasgow Herald.*

'One of the most complete legal monographs that has ever been written.'—*Journal of Jurisprudence.*

In One Volume royal 8vo, price 36s.,

TREATISE ON
MASTER AND SERVANT,
EMPLOYER AND WORKMAN, AND MASTER AND APPRENTICE.

BY THE SAME AUTHOR.

Third Edition
By WILLIAM CAMPBELL, M.A. *Advocate.*

This Edition embodies the whole changes effected in the law in recent years as to Employers' Liability; Factories; Miners, Seamen, and other workmen; together with Forms of Procedure in actions relative to Masters and Servants at Common Law, and under the various statutes applicable to workmen. It also contains the 'Summary Jurisdiction (Scotland) Act, 1881,' and the 'Summary Jurisdiction (Process) Act, 1881,' with a Commentary and Notes.

To Justices of the Peace, Magistrates, Country Gentlemen, Lawyers, Accountants, Parochial Boards, Clergymen, Merchants, etc. etc.

In One Volume demy 8vo, **Fourth Edition,** *price £1, 11s. 6d.,*

A DIGEST OF THE LAW OF SCOTLAND,

WITH SPECIAL REFERENCE TO THE

OFFICE AND DUTIES OF A JUSTICE OF THE PEACE.

BY

HUGH BARCLAY, LL.D.,
SHERIFF-SUBSTITUTE OF PERTHSHIRE.

Fourth Edition, Revised and Enlarged.

'The book appears, in its present form, to be brought down to date with care and accuracy, and it deserves to retain the good opinion of the special public to whom it is addressed.'—*Scotsman.*

'The most complete compendium of our law which, in the convenient form of a Dictionary, has yet appeared.'—*Dundee Advertiser.*

'The work may be cordially recommended as well fitted for the special object at which it aims—as a mine of information on legal matters for Justices of the Peace and other magistrates.'—*Courant.*

In crown 8vo, price 9s.,

A HANDBOOK OF THE LAW OF SCOTLAND.

BY

JAMES LORIMER, ADVOCATE, M.A., F.R.S.E.,
Professor of Public Law in the University of Edinburgh.

FIFTH EDITION.
BY
RUSSELL BELL, ADVOCATE.

'All the characteristics which have from the first given value to this compendium are retained, while it has been brought down to the present date.'—*Scotsman.*

'Within the compass of 576 pages, it presents an amount of information far exceeding what is afforded by many diffuse and unsystematic works of thrice its size.'—*Irish Law Times.*

'We appreciate the care with which Mr. Bell has brought the work abreast of the law of the day, and that not the least valuable feature of the treatise is the copious and intelligent index with which it is furnished.'—*Glasgow News.*

'It is hardly necessary, at this time of day, to say anything about Professor Lorimer's well-known handbook. . . . . Its size is extremely convenient, and there are few legal works which contain so much accurate information in so small a space.'—*Journal of Jurisprudence.*

In demy 8vo, Second Edition, price 21s.,

Private International Law
and the Retrospective Operation of Statutes.

A TREATISE
ON
THE CONFLICT OF LAWS,
AND THE LIMITS OF THEIR OPERATION IN RESPECT OF PLACE AND TIME.

By FRIEDRICH CARL VON SAVIGNY.

Translated, with Notes, by WILLIAM GUTHRIE, *Advocate.*

WITH AN APPENDIX CONTAINING THE TREATISES OF BARTOLUS, MOLINÆUS, PAUL VOET, AND HUBER.

'Savigny, for the first time in modern days, brought to this subject original thought. In Savigny's system of the Roman Private Law, as at the present time, he devotes a volume to the consideration of Private International Law, in which he exhibits all the genius and power which have placed him at the head of scientific jurists in modern days, and given him a place equal to that occupied in former times by Cujacius.'—*Fraser's Treatise on the Law of Parent and Child.*

'Savigny's *System of Modern Roman Law* is perhaps the greatest work on jurisprudence which our age has produced, and Mr. Guthrie has done good service by introducing one section of it in an English dress to English lawyers and students.'—*Law Times.*

'This second edition will obtain, as it deserves, the same favourable reception as the first; and Mr. Guthrie is entitled to no small thanks for the care which he has bestowed on the book.'—*Scotsman.*

In demy 8vo, price 20s.,

SELECT CASES
DECIDED IN THE
SHERIFF COURTS OF SCOTLAND.

COLLECTED BY WILLIAM GUTHRIE, ADVOCATE,
SHERIFF-SUBSTITUTE OF LANARKSHIRE.

'Mr. Guthrie has done his work of editing with his usual exemplary care and skill. He has printed no rubbish, he has wasted no words, he has fished with a long net, but classified judiciously, and he has always given the necessary information at the right place, keeping a steady eye to the readability and utility of his compendious compilation.'—*Scotsman.*

'We trust the present volume may have the wide circulation amongst Sheriffs and Sheriff Court practitioners which it unquestionably deserves.'—*Journal of Jurisprudence.*

In One Volume royal 8vo, Second Edition, price 21s.,

TREATISE ON THE LAW OF ARBITRATION IN SCOTLAND.

By JOHN MONTGOMERY BELL, ESQ., ADVOCATE.
WITH AN APPENDIX OF FORMS.

'Take it all in all, it is one of the most honest, accurate, and thorough of law books.—*Scotsman.*

'In this work is contained every information at all connected with arbitration. . We have much pleasure in recommending the second edition of this useful work to the attention of the profession.'—*Journal of Jurisprudence.*

Just published, in demy 8vo, price 7s. 6d.,

PROCEDURE AND APPEAL

IN

SUMMARY CRIMINAL CASES IN SCOTLAND,

WITH APPENDIX CONTAINING
FORMS OF COMPLAINTS AND APPEALS, AND STATUTES.

By R. W. RENTON, S.S.C.,

PROCURATOR-FISCAL OF FIFESHIRE.

'Terse, orderly, and accurate. It will be of great assistance to all prosecutors in Inferior Courts as well as to magistrates and general practitioners.'—*Journal of Jurisprudence.*

'This book is a new departure, and supplies a want in the profession. . . . We heartily recommend it for its clearness, point, and practical usefulness.'—*The Juridical Review.*

'Mr. Renton's book will be welcome to practitioners in the Inferior Courts as a concise and well-arranged digest of the rules of the statutes and decisions which regulate the manner of conducting prosecutions.'—*Scotsman.*

'It is a thoroughly good piece of workmanship. Not only is the matter clearly and orderly arranged, but concise digests of 'illustrative cases' are sandwiched between the sections of the expository text. The usefulness of such a manual is not confined to those actually engaged in the work of summary criminal courts: it provides also a short cut for the consulting lawyer in cases of difficulty to arrive at the sources of the law on a necessarily technical subject.'—*Scots Observer.*

Just published, in demy 8vo, price 18s.,

FOURTH EDITION, ENLARGED AND REVISED,

PROCEDURE IN THE COURT OF SESSION.

By JOHN P. COLDSTREAM, W.S.,

LECTURER IN THE UNIVERSITY OF EDINBURGH ON CIVIL AND CRIMINAL PROCEDURE IN THE SUPERIOR AND INFERIOR COURTS OF SCOTLAND;
EXTRAORDINARY MEMBER, FORMERLY ONE OF THE PRESIDENTS, OF THE JURIDICAL SOCIETY OF EDINBURGH.

'A Fourth Edition has been published of Mr. Coldstream's "Procedure in the Court of Session." For thoroughness and handiness combined, Mr. Coldstream's work is by far the best manual extant of the forms of procedure in our Supreme Court. . . . For the Law Agent's examination in especial it is the recognised preparative. The present edition has been carefully revised and largely added to, so as to bring it abreast with the latest reforms of the law.'—*Scottish Leader.*

'The rapidity with which the work has gone through so many editions since its first appearance is the best evidence of its value. Written originally as a text-book for students, it has come to be largely used by the legal profession as a guide and aid in practice.'—*Scotsman.*

'A book of value to the practitioner. . . . Affords the necessary information in all ordinary actions.'—*Journal of Jurisprudence.*

In demy 8vo, price 21s.,

The Institutes of Gaius and Ulpian's Rules.

THE FORMER AFTER STUDEMUND'S APOGRAPH OF THE VERONA MS.

With Translation and Notes, and a Copious Synoptical Index.

By JAMES MUIRHEAD,
PROFESSOR OF ROMAN LAW IN THE UNIVERSITY OF EDINBURGH.

'A thoroughly careful and scholarly work, aiming at the right sort of ends, and successfully accomplishing them. The Editor has taken in its full and simple sense the duty of editing a classical text of Roman Law, and has performed it with constant diligence, and with judgment seldom at fault.'—*Saturday Review.*

'The addition referred to is called a Digest, and is neither more nor less than a very complete treatise on the classical jurisprudence, under headings arranged in alphabetical order, and with special reference to the text of the work. The framing of such a compendium must have been a task involving much irksome labour. The result is, so far as we are aware, unique. It will be invaluable to the student of civil law.'—*Journal of Jurisprudence.*

'A most valuable contribution to the study of Roman law. . . . A work like this should be peculiarly acceptable to all students of our race and country whose aim is to acquire a practical grasp of legal ideas.'—*Scotsman.*

KANT'S PHILOSOPHY OF LAW.

In crown 8vo, price 5s.,

THE PHILOSOPHY OF LAW.

AN EXPOSITION OF THE FUNDAMENTAL PRINCIPLES OF JURISPRUDENCE AS THE SCIENCE OF RIGHT.

By IMMANUEL KANT.

Translated from the German
By W. HASTIE, B.D.

'Mr. Hastie has done a valuable service to the study of jurisprudence by the production of this work. His translation is admirably done, and his introductory chapter gives all the information necessary to enable a student to approach the main body of the work with sympathy and intelligence. The work supplies a defect hitherto regretted in the literature of jurisprudence in this country.'—*Scotsman.*

'An epoch-making book in the history of Continental jurisprudence.'—*Literary World.*

In crown 8vo, price 6s.,

OUTLINES OF THE SCIENCE OF JURISPRUDENCE.

AN INTRODUCTION TO THE SYSTEMATIC STUDY OF LAW.

Translated and Edited from the Juristic Encyclopædias of Puchta, Friedländer, Falck, and Ahrens.

By W. HASTIE, B.D.

'It ought to be useful, and I shall have pleasure in recommending it. The translator has a wonderful talent for rendering the foreign idea in English of the best class. With "Puchta" he has been extraordinarily successful.'—Professor J. MUIRHEAD.

'We had occasion some time ago to notice favourably Mr. Hastie's excellent translation of Kant's "Philosophy of Law." . . . He has now followed this up by a companion volume, entitled "Outlines of the Science of Jurisprudence," and made up of translations from the works of the chief German scientific jurists since the time of Kant. These two books are likely to exercise a considerable influence on the study of jurisprudence in England. . . . Every student of jurisprudence ought to read this preface carefully, for it is calculated to exercise a profound influence in enlarging and modifying his views.'—*Literary World.*

Just published, in demy 8vo, price 5s.,

LAW EXAMINATION MANUAL FOR STUDENTS;

Containing Conveyancing, Scots Law, and Court Practice, in the Form of Tables and Abstracts; The Latin Maxims in Bell's and Erskine's Principles; and Numerous Examples of the Examination Questions.

COMPILED BY WILLIAM WHYTE,
SOLICITOR SUPREME COURTS.

'There can be no question of its usefulness as a means of mastering the contents of the text-books.'—*Scotsman.*

'The student will find here, without the waste of many laborious days, a much more handy means of refreshing his memory on the salient points in each subject of examination than he could possibly expect to prepare for himself, and also a collection of questions sufficiently exhaustive to furnish a pretty effective test of his fitness for the "final."'—*Aberdeen Journal.*

'The pages devoted to giving outlines of Court of Session and Sheriff Court practice; the table of less familiar Latin maxims; the selections of questions from examination papers; and a copious index, add greatly to the ability of a manual which is evidently carefully compiled, and should be of great service to those for whom it is intended.'—*Fifeshire Journal.*

A NEW EDITION IN PREPARATION.

A TREATISE ON THE
LAW OF BANKRUPTCY IN SCOTLAND,

WITH AN APPENDIX CONTAINING THE EXISTING BANKRUPTCY STATUTES AND A COLLECTION OF FORMS.

By HENRY GOUDY, LL.B., ADVOCATE.

'Mr. Goudy's work is original, clear, and keeps strictly within the bounds of its stated subject. . . . At times improvements in the law are suggested, most of which would be undoubtedly advantageous. . . . Mr. Goudy's book will be found of the greatest possible value.'—*Scotsman.*

'He who devotes himself to a careful reading of this treatise will, we think, be able to gather from it a clearer understanding of the complicated laws it deals with than from any other work on the same subject.'—*Aberdeen Journal.*

In Two Volumes demy 4to, price £5, 5s.,

COMMENTARIES
ON
THE LAW OF SCOTLAND,
AND ON
THE PRINCIPLES OF MERCANTILE JURISPRUDENCE.

By GEORGE JOSEPH BELL, Esq., ADVOCATE,
PROFESSOR OF THE LAW OF SCOTLAND IN THE UNIVERSITY OF EDINBURGH.

Seventh Edition. Being a re-publication of the Fifth Edition, with additional Notes, adapting the work to the present state of the Law, and comprising abstracts of the more recent English authorities illustrative of the Law of Scotland.

By JOHN M'LAREN,
ONE OF THE SENATORS OF THE COLLEGE OF JUSTICE.

Scotch Appeals, 1851 to 1873.

In Two Volumes royal 8vo, pp. 2244, price £5, 5s.,

REPORTS OF SCOTCH APPEALS IN THE HOUSE OF LORDS,
A.D. 1851 TO 1873,

With Tables of all the Cases cited, Notes, and Copious Index.

By JAMES PATERSON, M.A., BARRISTER-AT-LAW,
AUTHOR OF 'A COMPENDIUM OF ENGLISH AND SCOTCH LAW, STATING THEIR DIFFERENCES,' ETC. ETC.

'These volumes may be relied upon for a particularly full and careful account of all the Appeal Cases during the period which they embrace. It is, indeed, one of the most valuable contributions to the legal literature of Scotland of recent years.'—*Scotsman.*

'The name of Mr. Paterson is itself a guarantee that the work is well done; nothing seems to have been left out that could in any way tend to the elucidation of the cases, or that would make reference to them more easy. The reports are a valuable addition to the case-law of our country, and we are sure that before long every practising lawyer will have them at his hand.'—*Journal of Jurisprudence.*

In One large Volume, demy 8vo, price 31s. 6d.,

MANUAL OF POLICE LAW AND PRACTICE,
COMPRISING

AN ANALYSIS OF THE GENERAL POLICE AND IMPROVEMENT (SCOTLAND) ACT, 1862, WITH NOTES OF DECIDED CASES AND RELATIVE STATUTES;

AND

AN APPENDIX,
CONTAINING

THE SCHEDULES APPENDED TO THE ACT, FORMS FOR CARRYING IT INTO OPERATION, INCORPORATED CLAUSES OF OTHER STATUTES, UNREPORTED DECISIONS, AND
A TABLE OF PARALLEL CLAUSES IN THE ACT AND THE POLICE AND IMPROVEMENT (SCOTLAND) ACT, 1850.

By JAMES CAMPBELL IRONS, M.A., S.S.C.
REVISED BY E. ERSKINE HARPER, ADVOCATE.
And of the Middle Temple, Barrister-at-Law, Joint Assessor-in-Law of the Burgh of Leith.

'To members of Local Authorities, Burgh Magistrates, and indeed to almost all who are personally interested in our municipal and local government, this book will be of great value.'—*Scotsman.*

'The work reflects the highest credit upon the author and those who have assisted him, being manifestly the result of minute and painstaking research, and of skilful selection and arrangement of materials.'—*Glasgow News.*

In demy 8vo, price 8s. 6d.,

FORMS OF PROCEEDINGS IN MARITIME CAUSES
BEFORE THE
SHERIFF COURTS IN SCOTLAND.

By ROBERT NEILL, SOLICITOR AND NOTARY-PUBLIC, GREENOCK.

'Mr. Neill's manual will be found to be of extreme value to lawyers in every mercantile community in Scotland; they will find in the text of the work a clear statement of what the rights of their clients are, and in the annexed forms a trustworthy example of how these may be enforced.'—*Glasgow News.*

'It is impossible to fail to recognise in every page the observations of a good lawyer, who knows the theory as well as the practice in this branch of law with a completeness and accuracy much beyond what is common.'—*Scotsman.*

In Three Volumes imperial 8vo, price £9, 9s.,

DIGEST OF CASES

DECIDED IN THE SUPREME COURTS OF SCOTLAND FROM 1800 TO 1868; AND, ON APPEAL, BY THE HOUSE OF LORDS, FROM 1726 TO 1868.

Being a New Edition of the *Digest* from 1800 to 1852, by Mr. SHAW; and from 1852 to 1862, by Messrs. MACPHERSON, BELL, and LAMOND, Advocates. Revised, Consolidated, and Continued to 1868 by ANDREW BEATSON BELL and WILLIAM LAMOND, Advocates.

'As this excellently designed and excellently executed handbook has already been the theme of a paper in the leading journal of Scotland, as remarkable for its great literary power as for its appreciation of the value of the book which it reviews, it is less necessary for us to encroach on our scanty space for the purpose of criticising the labours of Messrs. Bell and Lamond. No procurator-fiscal can want it, and every lawyer engaged in criminal practice must constantly refer to it. No book can be compared to it for utility in its own branch of the law.'—*Journal of Jurisprudence.*

The Article 'CRIME' in the above *Digest* may be had separately. price 5s.

In One Volume imperial 8vo, price 38s.,

AN ANALYTICAL DIGEST OF CASES

DECIDED IN THE SUPREME COURTS OF SCOTLAND; AND, ON APPEAL, BY THE HOUSE OF LORDS, FROM JULY 20, 1867, TO JULY 20, 1877.

Compiled from the Session Cases, with References to the Scottish Jurist and Justiciary Reports, by A. E. HENDERSON, DAVID GILLESPIE, and HENRY JOHNSTON, Advocates, assisted by J. PATTEN and G. R. GILLESPIE, Advocates.

And in continuation of the above, in One Vol. imperial 8vo, price 38s.,

FROM JULY 20, 1877, TO JULY 20, 1885.

Compiled from the Session Cases.

By HENRY JOHNSTON, C. C. MACONACHIE, AND H. J. E. FRASER, ADVOCATES.

In demy 8vo, Third Edition, price 18s.,

A DIGEST OF THE LAW OF SCOTLAND,

RELATING TO

THE POOR, THE PUBLIC HEALTH,

And other Matters managed by Parochial Boards.

By JOHN GUTHRIE SMITH, ADVOCATE.

'The value of the work as an epitome of all the statutory provisions with respect to the powers and duties of parochial boards, has long been recognised.'—*Scotsman.*

'The book has become in its former editions so well known and so much of a trusted guide and authority, and its author stands so high as one of the most efficient sheriffs in Scotland, and one of the most skilful, judicious lawyers at the bar, that it needs no commendation of ours.'—*Glasgow Herald.*

'This volume will be found very useful, not only by the professional lawyers, but by laymen, to whom, as members of parochial boards and inspectors, the administration of the Poor and Public Health Law is entrusted.'—*Journal of Jurisprudence.*

REPORTS.

REPORTS OF CASES DECIDED IN THE COURT OF SESSION, TEIND COURT, COURT OF EXCHEQUER, AND HOUSE OF LORDS.

SECOND SERIES, 24 vols. 1838 to 1862. £43, 15s. 6d.
THIRD SERIES, 11 vols. 1862 to 1873. £28, 8s. 6d.
FOURTH (CURRENT) SERIES. This Series commences with 20th July 1873.

HOUSE OF LORDS.

HOUSE OF LORDS REPORTS from 1726 to 1821. Reported by JOHN CRAIGIE, J. S. STEWART, and THOMAS S. PATON, Esqs., Advocates. 6 vols., £13.
From 1821 to 1838. By P. SHAW, J. WILSON, C. MACLEAN, Esqs. 12 vols., £19.
From 1840 to 1841. By G. ROBINSON, Esq. 2 vols., £2, 10s.

THE JUSTICIARY COURTS.

REPORTS OF CASES TRIED IN THE HIGH COURT OF JUSTICIARY, from 1826 to 1830. By DAVID SYME, Esq., Advocate. £1, 2s.
From 1835 to 1841. By ARCHIBALD SWINTON, Esq., LL.D., Advocate. 2 vols. royal 8vo, £3, 10s.
From 1841 to 1845. By ARCHIBALD BROUN, Esq., Advocate. 2 vols. royal 8vo, £3, 15s.
From January 1846 to December 1848. By PATRICK ARKLEY, Esq., Advocate. 1 vol. 8vo, £1, 14s. 6d.
From January 1849 to June 1852. By JOHN SHAW, Esq., Advocate. 1 vol. royal 8vo, £1, 16s. 6d.
From June 1852 to December 1867. By A. F. IRVINE, Esq., Advocate. 5 vols. royal 8vo, £10, 5s.
From January 1868 to December 1885. By C. T. COUPER, Esq., Advocate. 5 vols. royal 8vo, £11, 9s.
From December 1885 to March 1888. By J. Cathcart White, Esq., Advocate. Vol. I., £2, 3s. 6d. *Volume II. in course of publication.*

In demy 8vo, price 7s. 6d.,

AN ABRIDGEMENT OF
THE PROCEDURE ACTS
PASSED BY THE SUPREME COURTS IN SCOTLAND;

CONTAINING THE ACTS OF SEDERUNT
OF THE LORDS OF COUNCIL AND SESSION, FROM JANUARY 1852 TO OCTOBER 1886,
AND THE ACTS OF ADJOURNAL
OF THE HIGH COURT OF JUSTICIARY AT PRESENT IN FORCE.

With Notes and References

BY EDWIN ADAM, M.A., LL.B., ADVOCATE.

'These Acts are here collected for the first time. They deal with a number of points of great interest which constantly arise in criminal practice, and the authorities on which it is often difficult to find at a moment's notice. The present compilation will supply a felt want.'—*Aberdeen Journal.*

In demy 8vo, price 4s. (per post, 4s. 3d.),
Second Edition, with Additions.

PUBLIC-HOUSES STATUTES,

With Notes, Decided Cases in England and Scotland, and Extracts from Commissioners' Report. Arranged by HUGH BARCLAY, LL.D., Sheriff-Substitute of Perthshire.

'He who possesses this book will scarcely need any other.'—*Scotsman.*

'Will be found eminently serviceable to all who wish to know how matters at present stand in regard to the liquor laws.'—*Daily Review.*

'Will be found extremely useful to agents as well as justices.'—*Fife Advertiser.*

In demy 8vo, price 5s. (per post, 5s. 3d.),

MANUAL OF THE PUBLIC-HOUSES (SCOTLAND) ACTS,

With Decisions thereon, References to Cases under the English Public-Houses Statutes, Notes relative to Appeal and Review in Scotland, and Appendix containing the Acts and Relative Forms. By JAMES CAMPBELL IRONS, M.A., S.S.C., Edinburgh. Revised by E. ERSKINE HARPER, Advocate.

'We consider this little work a model. . . . The style is clear and concise, and the different points are put with much discrimination.'—*Daily Review.*

'Will be found specially valuable to those who have to do with the granting of public-house licences.'—*Courant.*

COOK'S CHURCH STYLES.

In demy 8vo, price 12s.,

STYLES OF WRITS,

FORMS OF PROCEDURE, AND PRACTICE OF THE CHURCH COURTS OF SCOTLAND.

BY THE LATE REV. J. COOK, D.D.

Fifth Edition.

Revised and adapted to the present state of the Law of the Church (1882).

BY REV. GEORGE COOK, B.D., MINISTER OF LONGFORMACUS.

'The work has already proved an almost indispensable guide in Church Court procedure, and we can confidently recommend this edition, as showing the way through the numerous changes and improvements of recent years.'—*Courant.*

Recently published. Third Edition, price 12s. 6d.,

TREATISE
ON THE
GAME LAWS OF SCOTLAND;
WITH APPENDIX CONTAINING THE PRINCIPAL STATUTES AND FORMS.

BY ALEXANDER FORBES IRVINE, ADVOCATE.

'This work may well claim to be the authority on the Game Laws of Scotland, not only on account of the exhaustive method in which the subject is treated, but also on account of the clear and learned manner in which the law has been laid down and expounded.'—*Glasgow Herald.*

In demy 8vo, price 12s.,

The Land Rights of Scotland: Being a Collection of the
Entail, Conveyancing, and other Statutes relating to Land; with Introductory Observations and Notes. By HUGH COWAN, Sheriff-Substitute of Renfrew and Bute. Second Edition. Revised and brought down to date by the Author.

In One Volume royal 8vo, price 26s.,

Sheriff Court Practice. Practical Notes on the Jurisdiction
and Forms of Process in Civil Causes of the Sheriff Courts of Scotland. By JOHN M'GLASHAN, Esq., Solicitor in the Supreme Courts and Sheriff Court of Edinburgh.—Fourth Edition, Revised, with Decided Cases, and an Appendix containing relative Enactments, Legislative and Judicial. By HUGH BARCLAY, Esq., LL.D., Sheriff-Substitute of Perthshire.

In One Volume royal 8vo, price 28s.,

A Treatise on the Law of Bills of Exchange, Promissory Notes,
BANK NOTES, BANKERS' NOTES, AND CHEQUES ON BANKERS IN SCOTLAND; including the latest English Decisions and Authorities applicable to the Law of Scotland. By ROBERT THOMSON, Advocate. Third Edition, edited by J. DOVE WILSON, Advocate, Sheriff-Substitute, Aberdeen.

'The subject is treated in this handsome volume with severe legal accuracy. Industry, patient consideration, a clear, neat, unambitious style, and quiet, well-balanced common sense, are disclosed in the work of the author or editor of this edition.'—*Scotsman.*

In demy 8vo, price 7s. 6d.,

The Erection of Parishes Quoad Sacra; and the Feuing of
Glebes, under Authority of the Court of Teinds. By NENION ELLIOT, S.S.C., Clerk and Extractor of the Court of Teinds.

'A thoroughly practical book on a little-known subject; and we have no doubt that it will be of the greatest assistance to many agents.'—*Journal of Jurisprudence.*

In demy 8vo, price 7s. 6d.,

Poor-Law Decisions. Decisions on the Poor Law of Scotland
in the Court of Session, and Awards by Arbitration. Condensed by WILLIAM HAY, Solicitor, Dundee.

In demy 8vo, price 10s. 6d.,

The Law of Highways in Scotland. By Hugh Barclay, LL.D.,
Sheriff-Substitute of Perthshire.

In demy 8vo, price 10s. 6d.,

Decisions of the Supreme Courts of England and Scotland on
the Liability of Proprietors, Masters and Servants, etc., for Reparation of Injuries arising from Accidents and the Negligence of Parties; including Cases of Railways, Coal Pits, Road and Harbour Trusts, and Public Corporations. Condensed and arranged by WILLIAM HAY, Solicitor.

In demy 8vo, price 3s. 6d.,

MONOMANIE SANS DÉLIRE.

An Examination of 'The Irresistible Criminal Impulse Theory.'

By A. WOOD RENTON, M.A., LL.B.,

OF GRAY'S INN, AND OF THE OXFORD CIRCUIT, BARRISTER-AT-LAW.

'This work will be read with interest by persons who have studied criminal jurisprudence.'—*Dundee Advertiser.*

'Mr. Renton's criticisms are very able, and deserving of attention.'—*Journal of Jurisprudence.*

In Two Volumes royal 8vo, price £2, 5s.,

A TREATISE ON THE LAW OF PARTNERSHIP AND JOINT-STOCK COMPANIES, ACCORDING TO THE LAW OF SCOTLAND;

Including Private Copartneries, Common Law Companies, Registered Companies, Chartered Companies, Railway Companies, and Others, formed under the Consolidation Acts.

By FRANCIS WILLIAM CLARK,
SHERIFF OF LANARKSHIRE.

'It is a book which every practising lawyer will find it for his interest to have beside him as a book of reference. The author's own ability and accuracy require no guarantee.'—*Scotsman.*

In demy 8vo, price 16s.,

THE LAW AND PRACTICE OF CITATION AND DILIGENCE,

On the basis of the late Mr. Darling's *Powers and Duties of Messengers-at-Arms and other Officers of the Law.*

By ROBERT CAMPBELL, M.A.,
ADVOCATE, FELLOW OF TRINITY HALL, CAMBRIDGE.

With a very copious Collection of Forms.

CABINET LIBRARY OF SCARCE AND CELEBRATED TRACTS.

'The whole of these rare gems are recommended by their neat form and cheapness, and will now have a large circulation.'—*Monthly Review.*

1. Sir James Mackintosh's Discourse on the Study of the Law of Nature and Nations. 1s. 6d.
2. Hon. Justice Story's Discourse on the Past History, Present State, and Future Prospects of the Law. 1s. 6d.
3. Sir W. Scott's (late Lord Stowell) Judgment pronounced in the Consistory Court of London, in the Case of Dalrymple the Wife *v.* Dalrymple the Husband. 2s.
4. Sir W. Scott's Judgments pronounced in the Case of—1. The Maria; 2. The Gratitudine. 2s.
5. Jenkinson, Earl of Liverpool, on the Conduct of the Government of Great Britain in respect to Neutral Nations. 2s.
6. Controversy respecting the Law of Nations; specially relative to Prussia's Attachment of British Funds by way of Reprisal for English Captures. 2s.
7. The Right Hon. Edmund Burke's Letter to a Noble Lord. 1s. 3d.
8. Warnkönig's Analysis of Savigny's Treatise on the Law of Possession. 1s. 8d.
9. Mittermaier on the Effect of Drunkenness on Criminal Responsibility. 1s. 6d.

'The ablest organ of legal criticism in Scotland.'—IRISH LAW TIMES.

THE
JOURNAL OF JURISPRUDENCE

AND

SCOTTISH LAW MAGAZINE.

Edited by JOHN CHISHOLM, M.A., LL.B., Advocate.

Published Monthly, Price 1s. 6d.; Per Annum, 18s.

'The Journal is accurately, clearly, and elegantly written, which is all that can be expected, and more than is often obtained, in writing on practical legal subjects. We have no hesitation in expressing an opinion that for legal intelligence, decisions in the Courts of Session and Justiciary, new Statutes passed or in process, legal promotions and appointments, etc.,—in short, most matters of the day that a professional man may require to know or be curious to know,—this periodical is most essential, and of a value not to be estimated by many times its small cost of 1s. 6d. per month.'—*Scotsman*.

In crown 8vo, price 2s. 6d.,

THE SOURCES OF THE LAW OF ENGLAND.
AN HISTORICAL INTRODUCTION TO THE STUDY OF ENGLISH LAW.

By Dr. H. BRUNNER.

PROFESSOR IN THE UNIVERSITY OF BERLIN.

TRANSLATED FROM THE GERMAN
By W. HASTIE, B.D.

'Remarkable for its clearness, its erudition, and the succinct and perspicuous form in which it embodies matter that might have been expanded into a considerable volume. ... It forms an attractive and instructive means of passing from the study of general jurisprudence to that of the special system of the English law.'—*Glasgow Herald*.

WORKS PREPARING FOR PUBLICATION.

A TREATISE
ON
THE LAW OF SALE IN SCOTLAND.
By JOHN WILSON, ADVOCATE.

THE LAW OF SCOTLAND
RELATING TO
LOCAL ADMINISTRATION IN COUNTIES AND PARISHES.
By HAY SHENNAN, ADVOCATE.

www.ingramcontent.com/pod-product-compliance
Lightning Source LLC
Chambersburg PA
CBHW022111230426
43672CB00008B/1343